EU
· Technology ·
Licensing

EU
· Technology ·
Licensing

Stephen Kinsella
MA (Cantab)
*Partner, Herbert Smith,
Brussels*

Palladian Law Publishing Ltd

© Stephen Kinsella
1998

Published by
Palladian Law Publishing Ltd
PO Box 15
Bembridge
Isle of Wight PO35 5NQ
www.palladianlaw.com

in association with
Lawfully Simple Communications Ltd
170 Tachbrook Street
London SW1V 2NE

ISBN 1 90255 802 2

Typeset by Cheryl Zimmerman
Printed in Great Britain

Part 1

· Introduction ·

This book deals with the application of European competition law to technology transfer agreements. In order to understand the implications of the detailed rules adopted by the Commission it is essential to have at least a general understanding of the basic principles of European competition law.

This section provides a general introduction to the concept of competition law and explains when EU competition rules are applicable.

1. What is competition law?

Competition law groups together those laws which have been adopted essentially on grounds of economic policy with the intention of regulating the conduct of business and thereby the market place.

From the perspective of industry, competition law creates a sort of commercial code of conduct, limiting the extent to which it can enter into certain types of agreement and in some cases the extent to which it can use its own economic power to achieve aims which are not perceived to be in the general interests of consumers. The two recurring themes of competition policy are therefore the protection of the interests of consumers and the needs of national or European industrial policy. In comparison with national competition laws, European competition rules have an additional overriding objective: to ensure that industry does not take steps of its own to prevent the creation of a single market for goods and services throughout the Member States of the European Union.

Competition rules exist at both a national and European level. This work is concerned primarily with the application of European competition rules. Increasingly it is these European rules which define the approach taken by national competition authorities. Many national laws now follow closely or simply reproduce the European rules.

2. Who decides?

This implementing legislation effectively defines the powers of the European Commission in competition cases. Council Regulation 17/62 established three essential features of EU competition law:

1. The Commission has specific powers of investigation and fining in order to enforce Articles 85 and 86.

2. To obtain the benefit of an exemption under Article 85(3), an agreement must be notified.

3. Only the Commission has power to grant an exemption and accordingly all notifications must be addressed to the Commission.

Subsequently, Council Regulation 19/65 gave additional powers to the Commission to adopt a general exemption for a specific category of agreement without the need for individual notification. These exemptions are known as **block exemptions**.

As Articles 85 and 86 are directly effective provisions of the Treaty, creating rights in individuals which can be enforced by national courts, national courts are also competent to rule on the applicability of Articles 85 and 86 and to impose penalties for their infringement. Although national courts can rule that an agreement is prohibited by Article 85(1) and is therefore void and unenforceable, they cannot grant an exemption under the terms of Article 85(3).

It follows from the above that the sources of European competition law are found in the following:

- the block exemption regulations and individual decisions of the Commission applying Articles 85 and 86;
- the notices and policy documents issued by the Commission on the way it intends to apply the competition rules to specific sectors or types of agreement;
- the judgments of the European Courts reviewing the legality of the decisions adopted by the Commission or in reply to preliminary references made by national courts in the context of domestic proceedings;
- the decisions of the national courts or competition authorities of the Member States in application of the EU competition rules.

In legal terms, only the judgments of the European Court (and in particular the Full Court of Justice where a judgment of the Court of

First Instance has been appealed) have the ultimate power to bind not only all national courts but also the Commission itself. The Full Court, being Europe's supreme court, is not however bound by such precedent.

3. Article 85

Article 85(1) establishes a prohibition against all types of agreement, formal and informal, which are entered into between undertakings which prevent, restrict or distort competition within the EU. Agreements which are prohibited can nevertheless be exempted where they are shown to be beneficial to consumers and meet the criteria set out in Article 85(3).

At first sight Article 85 appears to have an improbably wide scope of application. It covers:

- agreements, decisions or concerted practices, whether written or oral, between two or more undertakings;
- whose object or effect is to prevent, restrict, or distort competition.

The technical distinction between agreements, concerted practices and decisions is of limited practical importance. All forms of agreement between undertakings are caught and for ease of reference we will simply refer to "agreements" to encompass all three concepts.

Article 85(1) lists five examples of prohibited agreements. Although these examples are illustrations, each one could apply to a very wide variety of commercial arrangements. Take for example Article 85(1)(c), which confirms that the prohibition covers agreements under which markets or sources of supply are shared. On initial consideration we can conclude that this provision could cover all forms of exclusive distribution, exclusive supply agreements, various forms of non-exclusive distribution agreements and many licensing agreements which allot exclusive territories. Viewed at a wider perspective this provision is of particular relevance to all forms of co-operation agreements and joint ventures.

What is of vital practical importance is that the concept of an agreement extends far beyond the written word. An agreement for these purposes can thus be written or oral. Indeed the agreement can be evidenced solely by the conduct and actions of the parties to it.

Although Article 85 only applies to agreements between two or more parties, the Commission has on a number of occasions managed to identify bilateral conduct out of actions which appear to be unilateral.

For example, it has ruled that the standard terms and conditions of business imposed without negotiation by a supplier for all of its deliveries of goods can amount to an agreement with the purchaser of the goods where the purchaser has not objected to their use.

The prohibition in Article 85 only applies where there is an agreement between undertakings. The concept of an undertaking covers all entities whether corporate, public or private who carry out an economic activity. It is the economic status of the entity, not its legal structure that is important. What is vital is that the entity has the freedom to determine its own economic activity.

Thus, a sole trader, a company, a partnership as well as a co-operative will all be undertakings for the purposes of Article 85. Agreements between an employer and employee are not normally covered as the employee is not regarded as an undertaking in its own right - unless he is, for example, a professional footballer, an inventor or a major recording artist.

Agreements between a parent company and its subsidiaries as well as between companies within the same group are not considered to be agreements between independent undertakings. Such companies are considered to be part of the same economic entity and therefore the individual legal entities cannot be considered to be distinct undertakings. This rule, however, is not absolute. Where a subsidiary has the freedom to determine its own economic behaviour on a specific market, it could be considered to be an independent undertaking but in practice this has never happened.

The nationality of the undertaking is of no relevance in determining whether Article 85 is applicable. Thus, companies established outside the EU, in the United States or in Japan for example, are as equally capable of being undertakings for the purposes of Article 85 as is a company incorporated in England and Wales. If the agreement or act produces effects within the EU, and these effects are of sufficient economic significance, EU competition law will be applicable.

4. Appreciability

Not all agreements which meet the criteria of application of Article 85 are actually caught by its prohibition. For Article 85 to apply the agreement in question must create an appreciable effect on competition and on trade between Member States. This criterion also determines in effect whether European or national competition rules are applicable.

The European Commission has indicated through an administrative notice when it considers that an agreement will not be of sufficient economic importance to trigger the application of Article 85. The Commission considers that, save for exceptional cases, Article 85 will not be applicable where the parties to an agreement:

- operate at the same level of trade, that is, they are horizontally related and have a combined market share of less than 5% for the products concerned (and those other products which they produce which are actually competing products); or
- operate at different levels of trade, that is, they are only vertically related and have a combined market share of less than 10% for the products concerned.

Even where the direct impact of an agreement or act is confined to the territory of a single Member State, there may be sufficient indirect impact on the existing patterns of trade between that Member State and other Member States for EU competition rules to apply.

5. What are the consequences of infringement?

Article 85(2) states that agreements in breach of Article 85(1) are automatically void and unenforceable. Case law has confirmed that the voidness only attaches automatically to the infringing provisions of the agreement.

The commercial consequences of infringing Article 85 are therefore:

1. Those parts of the agreement which contain restrictions prohibited by Article 85 are automatically unenforceable. The parties will not be able to go before the courts to ensure the performance of the agreement. In addition, if (applying national law on severability) the remaining parts of the agreement lose all economic meaning, a court may rule that the whole agreement is unenforceable.

2. A court may make an award of damages against a party who has implemented an agreement in breach of Article 85(1) and thereby caused loss to another.

3. The European Commission may impose a fine on the undertakings participating in the infringement. The maximum fine that can be imposed by the Commission is limited to 10% of the world-wide turnover of the group of companies concerned.

Although the threat of fining by the Commission is both a real and powerful deterrent the administrative limits placed on the Commission mean that on average only about 12 fining decision are adopted each year. By far the greatest commercial impact arises as a result of the unenforceability of restrictive provisions before the courts. By their very definition restrictive terms of an agreement are the very ones that a party will most likely need to enforce if a dispute arises and the agreement is brought before the courts. Furthermore, although there has not yet been a successful claim in the UK courts a party which suffers loss as a result of a breach of Article 85 could have a claim for damages.

Unlike competition rules in the United States a breach of EU competition rules only creates civil liability. In the United States the officers of the company concerned also face the threat of criminal proceedings. This is also true for breaches of domestic competition law in a number of EU states such as the United Kingdom. Even without the additional sanction of the criminal law there are clearly good reasons for all undertakings to ensure that they do not infringe EU competition rules.

Apart from not entering into a prohibited agreement in the first place, there is only one way of entering into a valid agreement which contains provisions prohibited by Article 85(1), and that is by obtaining an exemption for the agreement under the terms of Article 85(3).

6. Commission exemptions

As we have already seen, the Commission alone has power to grant exemptions under Article 85(3). Exemptions come in two kinds: an individual exemption and an exemption provided by a Commission Block Exemption Regulation.

Article 85(3) sets out three clear tests that all agreements must satisfy before they can be exempted. The agreement must:

1. Contribute to improving the production or distribution of goods; or

2. Promote technical or economic progress; and in either case

3. Allow consumers a fair share of the resulting benefits.

Even if these criteria are satisfied, an agreement will not be capable of exemption where it contains:

 ■ restrictions on the undertakings which are not indispensable to achieving its objectives; or where

- the parties as a result would be able to eliminate competition in respect of a substantial part of the products in question.

6.1 Individual notification

Where an agreement is notified individually to the Commission, the notification must be made in the Commission's standard form, following Form A/B. The information required under Form A/B is needed by the Commission in order to make its evaluation of whether Article 85(1) applies at all and, if so, whether the conditions for exemption set out in Article 85(3) are satisfied.

Preparing and filing a notification is a complex and time-consuming task. It needs to be done properly because if a notification is incomplete the parties will not gain the benefit of making an individual notification: that from the date of notification the parties are granted an immunity from the Commission's powers to impose fines for breach of Article 85(1). In addition, subject to a limited exception, an exemption can only take effect from the date of valid notification.

6.2 Block exemptions

The Commission created block exemption regulations in order to avoid the huge administrative burden of having to review thousands of individual notifications each year, many of which would inevitably be in respect of generally standard form agreements.

The block exemption regulations in effect set out a statement of the Commission that certain agreements which fit within a standard format and which contain only certain specified restrictions of competition (the **White List**) and no others and do not contain any specified prohibited restrictions (the **Black List**) can be granted an exemption under Article 85(3) without the need for any notification. The block exemptions therefore set out a blueprint of what agreements the Commission accepts as satisfying the conditions of Article 85(3) in all cases and irrespective of the parties involved.

Each block exemption will contain:

- a description of the specific nature of the type of agreement that is covered;
- a **White List** of those restrictive provisions that can or must be included in the agreement;

- a **Black List** of restrictions which cannot under any circumstances be included, if the block exemption is to apply.

In some cases the block exemption will contain an opposition procedure. This procedure allows the parties to an agreement to use an accelerated notification procedure where the agreement in question contains restrictions in addition to those set out in the **White List** but nevertheless contains no **Black List** clauses. If the Commission does not object to the notification within a specific period of time, the agreement is deemed to be exempted.

Block exemptions are therefore of great commercial value because:

- they provide legal certainty;
- they are cost effective;
- they are highly effective.

7. **Which block exemption?**

The following is a list of the principal **block exemptions** that are currently in force:

- Exclusive distribution;
- Exclusive purchasing;
- Franchising;
- Technology transfer;
- Research & development;
- Specialisation.

In addition to these block exemptions which are of general application, that is, they apply to all sectors, the Commission has issued a series of block exemptions for the following sectors:

- Motor vehicle distribution;
- Shipping;
- Air transport;
- Insurance.

8. **Article 86**

Article 86 complements the provisions of Article 85 by applying a set of additional rules that must be observed by those undertakings who have such individual market power that they are regarded as dominant undertakings. Article 86 provides that:

"Any abuse by one or more undertakings of a dominant position within the common market or in a substantial part of it shall be prohibited as incompatible with the common market in so far as it may affect trade between Member States."

Although Article 86 primarily regulates the activities of individual undertakings, the actions of a few undertakings may still be considered a collective abuse under Article 86. Thus, even where more than one undertaking is implicated in potentially abusive conduct, bringing the agreement prima facie within the scope of Article 85, Article 86 may still be relevant.

8.1 Dominance

Complex economic analysis is required to determine whether an undertaking enjoys a dominant position. The Court of Justice has confirmed that a dominant position exists where an undertaking enjoys a position of economic strength which enables it to prevent effective competition being maintained in the relevant market, by giving it the power to behave to an appreciable extent independently of its suppliers, competitors, and ultimately of its customers. A business that is able to set prices without regard to its competitors would be a classic example of such independence from normal competitive constraints. However, in order to assess whether an undertaking is dominant, it is necessary to examine the undertaking in relation to a particular market or the "relevant market".

The relevant market is defined by reference to both the product market and the geographical market. The product market groups together all products of comparable nature, price and use. If there is no suitable alternative to the product, then it is generally accepted that the product in question can form a market on its own. As regards the geographic market, this is the area in which the same conditions of competition apply and in which the conduct creates its effects. Article 86 can apply where the undertaking is dominant in the common market or a substantial part of it. Where an undertaking is dominant within one single Member State, this will generally be regarded as being a substantial part of the common market.

When assessing market power, market share figures are often used as indicative of market power. Although there may be (and often is) a direct correlation between market share and market power, this is not always the case. A company controlling 40% of the market across the

EU for a product is very likely to have considerable market power and would in most cases be considered to be dominant, unless its sole competitor had the other 60%. A company controlling 90% of the UK market may have such power but may conversely have very little at all. The latter would apply if, for example, the company was not able to impose a small but significant price increase above the ruling price in other EU markets without immediately losing significant market share to imports.

8.2 Abuse

Article 86 does not prohibit an undertaking from merely holding or maintaining a dominant position. The prohibition relates only to the exploitation of such dominance in an abusive manner. As with Article 85, Article 86 lists five examples of types of behaviour which are to be considered as types of abuse and they are very similar to the Article 85 catalogue.

8.3 Procedure

Unlike Article 85, no exemption procedure is contained in Article 86. Individual exemptions and block exemptions are therefore irrelevant. Although it is possible to notify a practice to the Commission for negative clearance this happens very rarely and therefore most dominant companies trade in a state of considerable uncertainty. Moreover, a dominant company cannot assume that restrictions which are permitted in an agreement covered by a block exemption will not amount to abusive conduct if committed by a dominant undertaking. Article 86 requires special care. If an undertaking is found to be in breach of the provisions of Article 86, then the Commission has the power to fine the undertaking.

Part 2

Technology Transfer Block Exemption

1. Structure of this book

This book was conceived as a practical and portable guide to the Regulation, intended to answer questions which would occur to those seeking to make use of the block exemption. For that reason the approach adopted has been, having set out **the text of the Regulation,** to proceed with a clause by clause analysis of the Regulation with appropriate cross references to other parts of the Regulation or of this book. The **Analysis** Section is then followed by a **Commentary** in which a number of broader themes are discussed, again with appropriate cross references (and those less familiar with the Regulation or EU competition law may decide to turn to the Commentary Section first). The book concludes with a number of **summaries of key Commission decisions and court cases** which are used to illustrate the points made elsewhere.

The structure of the Regulation is such that, in the main, issues are dealt with in the same order in which they would by a practitioner drafting an agreement to comply with the Regulation. Therefore, the Regulation begins with the main criteria as to what is a qualifying agreement and what are the principal restrictions which can be included, proceeding then through various exceptions and the special cases in which the exemption might or might not apply. However, not all of the provisions are where one might expect to find them and there is always a risk that those unfamiliar with the entire Regulation could be tripped up by overlooking a clause which could exclude their agreement. There is no substitute for familiarity with the Regulation as a whole. In an effort to make matters easier, there follows a flowchart which, so far as possible in diagrammatic form, takes the reader through the key questions in determining applicability of the Regulation and cross refers to those sections of this book in which the relevant provisions are discussed.

The technology transfer block exemption

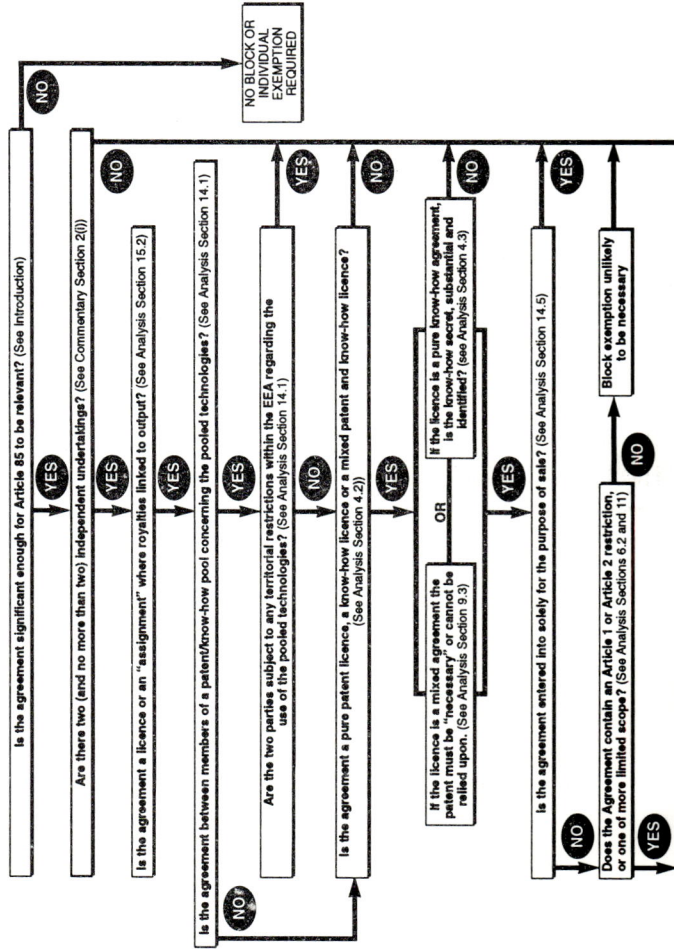

Is the agreement significant enough for Article 85 to be relevant? (See Introduction)

NO → NO BLOCK OR INDIVIDUAL EXEMPTION REQUIRED

YES

Are there two (and no more than two) independent undertakings? (See Commentary Section 2(i))

NO

YES

Is the agreement a licence or an "assignment" where royalties linked to output? (See Analysis Section 15.2)

YES

Is the agreement between members of a patent/know-how pool concerning the pooled technologies? (See Analysis Section 14.1)

NO

YES

Are the two parties subject to any territorial restrictions within the EEA regarding the use of the pooled technologies? (See Analysis Section 14.1)

YES

NO

Is the agreement a pure patent licence, a know-how licence or a mixed patent and know-how licence? (See Analysis Section 4.2))

NO

YES

If the licence is a mixed agreement the patent must be "necessary" or cannot be relied upon. (See Analysis Section 9.3)

OR

If the licence is a pure know-how agreement, is the know-how secret, substantial and identified? (see Analysis Section 4.3)

NO

YES

Is the agreement entered into solely for the purpose of sale? (See Analysis Section 14.5)

YES → Block exemption unlikely to be necessary

NO

Does the Agreement contain an Article 1 or Article 2 restriction, or one of more limited scope? (See Analysis Sections 6.2 and 11)

NO

YES

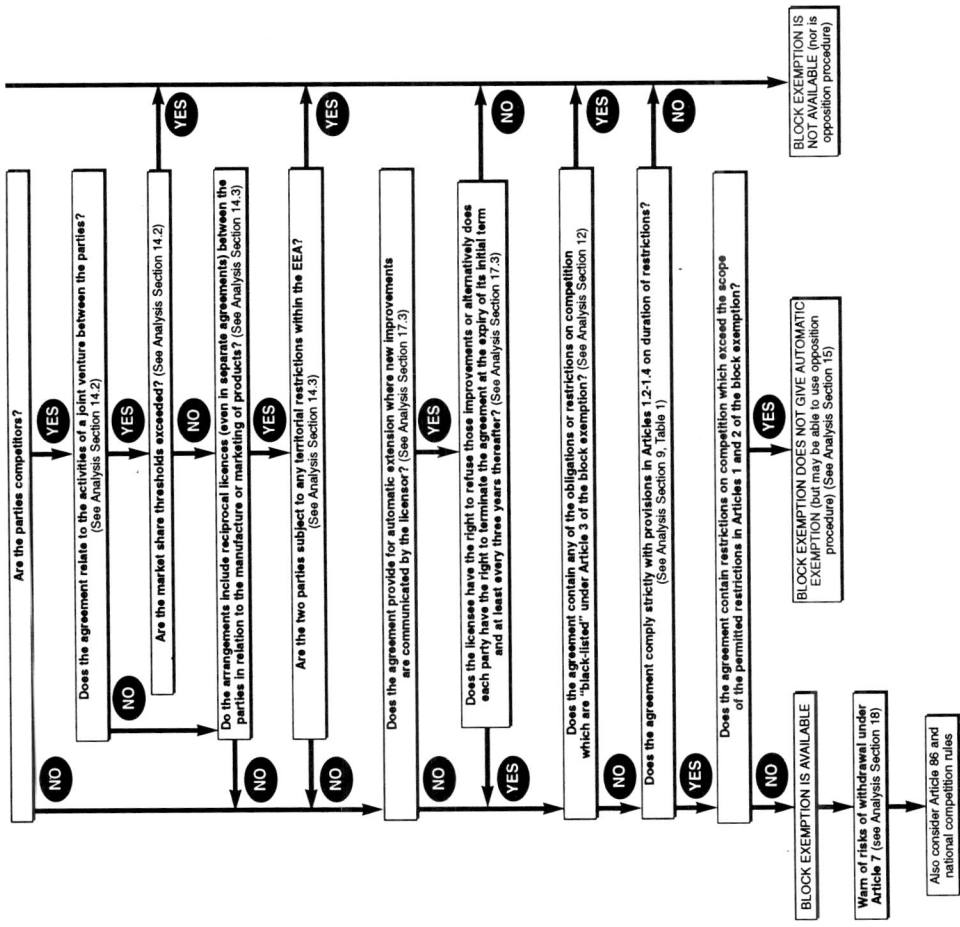

2. Block exemption text: EU version

Commission Regulation (EC) No 240/96[1]

of 31 January 1996

on the application of Article 85(3) of the Treaty to certain categories of technology transfer agreements

(Text with EEA relevance)

THE COMMISSION OF THE EUROPEAN COMMUNITIES,

Having regard to the Treaty establishing the European Community,

Having regard to Council Regulation No 19/65/EEC of 2 March 1965 on the application of Article 85(3) of the Treaty to certain categories of agreements and concerted practices, as last amended by the Act of Accession of Austria, Finland and Sweden, and in particular Article 1 thereof,

Having published a draft of this Regulation,

After consulting the Advisory Committee on Restrictive Practices and Dominant Positions,

Whereas:

(1) Regulation No 19/65/EEC empowers the Commission to apply Article 85(3) of the Treaty by regulation to certain categories of agreements and concerted practices falling within the scope of Article 85(1) which include restrictions imposed in relation to the acquisition or use of industrial property rights – in particular of patents, utility models, designs or trade marks – or to the rights arising out of contracts for assignment of, or the right to use, a method of manufacture or knowledge relating to use or to the application of industrial processes.

(2) The Commission has made use of this power by adopting Regulation (EEC) No 2349/84 of 23 July 1984 on the application of Article 85(3) of the Treaty to certain categories of patent licensing agreements, as last amended by Regulation (EC) No 2131/95, and Regulation (EEC) No 556/89 of 30 November 1988 on the application of Article 85(3) of the Treaty to certain categories of know-how licensing agreements, as last amended by the Act of Accession of Austria, Finland and Sweden.

(3) These two block exemptions ought to be combined into a single regulation covering technology transfer agreements, and the rules governing patent licensing agreements and agreements for the licensing of know-how ought to be harmonised and simplified as far as possible, in order to encourage

---

1   OJ 1996 L31/2. Minor typograpical errors in OJ version have been corrected.

the dissemination of technical knowledge in the Community and to promote the manufacture of technically more sophisticated products. In those circumstances Regulation (EEC) No 556/89 should be repealed.

(4) This Regulation should apply to the licensing of Member States' own patents, Community patents and European patents ("pure" patent licensing agreements). It should also apply to agreements for the licensing of non-patented technical information such as descriptions of manufacturing processes, recipes, formulae, designs or drawings, commonly termed "know-how" ("pure" know-how licensing agreements), and to combined patent and know-how licensing agreements ("mixed" agreements), which are playing an increasingly important role in the transfer of technology. For the purposes of this Regulation, a number of terms are defined in Article 10.

(5) Patent or know-how licensing agreements are agreements whereby one undertaking which holds a patent or know-how ("the licensor") permits another undertaking ("the licensee") to exploit the patent thereby licensed, or communicates the know-how to it, in particular for purposes of manufacture, use or putting on the market. In the light of experience acquired so far, it is possible to define a category of licensing agreements covering all or part of the common market which are capable of falling within the scope of Article 85(1) but which can normally be regarded as satisfying the conditions laid down in Article 85(3), where patents are necessary for the achievement of the objects of the licensed technology by a mixed agreement or where know-how – whether it is ancillary to patents or independent of them – is secret, substantial and identified in any appropriate form. These criteria are intended only to ensure that the licensing of the know-how or the grant of the patent licence justifies a block exemption of obligations restricting competition. This is without prejudice to the right of the parties to include in the contract provisions regarding other obligations, such as the obligation to pay royalties, even if the block exemption no longer applies.

(6) It is appropriate to extend the scope of this Regulation to pure or mixed agreements containing the licensing of intellectual property rights other than patents (in particular, trade marks, design rights and copyright, especially software protection), when such additional licensing contributes to the achievement of the objects of the licensed technology and contains only ancillary provisions.

(7) Where such pure or mixed licensing agreements contain not only obligations relating to territories within the common market but also obligations relating to non-member countries, the presence of the latter does not prevent this Regulation from applying to the obligations relating to territories within the common market. Where licensing agreements for non-member countries or for territories which extend beyond the

frontiers of the Community have effects within the common market which may fall within the scope of Article 85(1), such agreements should be covered by this Regulation to the same extent as would agreements for territories within the common market.

(8) The objective being to facilitate the dissemination of technology and the improvement of manufacturing processes, this Regulation should apply only where the licensee himself manufactures the licensed products or has them manufactured for his account, or where the licensed product is a service, provides the service himself or has the service provided for his account, irrespective of whether or not the licensee is also entitled to use confidential information provided by the licensor for the promotion and sale of the licensed product. The scope of this Regulation should therefore exclude agreements solely for the purpose of sale. Also to be excluded from the scope of this Regulation are agreements relating to marketing know-how communicated in the context of franchising arrangements and certain licensing agreements entered into in connection with arrangements such as joint ventures or patent pools and other arrangements in which a licence is granted in exchange for other licences not related to improvements to or new applications of the licensed technology. Such agreements pose different problems which cannot at present be dealt with in a single regulation (Article 5).

(9) Given the similarity between sale and exclusive licensing, and the danger that the requirements of this Regulation might be evaded by presenting as assignments what are in fact exclusive licences restrictive of competition, this Regulation should apply to agreements concerning the assignment and acquisition of patents or know-how where the risk associated with exploitation remains with the assignor. It should also apply to licensing agreements in which the licensor is not the holder of the patent or know-how but is authorised by the holder to grant the licence (as in the case of sub-licences) and to licensing agreements in which the parties' rights or obligations are assumed by connected undertakings (Article 6).

(10) Exclusive licensing agreements, i.e. agreements in which the licensor undertakes not to exploit the licensed technology in the licensed territory himself or to grant further licences there, may not be in themselves incompatible with Article 85(1) where they are concerned with the introduction and protection of a new technology in the licensed territory, by reason of the scale of the research which has been undertaken, of the increase in the level of competition, in particular inter-brand competition, and of the competitiveness of the undertakings concerned resulting from the dissemination of innovation within the Community. In so far as agreements of this kind fall, in other circumstances, within the scope of Article 85(1), it is appropriate to include them in Article 1 in order that they may also benefit from the exemption.

(11) The exemption of export bans on the licensor and on the licensees does not prejudice any developments in the case law of the Court of Justice in relation to such agreements, notably with respect to Articles 30 to 36 and Article 85(1). This is also the case, in particular, regarding the prohibition on the licensee from selling the licensed product in territories granted to other licensees (passive competition).

(12) The obligations listed in Article 1 generally contribute to improving the production of goods and to promoting technical progress. They make the holders of patents or know-how more willing to grant licences and licensees more inclined to undertake the investment required to manufacture, use and put on the market a new product or to use a new process. Such obligations may be permitted under this Regulation in respect of territories where the licensed product is protected by patents as long as these remain in force.

(13) Since the point at which the know-how ceases to be secret can be difficult to determine, it is appropriate, in respect of territories where the licensed technology comprises know-how only, to limit such obligations to a fixed number of years. Moreover, in order to provide sufficient periods of protection, it is appropriate to take as the starting point for such periods the date on which the product is first put on the market in the Community by a licensee.

(14) Exemption under Article 85(3) of longer periods of territorial protection for know-how agreements, in particular in order to protect expensive and risky investment or where the parties were not competitors at the date of the grant of the licence, can be granted only by individual decision. On the other hand, parties are free to extend the term of their agreements in order to exploit any subsequent improvement and to provide for the payment of additional royalties. However, in such cases, further periods of territorial protection may be allowed only starting from the date of licensing of the secret improvements in the Community, and by individual decision. Where the research for improvements results in innovations which are distinct from the licensed technology the parties may conclude a new agreement benefiting from an exemption under this Regulation.

(15) Provision should also be made for exemption of an obligation on the licensee not to put the product on the market in the territories of other licensees, the permitted period for such an obligation (this obligation would ban not just active competition but passive competition too) should, however, be limited to a few years from the date on which the licensed product is first put on the market in the Community by a licensee, irrespective of whether the licensed technology comprises know-how, patents or both in the territories concerned.

(16) The exemption of territorial protection should apply for the whole duration of the periods thus permitted, as long as the patents remain in force or the know-how remains secret and substantial. The parties to a mixed patent and know-how licensing agreement must be able to take advantage in a particular territory of the period of protection conferred by a patent or by the know-how, whichever is the longer.

(17) The obligations listed in Article 1 also generally fulfil the other conditions for the application of Article 85(3). Consumers will, as a rule, be allowed a fair share of the benefit resulting from the improvement in the supply of goods on the market. To safeguard this effect, however, it is right to exclude from the application of Article 1 cases where the parties agree to refuse to meet demand from users or resellers within their respective territories who would resell for export, or to take other steps to impede parallel imports. The obligations referred to above thus only impose restrictions which are indispensable to the attainment of their objectives.

(18) It is desirable to list in this Regulation a number of obligations that are commonly found in licensing agreements but are normally not restrictive of competition, and to provide that in the event that because of the particular economic or legal circumstances they should fall within Article 85(1), they too will be covered by the exemption. This list, in Article 2, is not exhaustive.

(19) This Regulation must also specify what restrictions or provisions may not be included in licensing agreements if these are to benefit from the block exemption. The restrictions listed in Article 3 may fall under the prohibition of Article 85(1), but in their case there can be no general presumption that, although they relate to the transfer of technology, they will lead to the positive effects required by Article 85(3), as would be necessary for the granting of a block exemption. Such restrictions can be declared exempt only by an individual decision, taking account of the market position of the undertakings concerned and the degree of concentration on the relevant market.

(20) The obligations on the licensee to cease using the licensed technology after the termination of the agreement (Article 2(1)(3)) and to make improvements available to the licensor (Article 2(1)(4)) do not generally restrict competition. The post-term use ban may be regarded as a normal feature of licensing, as otherwise the licensor would be forced to transfer his know-how or patents in perpetuity. Undertakings by the licensee to grant back to the licensor a licence for improvements to the licensed know-how and/or patents are generally not restrictive of competition if the licensee is entitled by the contract to share in future experience and inventions made by the licensor. On the other hand, a restrictive effect on competition arises where the agreement obliges the licensee to assign to

the licensor rights to improvements of the originally licensed technology that he himself has brought about (Article 3(6)).

(21) The list of clauses which do not prevent exemption also includes an obligation on the licensee to keep paying royalties until the end of the agreement independently of whether or not the licensed know-how has entered into the public domain through the action of third parties or of the licensee himself (Article 2(1)(7)). Moreover, the parties must be free, in order to facilitate payment, to spread the royalty payments for the use of the licensed technology over a period extending beyond the duration of the licensed patents, in particular by setting lower royalty rates. As a rule, parties do not need to be protected against the foreseeable financial consequences of an agreement freely entered into, and they should therefore be free to choose the appropriate means of financing the technology transfer and sharing between them the risks of such use. However, the setting of rates of royalty so as to achieve one of the restrictions listed in Article 3 renders the agreement ineligible for the block exemption.

(22) An obligation on the licensee to restrict his exploitation of the licensed technology to one or more technical fields of application ("fields of use") or to one or more product markets is not caught by Article 85(1) either, since the licensor is entitled to transfer the technology only for a limited purpose (Article 2(1)(8)).

(23) Clauses whereby the parties allocate customers within the same technological field of use or the same product market, either by an actual prohibition on supplying certain classes of customer or through an obligation with an equivalent effect, would also render the agreement ineligible for the block exemption where the parties are competitors for the contract products (Article 3(4)). Such restrictions between undertakings which are not competitors remain subject to the opposition procedure. Article 3 does not apply to cases where the patent or know-how licence is granted in order to provide a single customer with a second source of supply. In such a case, a prohibition on the second licensee from supplying persons other than the customer concerned is an essential condition for the grant of a second licence, since the purpose of the transaction is not to create an independent supplier in the market. The same applies to limitations on the quantities the licensee may supply to the customer concerned (Article 2(1)(13)).

(24) Besides the clauses already mentioned, the list of restrictions which render the block exemption inapplicable also includes restrictions regarding the selling prices of the licensed product or the quantities to be manufactured or sold, since they seriously limit the extent to which the licensee can exploit the licensed technology and since quantity restrictions

particularly may have the same effect as export bans (Article 3(1) and (5)). This does not apply where a licence is granted for use of the technology in specific production facilities and where both a specific technology is communicated for the setting up, operation and maintenance of these facilities and the licensee is allowed to increase the capacity of the facilities or to set up further facilities for its own use on normal commercial terms. On the other hand, the licensee may lawfully be prevented from using the transferred technology to set up facilities for third parties, since the purpose of the agreement is not to permit the licensee to give other producers access to the licensor's technology while it remains secret or protected by patent (Article 2(1)(12)).

(25) Agreements which are not automatically covered by the exemption because they contain provisions that are not expressly exempted by this Regulation and not expressly excluded from exemption, including those listed in Article 4(2), may, in certain circumstances, nonetheless be presumed to be eligible for application of the block exemption. It will be possible for the Commission rapidly to establish whether this is the case on the basis of the information undertakings are obliged to provide under Commission Regulation (EC) No 3385/94. The Commission may waive the requirement to supply specific information required in Form A/B but which it does not deem necessary. The Commission will generally be content with communication of the text of the agreement and with an estimate, based on directly available data, of the market structure and of the licensee's market share. Such agreements should therefore be deemed to be covered by the exemption provided for in this Regulation where they are notified to the Commission and the Commission does not oppose the application of the exemption within a specified period of time.

(26) Where agreements exempted under this Regulation nevertheless have effects incompatible with Article 85(3), the Commission may withdraw the block exemption, in particular where the licensed products are not faced with real competition in the licensed territory (Article 7). This could also be the case where the licensee has a strong position on the market. In assessing the competition the Commission will pay special attention to cases where the licensee has more than 40% of the whole market for the licensed products and of all the products or services which customers consider interchangeable or substitutable on account of their characteristics, prices and intended use.

(27) Agreements which come within the terms of Articles 1 and 2 and which have neither the object nor the effect of restricting competition in any other way need no longer be notified. Nevertheless, undertakings will still have the right to apply in individual cases for negative clearance or for exemption under Article 85(3) in accordance with Council Regulation

No 17, as last amended by the Act of Accession of Austria, Finland and Sweden. They can in particular notify agreements obliging the licensor not to grant other licences in the territory, where the licensee's market share exceeds or is likely to exceed 40%.

HAS ADOPTED THIS REGULATION:

Article 1

1. Pursuant to Article 85(3) of the Treaty and subject to the conditions set out below, it is hereby declared that Article 85(1) of the Treaty shall not apply to pure patent licensing or know-how licensing agreements and to mixed patent and know-how licensing agreements, including those agreements containing ancillary provisions relating to intellectual property rights other than patents, to which only two undertakings are party and which include one or more of the following obligations:

   (1)   an obligation on the licensor not to license other undertakings to exploit the licensed technology in the licensed territory;

   (2)   an obligation on the licensor not to exploit the licensed technology in the licensed territory himself;

   (3)   an obligation on the licensee not to exploit the licensed technology in the territory of the licensor within the common market;

   (4)   an obligation on the licensee not to manufacture or use the licensed product, or use the licensed process, in territories within the common market which are licensed to other licensees;

   (5)   an obligation on the licensee not to pursue an active policy of putting the licensed product on the market in the territories within the common market which are licensed to other licensees, and in particular not to engage in advertising specifically aimed at those territories or to establish any branch or maintain a distribution depot there;

   (6)   an obligation on the licensee not to put the licensed product on the market in the territories licensed to other licensees within the common market in response to unsolicited orders;

   (7)   an obligation on the licensee to use only the licensor's trade mark or get up to distinguish the licensed product during the term of the agreement, provided that the licensee is not prevented from identifying himself as the manufacturer of the licensed products;

   (8)   an obligation on the licensee to limit his production of the licensed product to the quantities he requires in manufacturing his own products and to sell the licensed product only as an integral part of

or a replacement part for his own products or otherwise in connection with the sale of his own products, provided that such quantities are freely determined by the licensee.

2.   Where the agreement is a pure patent licensing agreement, the exemption of the obligations referred to in paragraph 1 is granted only to the extent that and for as long as the licensed product is protected by parallel patents, in the territories respectively of the licensee (points (1), (2), (7) and (8)), the licensor (point (3)) and other licensees (points (4) and (5)). The exemption of the obligation referred to in point (6) of paragraph 1 is granted for a period not exceeding five years from the date when the licensed product is first put on the market within the common market by one of the licensees, to the extent that and for as long as, in these territories, this product is protected by parallel patents.

3.   Where the agreement is a pure know-how licensing agreement, the period for which the exemption of the obligations referred to in points (1) to (5) of paragraph 1 is granted may not exceed ten years from the date when the licensed product is first put on the market within the common market by one of the licensees.

The exemption of the obligation referred to in point (6) of paragraph 1 is granted for a period not exceeding five years from the date when the licensed product is first put on the market within the common market by one of the licensees.

The obligations referred to in points (7) and (8) of paragraph 1 are exempted during the lifetime of the agreement for as long as the know-how remains secret and substantial.

However, the exemption in paragraph 1 shall apply only where the parties have identified in any appropriate form the initial know-how and any subsequent improvements to it which become available to one party and are communicated to the other party pursuant to the terms of the agreement and to the purpose thereof, and only for as long as the know-how remains secret and substantial.

4.   Where the agreement is a mixed patent and know-how licensing agreement, the exemption of the obligations referred to in points (1) to (5) of paragraph 1 shall apply in Member States in which the licensed technology is protected by necessary patents for as long as the licensed product is protected in those Member States by such patents if the duration of such protection exceeds the periods specified in paragraph 3.

The duration of the exemption provided in point (6) of paragraph 1 may not exceed the five-year period provided for in paragraphs 2 and 3.

However, such agreements qualify for the exemption referred to in paragraph 1 only for as long as the patents remain in force or to the extent that the know-how is identified and for as long as it remains secret and substantial whichever period is the longer.

5. The exemption provided for in paragraph 1 shall also apply where in a particular agreement the parties undertake obligations of the types referred to in that paragraph but with a more limited scope than is permitted by that paragraph.

Article 2

1. Article 1 shall apply notwithstanding the presence in particular of any of the following clauses, which are generally not restrictive of competition:

    (1) an obligation on the licensee not to divulge the know-how communicated by the licensor; the licensee may be held to this obligation after the agreement has expired;

    (2) an obligation on the licensee not to grant sublicences or assign the licence;

    (3) an obligation on the licensee not to exploit the licensed know-how or patents after termination of the agreement in so far and as long as the know-how is still secret or the patents are still in force;

    (4) an obligation on the licensee to grant to the licensor a licence in respect of his own improvements to or his new applications of the licensed technology, provided:

    –   that, in the case of severable improvements, such a licence is not exclusive, so that the licensee is free to use his own improvements or to license them to third parties, in so far as that does not involve disclosure of the know-how communicated by the licensor that is still secret,

    –   and that the licensor undertakes to grant an exclusive or non-exclusive licence of his own improvements to the licensee;

    (5) an obligation on the licensee to observe minimum quality specifications, including technical specifications, for the licensed product or to procure goods or services from the licensor or from an undertaking designated by the licensor, in so far as these quality specifications, products or services are necessary for:

    (a) a technically proper exploitation of the licensed technology; or

    (b) ensuring that the product of the licensee conforms to the minimum quality specifications that are applicable to the licensor and other licensees;

    and to allow the licensor to carry out related checks;

(6)   obligations:

   (a)   to inform the licensor of misappropriation of the know-how or of infringements of the licensed patents; or

   (b)   to take or to assist the licensor in taking legal action against such misappropriation or infringements;

(7)   an obligation on the licensee to continue paying the royalties:

   (a)   until the end of the agreement in the amounts, for the periods and according to the methods freely determined by the parties, in the event of the know-how becoming publicly known other than by action of the licensor, without prejudice to the payment of any additional damages in the event of the know-how becoming publicly known by the action of the licensee in breach of the agreement;

   (b)   over a period going beyond the duration of the licensed patents, in order to facilitate payment;

(8)   an obligation on the licensee to restrict his exploitation of the licensed technology to one or more technical fields of application covered by the licensed technology or to one or more product markets;

(9)   an obligation on the licensee to pay a minimum royalty or to produce a minimum quantity of the licensed product or to carry out a minimum number of operations exploiting the licensed technology;

(10)   an obligation on the licensor to grant the licensee any more favourable terms than the licensor may grant to another undertaking after the agreement is entered into;

(11)   an obligation on the licensee to mark the licensed product with an indication of the licensor's name or of the licensed patent;

(12)   an obligation on the licensee not to use the licensor's technology to construct facilities for third parties; this is without prejudice to the right of the licensee to increase the capacity of his facilities or to set up additional facilities for his own use on normal commercial terms, including the payment of additional royalties;

(13)   an obligation on the licensee to supply only a limited quantity of the licensed product to a particular customer, where the licence was granted so that the customer might have a second source of supply inside the licensed territory; this provision shall also apply where the customer is the licensee, and the licence which was granted in order to provide a second source of supply provides that the

customer is himself to manufacture the licensed products or to have them manufactured by a subcontractor;

(14) a reservation by the licensor of the right to exercise the rights conferred by a patent to oppose the exploitation of the technology by the licensee outside the licensed territory;

(15) a reservation by the licensor of the right to terminate the agreement if the licensee contests the secret or substantial nature of the licensed know-how or challenges the validity of licensed patents within the common market belonging to the licensor or undertakings connected with him;

(16) a reservation by the licensor of the right to terminate the licence agreement of a patent if the licensee raises the claim that such a patent is not necessary;

(17) an obligation on the licensee to use his best endeavours to manufacture and market the licensed product;

(18) a reservation by the licensor of the right to terminate the exclusivity granted to the licensee and to stop licensing improvements to him when the licensee enters into competition within the common market with the licensor, with undertakings connected with the licensor or with other undertakings in respect of research and development, production, use or distribution of competing products, and to require the licensee to prove that the licensed know-how is not being used for the production of products and the provision of services other than those licensed.

2. In the event that, because of particular circumstances, the clauses referred to in paragraph 1 fall within the scope of Article 85(1), they shall also be exempted even if they are not accompanied by any of the obligations exempted by Article 1.

3. The exemption in paragraph 2 shall also apply where an agreement contains clauses of the types referred to in paragraph 1 but with a more limited scope than is permitted by that paragraph.

Article 3

Article 1 and Article 2 (2) shall not apply where:

(1) one party is restricted in the determination of prices, components of prices or discounts for the licensed products;

(2) one party is restricted from competing within the common market with the other party, with undertakings connected with the other party or with other undertakings in respect of research and development, production,

use or distribution of competing products without prejudice to the provisions of Article 2(1)(17) and (18);

(3)   one or both of the parties are required without any objectively justified reason:

   (a)   to refuse to meet orders from users or resellers in their respective territories who would market products in other territories within the common market;

   (b)   to make it difficult for users or resellers to obtain the products from other resellers within the common market, and in particular to exercise intellectual property rights or take measures so as to prevent users or resellers from obtaining outside, or from putting on the market in the licensed territory products which have been lawfully put on the market within the common market by the licensor or with his consent;

   or do so as a result of a concerted practice between them;

(4)   the parties were already competing manufacturers before the grant of the licence and one of them is restricted, within the same technical field of use or within the same product market, as to the customers he may serve, in particular by being prohibited from supplying certain classes of user, employing certain forms of distribution or, with the aim of sharing customers, using certain types of packaging for the products, save as provided in Article 1(1)(7) and Article 2(1)(13);

(5)   the quantity of the licensed products one party may manufacture or sell or the number of operations exploiting the licensed technology he may carry out are subject to limitations, save as provided in Article 1(8) and Article 2(1)(13);

(6)   the licensee is obliged to assign in whole or in part to the licensor rights to improvements to or new applications of the licensed technology;

(7)   the licensor is required, albeit in separate agreements or through automatic prolongation of the initial duration of the agreement by the inclusion of any new improvements, for a period exceeding that referred to in Article 1(2) and (3) not to license other undertakings to exploit the licensed technology in the licensed territory, or a party is required for a period exceeding that referred to in Article 1(2) and (3) or Article 1(4) not to exploit the licensed technology in the territory of the other party or of other licensees.

Article 4

1.   The exemption provided for in Articles 1 and 2 shall also apply to agreements containing obligations restrictive of competition which are

not covered by those Articles and do not fall within the scope of Article 3, on condition that the agreements in question are notified to the Commission in accordance with the provisions of Articles 1, 2 and 3 of Regulation (EC) No 3385/94 and that the Commission does not oppose such exemption within a period of four months.

2. Paragraph 1 shall apply, in particular, where:

    (a) the licensee is obliged at the time the agreement is entered into to accept quality specifications or further licences or to procure goods or services which are not necessary for a technically satisfactory exploitation of the licensed technology or for ensuring that the production of the licensee conforms to the quality standards that are respected by the licensor and other licensees;

    (b) the licensee is prohibited from contesting the secrecy or the substantiality of the licensed know-how or from challenging the validity of patents licensed within the common market belonging to the licensor or undertakings connected with him.

3. The period of four months referred to in paragraph 1 shall run from the date on which the notification takes effect in accordance with Article 4 of Regulation (EC) No 3385/94.

4. The benefit of paragraphs 1 and 2 may be claimed for agreements notified before the entry into force of this Regulation by submitting a communication to the Commission referring expressly to this Article and to the notification. Paragraph 3 shall apply *mutatis mutandis.*

5. The Commission may oppose the exemption within a period of four months. It shall oppose exemption if it receives a request to do so from a Member State within two months of the transmission to the Member State of the notification referred to in paragraph 1 or of the communication referred to in paragraph 4. This request must be justified on the basis of considerations relating to the competition rules of the Treaty.

6. The Commission may withdraw the opposition to the exemption at any time. However, where the opposition was raised at the request of a Member State and this request is maintained, it may be withdrawn only after consultation of the Advisory Committee on Restrictive Practices and Dominant Positions.

7. If the opposition is withdrawn because the undertakings concerned have shown that the conditions of Article 85(3) are satisfied, the exemption shall apply from the date of notification.

8. If the opposition is withdrawn because the undertakings concerned have amended the agreement so that the conditions of Article 85(3) are

satisfied, the exemption shall apply from the date on which the amendments take effect.

9.   If the Commission opposes exemption and the opposition is not withdrawn, the effects of the notification shall be governed by the provisions of Regulation No 17.

Article 5

1.   This Regulation shall not apply to:

   (1)   agreements between members of a patent or know-how pool which relate to the pooled technologies;

   (2)   licensing agreements between competing undertakings which hold interests in a joint venture, or between one of them and the joint venture, if the licensing agreements relate to the activities of the joint venture;

   (3)   agreements under which one party grants the other a patent and/or know-how licence and in exchange the other party, albeit in separate agreements or through connected undertakings, grants the first party a patent, trade mark or know-how licence or exclusive sales rights, where the parties are competitors in relation to the products covered by those agreements;

   (4)   licensing agreements containing provisions relating to intellectual property rights other than patents which are not ancillary;

   (5)   agreements entered into solely for the purpose of sale.

2.   This Regulation shall nevertheless apply:

   (1)   to agreements to which paragraph 1(2) applies, under which a parent undertaking grants the joint venture a patent or know-how licence, provided that the licensed products and the other goods and services of the participating undertakings which are considered by users to be interchangeable or substitutable in view of their characteristics, price and intended use represent:

   –   in case of a licence limited to production, not more than 20%, and

   –   in case of a licence covering production and distribution, not more than 10%;

   of the market for the licensed products and all interchangeable or substitutable goods and services;

   (2)   to agreements to which paragraph 1(1) applies and to reciprocal licences within the meaning of paragraph 1(3), provided the parties

are not subject to any territorial restriction within the common market with regard to the manufacture, use or putting on the market of the licensed products or to the use of the licensed or pooled technologies.

3. This Regulation shall continue to apply where, for two consecutive financial years, the market shares in paragraph 2(1) are not exceeded by more than one-tenth; where that limit is exceeded, this Regulation shall continue to apply for a period of six months from the end of the year in which the limit was exceeded.

Article 6

This Regulation shall also apply to:

(1)   agreements where the licensor is not the holder of the know-how or the patentee, but is authorised by the holder or the patentee to grant a licence;

(2)   assignments of know-how, patents or both where the risk associated with exploitation remains with the assignor, in particular where the sum payable in consideration of the assignment is dependent on the turnover obtained by the assignee in respect of products made using the know-how or the patents, the quantity of such products manufactured or the number of operations carried out employing the know-how or the patents;

(3)   licensing agreements in which the rights or obligations of the licensor or the licensee are assumed by undertakings connected with them.

Article 7

The Commission may withdraw the benefit of this Regulation, pursuant to Article 7 of Regulation No 19/65/EEC, where it finds in a particular case that an agreement exempted by this Regulation nevertheless has certain effects which are incompatible with the conditions laid down in Article 85(3) of the Treaty, and in particular where:

(1)   the effect of the agreement is to prevent the licensed products from being exposed to effective competition in the licensed territory from identical goods or services or from goods or services considered by users as interchangeable or substitutable in view of their characteristics, price and intended use, which may in particular occur where the licensee's market share exceeds 40%;

(2)   without prejudice to Article 1(1)(6), the licensee refuses, without any objectively justified reason, to meet unsolicited orders from users or resellers in the territory of other licensees;

(3)   the parties:

  (a)   without any objectively justified reason, refuse to meet orders from users or resellers in their respective territories who would market the products in other territories within the common market; or

  (b)   make it difficult for users or resellers to obtain the products from other resellers within the common market, and in particular where they exercise intellectual property rights or take measures so as to prevent resellers or users from obtaining outside, or from putting on the market in the licensed territory products which have been lawfully put on the market within the common market by the licensor or with his consent;

(4)   the parties were competing manufacturers at the date of the grant of the licence and obligations on the licensee to produce a minimum quantity or to use his best endeavours as referred to in Article 2(1), (9) and (17) respectively have the effect of preventing the licensee from using competing technologies.

Article 8

1.   For purposes of this Regulation:

  (a)   patent applications;

  (b)   utility models;

  (c)   applications for registration of utility models;

  (d)   topographies of semiconductor products;

  (e)   *certificats d'utilité* and *certificats d'addition* under French law;

  (f)   applications for *certificats d'utilité* and *certificats d'addition* under French law;

  (g)   supplementary protection certificates for medicinal products or other products for which such supplementary protection certificates may be obtained;

  (h)   plant breeder's certificates,

shall be deemed to be patents.

2.   This Regulation shall also apply to agreements relating to the exploitation of an invention if an application within the meaning of paragraph 1 is made in respect of the invention for a licensed territory after the date when the agreements were entered into but within the time limits set by the national law or the international convention to be applied.

3. This Regulation shall furthermore apply to pure patent or know-how licensing agreements or to mixed agreements whose initial duration is automatically prolonged by the inclusion of any new improvements, whether patented or not, communicated by the licensor, provided that the licensee has the right to refuse such improvements or each party has the right to terminate the agreement at the expiry of the initial term of an agreement and at least every three years thereafter.

Article 9

1. Information acquired pursuant to Article 4 shall be used only for the purposes of this Regulation.

2. The Commission and the authorities of the Member States, their officials and other servants shall not disclose information acquired by them pursuant to this Regulation of the kind covered by the obligation of professional secrecy.

3. The provisions of paragraphs 1 and 2 shall not prevent publication of general information or surveys which do not contain information relating to particular undertakings or associations of undertakings.

Article 10

For purposes of this Regulation:

(1) "know-how" means a body of technical information that is secret, substantial and identified in any appropriate form;

(2) "secret" means that the know-how package as a body or in the precise configuration and assembly of its components is not generally known or easily accessible, so that part of its value consists in the lead which the licensee gains when it is communicated to him; it is not limited to the narrow sense that each individual component of the know-how should be totally unknown or unobtainable outside the licensor's business;

(3) "substantial" means that the know-how includes information which must be useful, i.e. can reasonably be expected at the date of conclusion of the agreement to be capable of improving the competitive position of the licensee, for example by helping him to enter a new market or giving him an advantage in competition with other manufacturers or providers of services who do not have access to the licensed secret know-how or other comparable secret know-how;

(4) "identified" means that the know-how is described or recorded in such a manner as to make it possible to verify that it satisfies the criteria of secrecy and substantiality and to ensure that the licensee is not unduly restricted in his exploitation of his own technology. To be identified the know-how can either be set out in the licence agreement or in a separate

document or recorded in any other appropriate form at the latest when the know-how is transferred or shortly thereafter, provided that the separate document or other record can be made available if the need arises;

(5)   "necessary patents" are patents where a licence under the patent is necessary for the putting into effect of the licensed technology in so far as, in the absence of such a licence, the realisation of the licensed technology would not be possible or would be possible only to a lesser extent or in more difficult or costly conditions. Such patents must therefore be of technical, legal or economic interest to the licensee;

(6)   "licensing agreement" means pure patent licensing agreements and pure know-how licensing agreements as well as mixed patent and know-how licensing agreements;

(7)   "licensed technology" means the initial manufacturing know-how or the necessary product and process patents, or both, existing at the time the first licensing agreement is concluded, and improvements subsequently made to the know-how or patents, irrespective of whether and to what extent they are exploited by the parties or by other licensees;

(8)   "the licensed products" are goods or services the production or provision of which requires the use of the licensed technology;

(9)   "the licensee's market share" means the proportion which the licensed products and other goods or services provided by the licensee, which are considered by users to be interchangeable or substitutable for the licensed products in view of their characteristics, price and intended use, represent of the entire market for the licensed products and all other interchangeable or substitutable goods and services in the common market or a substantial part of it;

(10) "exploitation" refers to any use of the licensed technology in particular in the production, active or passive sales in a territory even if not coupled with manufacture in that territory, or leasing of the licensed products;

(11) "the licensed territory" is the territory covering all or at least part of the common market where the licensee is entitled to exploit the licensed technology;

(12) "territory of the licensor" means territories in which the licensor has not granted any licences for patents and/or know-how covered by the licensing agreement;

(13) "parallel patents" means patents which, in spite of the divergences which remain in the absence of any unification of national rules concerning industrial property, protect the same invention in various Member States;

(14) "connected undertakings" means:

- (a) undertakings in which a party to the agreement, directly or indirectly:

  - owns more than half the capital or business assets, or

  - has the power to exercise more than half the voting rights, or

  - has the power to appoint more than half the members of the supervisory board, board of directors or bodies legally representing the undertaking, or

  - has the right to manage the affairs of the undertaking;

- (b) undertakings which, directly or indirectly, have in or over a party to the agreement the rights or powers listed in (a);

- (c) undertakings in which an undertaking referred to in (b), directly or indirectly, has the rights or powers listed in (a);

- (d) undertakings in which the parties to the agreement or undertakings connected with them jointly have the rights or powers listed in (a): such jointly controlled undertakings are considered to be connected with each of the parties to the agreement;

(15) "ancillary provisions" are provisions relating to the exploitation of intellectual property rights other than patents, which contain no obligations restrictive of competition other than those also attached to the licensed know-how or patents and exempted under this Regulation;

(16) "obligation" means both contractual obligation and a concerted practice;

(17) "competing manufacturers" or manufacturers of "competing products" means manufacturers who sell products which, in view of their characteristics, price and intended use, are considered by users to be interchangeable or substitutable for the licensed products.

Article 11

1. Regulation (EEC) No 556/89 is hereby repealed with effect from 1 April 1996.

2. Regulation (EEC) No 2349/84 shall continue to apply until 31 March 1996.

3. The prohibition in Article 85(1) of the Treaty shall not apply to agreements in force on 31 March 1996 which fulfil the exemption requirements laid down by Regulations (EEC) No 2349/84 or (EEC) No 556/89.

Article 12

1.   The Commission shall undertake regular assessments of the application of this Regulation, and in particular of the opposition procedure provided for in Article 4.

2.   The Commission shall draw up a report on the operation of this Regulation before the end of the fourth year following its entry into force and shall, on that basis, assess whether any adaptation of the Regulation is desirable.

Article 13

This Regulation shall enter into force on 1 April 1996.

It shall apply until 31 March 2006.

Article 11(2) of this Regulation shall, however, enter into force on 1 January 1996.

This Regulation shall be binding in its entirety and directly applicable in all Member States.

Done at Brussels 31 January 1996

3.   Block exemption text: EEA version

The EEA version of the technology transfer block exemption came into force on 1 April 1997. Attached is a copy of the adaptations which should be read in conjunction with the EC block exemption. There is no full text of the EEA version.

Annex XIV to the EEA Agreement

Technology Transfer Agreements

The provisions of the Regulation shall, for the purposes of the Agreement, be read with the following adaptations:

(a)   In **Article 1(4)** the term "Member States" shall read "EC Member States or EFTA States".

(b)   In **Article 1(4)**, the phrase "on condition that the agreements in question are notified to the Commission in accordance with the provisions of Articles 1, 2 and 3 of Regulation (EC) No 3385/94 and that the Commission does not oppose such exemption within a period of four months" shall read "on condition that agreements in question are notified to the EC Commission or the EFTA Surveillance Authority in accordance with Articles 1, 2 and 3 of Regulation (EC) No 3385/94, and the corresponding provisions envisaged in Protocol 21 to the EEA Agreement and Chapter III of Protocol 4 to the Agreement on the Establishment of a Surveillance Authority and a Court of Justice, and that the competent surveillance authority does not oppose such exemption within a period of four months."

(c) In **Article 4(3)**, the phrase "in accordance with Article 4 of Regulation (EC) No 3385/94" shall read "in accordance with Article 4 of Regulation (EC) No 3385/94, and the corresponding provisions envisaged in Protocol 21 to the EEA Agreement and Chapter III of Protocol 4 to the Agreement on the Establishment of a Surveillance Authority and a Court of Justice".

(d) In **Article 4(5)**, the second sentence shall be replaced by the following:

"It shall oppose exemption if it receives a request to do so from a State falling within its competence within two months of the transmission to the States of the notification referred to in paragraph 1 or of the communication referred to in paragraph 4."

(e) In **Article 4(6)** the second sentence shall be replaced by the following:

"However, where the opposition was raised at the request of a State falling within its competence and this request is maintained, it may be withdrawn only after consultation of its Advisory Committee on Restrictive Practices and Dominant Position."

(f) The following shall be added at the end of **Article 4(9)**:

"or the corresponding provisions in Protocol 21 to the EEA Agreement and Chapter II of Protocol 4 of the Agreement on the Establishment of a Surveillance Authority and a Court of Justice."

(g) In **Article 7**, introductory paragraph, the phrase "pursuant to Article 7 of Regulation No 19/65/EEC" shall read "either on its own initiative or at the request of the other surveillance authority or a State falling within its competence or of natural or legal persons claiming a legitimate interest;"

(h) The following paragraph shall be added at the end of **Article 7**:

"The competent authority may in such cases issue a decision in accordance with Articles 6 and 8 of Regulation (EEC) No 17/62 or the corresponding provisions in Protocol 21 to the EEA Agreement and Chapter II of Protocol 4 to the Agreement on the Establishment of a Surveillance Authority and a Court of Justice, without any prior notification being required."

(i) In **Article 10(13)**, the term "Member States" shall read "EC Member State or EFTA State".

Part 3

· Analysis ·

1. Introduction

1.1 Commission Regulation 240/96 of 31 January 1996 ("the Regulation" or occasionally the "Technology Regulation" where necessary to avoid confusion with other regulations) provides a block exemption for a defined category of technology transfer agreements. Any agreement which satisfies the criteria for applicability of the Regulation will be deemed to benefit from an automatic exemption from the prohibition of Article 85(1) of the Treaty. The justification for this automatic exemption is that such agreements can be assumed to satisfy the criteria laid down in Article 85(3) *i.e.* to result in certain improvements from which consumers derive a fair share of the benefits without containing any excessive restrictions or leading to an undue restriction of competition.

1.2 Although there is no obligation to follow the Technology Regulation when drafting a technology licence within the EU (see the discussion in the **Commentary Section 7**, below) it is likely, for a range of reasons, that the Regulation will significantly influence the structure and content of many such agreements. For this reason an understanding of the provisions and philosophy of the Regulation is extremely important.

1.3 A further point to bear in mind when reading the Analysis Section is that references throughout, consistent with the wording of the Regulation itself, are to the EU, the common market and to the Member States of the Community. There is, however, an agreement between the EU and the remaining Member States of EFTA (Norway, Iceland and Liechtenstein) who together comprise the European Economic Area ("the EEA"). Under the EEA Agreement, the Technology Regulation now applies across all 18 Member States of the EEA and therefore all references in the text to the common market or to Member States should be understood to refer to all 18 of the EEA Member States. There is no consolidated text of a regulation for the EFTA States but an Annex to the EEA Agreement showing the relatively minor amendments to the Technology Regulation is attached after the text of the Regulation at page 34, above.

1.4 The substantive law is therefore the same whether one is dealing with an agreement between a licensor in the United Kingdom and a licensee in Spain or between a Norwegian licensor and his Icelandic licensee. If an agreement is drafted to comply with the wording of the block exemption, the parties will not have to concern themselves with whether in fact an agreement has an effect on trade within the EU, just within EFTA or between certain EU and EFTA states. On the other hand, if they wish to draft an agreement falling outside the Regulation they will need to consider the other issues raised in this book, such as whether the agreement could be caught by Article 85 of the Treaty because it has an effect on trade between Member States or whether it might be caught by the matching provision of Article 53 of the EEA Treaty, which deals with agreements having effects between EFTA Member States or between EFTA and EU Member States. Finally, if they wish to notify an agreement for exemption they will need to consider whether it is the European Commission or the EFTA Surveillance Authority which has jurisdiction but the requirements, procedures and consequences of notification will be similar if not identical.

2. **Key elements**

The key criteria for application of the Regulation are as follows:

- The licence must be a technology transfer agreement. This term, which is not itself defined in the Regulation, is a convenient shorthand to cover agreements relating to the licensing of either patents or know-how. This reflects the fact that the Regulation replaces two earlier regulations which dealt separately with patent licences and know-how licences: the Patent Regulation and the Know-how Regulation (for a discussion of the principal differences between these regulations and the Technology Regulation see **Commentary Section 10**).
- Only two undertakings may be a party to the licence.
- The licence will normally contain at least one of the obligations listed in Article 1.1 of the Regulation, or a provision of that type with a more limited scope.
- The licence may additionally include further restrictions of the type identified in Article 2.1 of the Regulation.
- The exemption will not apply if the licence contains one or more of the restrictions identified in Article 3 of the Regulation

and neither will it apply to the types of agreement identified in Article 5.1.

- Even if all of the above conditions are satisfied, the Commission still reserves the right to withdraw the benefit of the Regulation in particular circumstances.

3. **Recitals**

3.1 As for all Commission block exemption regulations, the Recitals form an important part of the Regulation. As well as explaining the purpose and context of the Regulation, they are of considerable benefit in interpreting the substantive provisions of the Regulation. For instance, Recital 8 clarifies that the Regulation applies to agreements which facilitate the provision of services as well as the production of goods: thus a licence to exploit a process to purify water would be covered in the same way as a licence for the production of water purification tablets. Where appropriate when discussing the Articles of the Regulation, reference will be made to the corresponding Recitals.

3.2 It also important to point out that the interpretation of Commission regulations cannot be approached in the same way as one would interpret national law. Commission drafting is not always as precise as one might wish. Terminology is sometimes used loosely and inconsistently; defined terms are not always followed slavishly. It is therefore always important to bear in mind the overall purpose and context of the Regulation, which can be derived in part from the Recitals. It is also advisable to take some time to read the Regulation as a whole from start to finish, so as to get a feel for the structure and some appreciation of the inter-relationship between various clauses and recitals.

The Exemption – key criteria (Art 1)

4. Type of agreement

4.1 Article 1.1 is the basis for the exemption granted by the Regulation. It fulfils two main functions:

- it sets out the basic criteria which a qualifying agreement must satisfy in order to be eligible for exemption;
- it lists the eight key restrictions of competition, some or all of which might be expected to appear in a technology licensing regulation, and which are specifically granted an exemption.

4.2 Article 1.1 provides that Article 85(1) of the Treaty shall not apply to agreements which fall within the Regulation. The exemption covers:

- pure patent licensing agreements;
- pure know-how licensing agreements; and
- mixed patent and know-how licensing agreements.

These terms are defined in Recital 4 and by reference to the definitions in Article 10.

4.3 Recital 4 explains that a pure patent licensing agreement is one for the licensing of Member State patents, Community patents and European patents.* The definition of what constitutes a patent for the purposes of the Regulation is surprisingly wide and is defined in Article 8 to include topographies of semiconductor products and plant breeders' certificates. A pure know-how licensing agreement is one relating to non-patented technical information. In order for an agreement to qualify as a know-how licence it must meet the criteria of the definitions in Article 10, which require that there be a body of technical information which is secret, substantial and identified, which terms are further defined in that Article. (For a more detailed discussion see **Commentary Section 8.4.**) A combined patent and know-how agreement is described as a mixed agreement.

4.4 Recital 5 provides a further definition of what is meant by a patent or know-how licensing agreement. These are defined as agreements whereby one undertaking which holds a patent or owns know-how, permits another to exploit it for the purposes of manufacture, use or putting certain goods on the market or providing certain services. This ties in with the clear statement in Article 5.1(5) that licences granted to allow only sale rather than manufacture are not exempted (see **Section 14.5**).

4.5 In addition to provisions relating to the patents and know-how, Article 1.1 provides that such agreements may contain ancillary provisions relating to intellectual property rights other than patents. These are defined in Article 10(15) as provisions which contain obligations no more restrictive than those already permitted in respect

---

*The reference to Member State patents is self explanatory. "European Patents" are those granted under the 1973 Convention of European Patents and could include territories outside the EU. In 1989 the then EU Member States concluded an Agreement to that effect that, with certain exceptions, "European Patents" for the Member States should be re-designated as "Community Patents" having uniform effect throughout the relevant territories and capable of being granted, transferred or revoked only in respect of those territories.

of the know-how and patents. For example, an obligation to affix the trade mark only to goods manufactured according to the specifications does not involve a further restriction beyond that which already arises from the duty to adhere to those specifications (see further discussion in **Commentary Section 8.5**).

4.6 Finally, there is no definition in the Regulation of what is meant by an "agreement". It is clear from prior case law that for the purposes of EU competition law an agreement can be oral or in writing and could comprise a mere understanding between the parties (see discussion in the Introduction). Therefore a technology licence could comprise a number of documents (as long as they are only between the same two parties, see **Section 5**, below) as well as any other evidence which can be produced of the understanding reached between the parties. The definition of the "agreement" would certainly include any side letters, so there is no benefit in moving sensitive or restrictive provisions into side letters in order to try to claim that the "public" version of the agreement complies with the Regulation.

4.7 When it comes to drafting an agreement, if you wish to avoid the allegation that there are any other restrictions forming part of the overall arrangement (either for simple commercial reasons or because you do not want to risk the agreement then falling outside the Regulation) it would be wise to include an "entire agreement" clause in the principal document.

5.   **Only two undertakings**

5.1 The next criterion in Article 1.1 is that an exempt agreement may include no more than two *undertakings*. The Regulation itself contains no definition of an undertaking but case law on Article 85 has confirmed that it refers to a single economic entity so that a parent and subsidiary, two sister companies or two individuals working in partnership would be treated as a single undertaking. Article 10(14) contains a definition of "collective undertaking" which corresponds to the normal definition of companies forming part of a single group.

5.2 The requirement that there should be no more than two undertakings does not prevent a licensor concluding a number of distinct agreements with individual licensees. These may be in standard form and it is clear that Licensee A may conclude an agreement in full knowledge of the terms of an earlier agreement concluded with

Licensee B. It is also implicit in the Regulation (*e.g.* Recital 15) that Licensee A may be relying upon the fact that the licensor will enforce certain territorial restrictions against Licensee B (but note the limitations discussed in **Section 8.6**, below). There would be a risk if the parties went further, so that Licensee A and Licensee B were effectively negotiating the terms to be inserted in each other's licences, that the whole would be treated as a tripartite arrangement and both licences would fall outside the Regulation.

5.3 Special rules apply if the parties are involved in a patent pool or one of the parties is a joint venture company (see **Section 14**, below).

6. Essential restrictions

6.1 Finally, for the exemption in Article 1.1 to apply to the agreement as a whole, it is stated that the agreement should include one or more of the restrictions (referred to in the Regulation as "obligations") listed in **Section 8**, below.

6.2 This requirement follows from Regulation 19/65 which, as Recital 1 relates, empowers the Commission to grant block exemptions to certain categories of agreements which "include restrictions imposed in relation to acquisition or use of industrial property rights". It also provides that any block exemption regulation must specify the clauses which must be contained in the agreements. Therefore, one would assume that if the agreement does not contain any of the restrictions listed in Article 1.1 it cannot benefit from the block exemption, even if it is less restrictive of competition than other agreements which are exempt. However, this pre-condition is qualified by Article 1.5, which provides that the exemption "shall also apply" where the parties accept restrictions of the type listed but with a more limited scope than permitted by that paragraph. This significantly qualifies the requirement to include one of those restrictions and probably means in effect that any agreement which satisfies the definition of a technology licensing agreement will, even if it contains nothing resembling a restriction of competition, be covered by the block exemption for the avoidance of doubt.

6.3 Moreover, given that Article 2.2 and 2.3 extend the exemption to cover provisions of the type listed in Article 2.1 even if not accompanied by an Article 1 restriction, the Regulation is clearly extremely flexible. It might be possible to imagine circumstances in which an agreement would still infringe Article 85 while containing no provisions falling within the scope of Articles 1, 2 or 3, but the likelihood of such an agreement being commercially attractive must be extremely remote.

6.4 Article 10(16) has a definition of "obligation" as meaning both a contractual obligation (it is unfortunate that the Commission uses the term in order to define itself) and a concerted practice. In fact it will be seen from the discussion of the specific permitted restrictions below, that most of them will by their nature need to be spelt out in the contract. However, to the extent that they may not have been incorporated into a written agreement, Article 10(16) confirms that any such restrictions which arise from a simple understanding between the parties will also be covered by the exemption (see **Section 4.7**, above on the advisability of "entire agreement" clauses).

7.   Summary

- If the agreement contains one of the restrictions which appears in Article 1 or a provision of a similar type but a more limited scope, the exemption is capable of applying to the agreement as a whole.
- If the agreement does not contain an Article 1 type restriction, the exemption will still apply to any restrictions of the type listed in Article 2.
- If the agreement contains restrictions falling with Article 1 and also restrictions of competition of a type not covered by Article 1 or 2, the block exemption will not automatically apply but it will be possible to use the opposition procedure under Article 4 (see below) as long as the agreement does not contain any restrictions of the type identified in Article 3 (the "Black List").
- If the agreement contains one or more of the restrictions of the type black-listed in Article 3, the block exemption will not apply and the opposition procedure will not be available and the only possibility for exemption is by way of individual notification (see **Commentary Section 7**).

8.   Permitted restrictions

Article 1.1 lists eight restrictions, any one or more of which may be included in an exempt agreement. It is also important to consider

Article 1.2, 1.3 and 1.4 (dealt with below) which place limits on the duration of these restrictions. The eight restrictions (some of which are paraphrased slightly in the headings below: always refer to the full text of the Regulation on pages 14-34) are as follows:

8.1 Restriction I

An obligation on the licensor not to license other undertakings to exploit the licensed technology in the licensed territory (Art 1.1(1))

A licensee who is granted a territory within which to exploit the licensed technology will often want a degree of exclusivity to encourage him to invest. Community law recognises that particularly where the agreement involves the introduction of new technology and significant investment, an exclusive licence may not be incompatible with Article 85(1) *i.e.* it may not require exemption. This is underlined in Recital 10 (and see discussion in **Commentary Section 2**). However, given the inevitable uncertainty as to whether an agreement satisfies these criteria of novelty and risk, the grant of exclusivity has often required an individual exemption (see *Jus-rol*, **Case Note** 8) and is specifically exempted by Article 1.1(1).

The scope of the restriction is clarified in Article 10(10), which defines exploitation as any use of the licensed technology including production and sale (whether active or passive) or leasing of products. The definition of "exploitation" is a key definition when it comes to understanding the other restrictions which may be imposed. The effect is that the licensor may not license others to engage in these activities in the licensee's exclusive territory but there are still limits on how far the licensor may go to *prevent* other licensees selling into that territory (see **Section 9.5**).

It is extremely important to understand the limitations on the scope of this restriction. The licensor may agree not to grant to any other person a licence to work the patent so as to manufacture the products (or carry out the process) within the licensed territory. It follows logically that he will not grant one of his other licensees, who may be manufacturing in another territory, a specific "licence" to sell those products in the territory of the first licensee. However, as a matter of Community law (under Arts 30-36 of the Treaty), where products have been lawfully put on the market anywhere in the European Union they will be capable of being sold by a third party, such as a parallel importer, into the licensed territory without the need for any further permission from the licensor. This stems from the principle of "exhaustion of rights" under which an owner of intellectual property is entitled to assert his right to benefit from the monopoly conferred by that intellectual property by authorising the first manufacture or sale of the products within the European Union but is not allowed to enforce those rights so as to prevent any subsequent sales. This principle is reinforced in competition law by a prohibition on contractual attempts to prevent or deter any parallel sales. Therefore, although not expected actively to encourage encroachment by third parties on the exclusive territory allocated to the licensee, the licensor may not take steps to prevent it (see for instance the prohibition in Art 3(3)(b)). The furthest he may go are the active/passive restrictions discussed below in relation to Article 1.1(5) and (6).

8.2 Restriction II

An obligation on the licensor not to exploit the licensed technology in the licensed territory himself (Art 1.1(2))

The licensor may be placed under an obligation not to manufacture the goods, provide the service or in any other way work the licensed technology in the licensee's territory and neither may he sell into the licensed territory any goods or supply any services which utilise that technology. As mentioned above, Recital 10 confirms that such exclusivity may not require exemption in all cases but is covered for the avoidance of doubt. However, there is again a limitation imposed by Community law, in that the exemption of this restriction does not mean that the licensor can be prevented from selling the goods or providing the services to persons situated *outside* the confines of the licensee's territory, even if he knows they intend to import the goods or the benefits of those services into the licensed territory.

8.3 Restriction III

An obligation on the licensee not to exploit the licensed technology in the territory of the licensor within the common market (Art 1.1(3))

Article 1.1(3) is the counterpart of the obligation in Article 1.1(2) and prevents the licensee either working the technology or selling the goods into any territory which the licensor has reserved to himself. The fact that the licensee could not have engaged in these activities at all without the licence has not prevented the Commission ruling that the limitation of the licence requires exemption (see *Jus-rol*, **Case Note 8**). The licensor would normally want the reserved territory to be defined in his licence as the whole world, less those parts which are the subject of other licences. The definition of "territory reserved to the licensor" in Article 10(12) contains a minor improvement on the corresponding provision in the Know-how Regulation: defining it as all territories in which he has not granted a licence but not requiring him to have expressly reserved those territories to himself. In practice he would probably make an express reservation so as to make clear the scope of the restrictions.

However, it is unfortunate that Article 1.1.(3) is qualified by a reference to the common market. In most cases a restriction upon the licensee manufacturing in or selling into territories outside the common market is unlikely to involve an appreciable restriction of competition within the common market or to harm trade between Member States and therefore one can take the view that it does not need an exemption (see *Schlegel*, **Case Note 4**). Nevertheless, it is perfectly foreseeable that the licensor might want to prevent the licensee from selling products into a territory adjoining the common market which the licensor had reserved to himself, and that this could have an indirect effect on trade within the common market. For instance, if his reserved territory included Switzerland as well as Italy and Germany, a licensee might later claim that the restriction on selling into Switzerland where prices happen to be low was preventing those goods from being purchased and then resold into France from which they would then be further sold into other Member States.

It would be an absurd result if the consequence of extending the prohibition to cover a territory outside the common market, were that the benefit of the block exemption were lost and one had to utilise the opposition procedure (see **Section 13**, below). However, this does appear to be the consequence if the restriction on sales into a part of the licensor's territory outside the common market could be argued to have an effect on trade and competition within the EU. It does not seem possible to argue that the prohibition comes within the "safety net" provision of Article 1.5, since it is difficult to argue that this would constitute a clause with a "more limited scope": on the contrary, the "scope" is clearly wider in geographical terms than the exemption in Article 1.1(3) permits. There is also a clear conflict with Recital 7. This states that the inclusion of restrictions relating to countries outside the common market does not itself prevent the Regulation from applying to those restrictions which relate to territories within the common market (but see **Commentary Section 8.1**). It does go on to say that where agreements are concluded for territories which extend beyond the frontiers of the Community but have effects within the common market, then such agreements "<u>should</u> be covered by the Regulation to the same extent as would agreements for territories within the common market". This strongly suggests therefore that the exemption, to the extent it is needed, is intended to apply for the benefit of the entire territory whether within or outside the common market (and, logically, all of the "territories" whether of the licensor, licensee or other licensees) but this still does not explain why the Commission thought it necessary to insert the qualification in Article 1.1(3). Some clarification by the Commission or European Court would be welcome.

A further point to make is that the corresponding obligation upon the *licensor* in Article 1.1(2) does not include this reference to the common market, even though it appears from the definition of "licensed territory" in Article 10(11) that the territory licensed to the licensee could include countries both within and outside the common market. All that one can do is point out this inconsistency so that the parties can consider, in the circumstances, whether they might feel happier seeking the security of the opposition procedure.

8.4 Restriction IV

An obligation on the licensee not to manufacture or use the licensed product or process in territories within the common market which are licensed to other licensees (Art 1.1(4))

This provision appears quite straightforward. It is directed only towards a prohibition on those types of exploitation which involve use of the licensed technology. It does not itself exempt a prohibition of products on sale into the territories of other licensees (for which, see Restrictions V and VI, below).

It is important to emphasise that the licensor would in any event, where patents are concerned, be able to exercise those patent rights to prevent their infringement by the licensee outside the territory which has been licensed, against any use or processing which would constitute an infringing act under the law of the relevant country. Therefore, although this provision allows a direct contractual remedy rather than having to rely on the patent rights themselves, it does not add any appreciable restriction of competition. The same can be argued in respect of the know-how, to the extent that the licensee was not in a position prior to the agreement to exploit the know-how at all and therefore this provision amounts simply to a limitation of the grant, rather than a fetter on a pre-existing possibility of competing. It is therefore far less likely that such a prohibition in relation to territories outside the common market would be viewed as an appreciable restriction of competition, so that the problems identified above in relation to Article 1.1(3) may be even less likely to arise.

8.5 Restriction V

An obligation on the licensee not to pursue an active sales policy in relation to the licensed product (including advertising, branches or distribution depots) within territories within the common market which are licensed to other licensees (Art 1.1(5))

The Commission recognises an important distinction between *active* and *passive* selling, which appears in a number of other block exemption regulations and was in the previous Patent and Know-how Regulations. The terms active and passive (which are not properly defined in the Regulation) are understood to distinguish between situations where the vendor has taken steps to encourage sales or publicise the availability of products, as opposed to simply responding to unsolicited orders. (See above under Restriction III for discussion of the significance of the reference to "territories within the common market".) Restrictions on active selling are invariably accepted as deserving exemption (see *Mitchell Cotts*, **Case Note 6**).

A recurring difficulty is that the dividing line between active and passive sales activity can often be hard to identify. Article 1.1(5) gives examples of active sales activities and provides that the licensee can be prevented from engaging in advertising aimed at the territories of other licensees, from establishing a branch or maintaining a distribution depot. Those examples have been in block exemption regulations for over 30 years. However, they are becoming increasingly anachronistic, referring as they do to a time when the common market itself was not so integrated and when "selling" was much more closely linked to a physical presence. Nowadays, with developments including increases in cross frontier broadcasting and the use of the Internet, it is far harder to determine when a "domestic" sales activity might stray into international sales activity. For instance, if a UK licensee sets up a web site accessible from anywhere in the world which includes its sales prices and details of how to order, is it engaging in active sales efforts merely because it takes no steps to prevent Irish or French potential customers from accessing that information? Would adding to the site a page in French go too far, even if it were claimed that it were intended for the benefit of French speaking customers resident in the United Kingdom? If not, does the licensee step over the line if it has a French affiliate which, within its own marketing literature, includes the web site address at which information on UK terms and prices can be found? Certainly it is not unknown for licensors to prohibit <u>any</u> internet advertising, on the basis that it has no territorial boundaries and must therefore inevitably infringe the active sales prohibition.

It must be obvious that there are many opportunities for a licensee to undermine the protection which appears to be conferred on other licensees by the active sales ban. There could be some debate over whether a single act is evidence of a sales "policy" (see **Section 8.6**, below). Even if the licensee is wholly "innocent", there will be many situations where the market is relatively mature and where potential customers in the territory of one licensee are sufficiently sophisticated to know where there exist other licensees from whom better terms might be available. Without needing to be targeted by an unscrupulous licensee they will be able to seek out and place orders with those other licensees for delivery direct to them. In partial recognition of this problem, the Commission has permitted the following additional restriction.

8.6 Restriction VI

An obligation on the licensee not to put the licensed product on the market in territories licensed to other licensees within the common market in response to unsolicited orders (Art 1.1(6))

Recitals 11 and 15 refer to this clause as granting an exemption for a prohibition on *passive* competition. The licensee may be <u>absolutely</u> prohibited, for a short period governed by Article 1.2-1.4, from delivering the product to customers located in the territory of other licensees within the common market. (See above under Restriction III for discussion of the significance of the reference to "territories within the common market".)

A curiosity of the drafting of this provision is the addition of the words "in response to unsolicited orders". This wording did not appear in the corresponding provisions of the Patent or Know-how Regulations and has not been well thought through. The words are at best unnecessary and at worst counter-productive. It would have been preferable to omit those words and to distinguish between Article 1.1(5) and (6) solely by reference to their permitted durations in Article 1.2-1.4. However, the effect of adding these words is to limit the absolute prohibition (on selling into the territories of other licensees for a five-year period) to circumstances where the particular order is an unsolicited one.

It is possible that the licensee might have solicited such an order without that conduct being sufficient to breach the Article 1.1(5) prohibition on pursuing an "active policy of putting the licensed product on the market in the territories ... licensed to other licensees". For instance, a one-off approach to a customer in the territory of another licensee would be a solicitation but might fall short of being the "pursuit of an active policy". It might even have been made inadvertently; for instance because the licensee did not know that the customer was located in the territory of another licensee or did not know that the territory concerned had recently been the subject of a new licence agreement. The Commission will probably want to leave it to the national courts to establish common-sense guidelines as to when a licensee knew or should have known that he was encroaching. The Commission may well argue against an over-literal approach to interpretation of this provision. However, those courts may assume that, as the words have been added in this Regulation, they were intended in some way to limit the exemption to which they refer.

A further question which arises in relation to both Article 1.1(5) and (6), is whether the licensor can be obliged to agree to impose matching restrictions in contracts which he concludes with other licensees (which seems to have been the case in *Boussois*, **Case Note 7**). It could be said that this is a restriction of competition upon the licensor which is not specifically permitted anywhere else in the Regulation. However, the entire scheme of the Regulation appears to assume that such obligations will be reciprocal, even though each licensee will have (and can have: see **Section 5.2**, above) no direct contractual right as against other licensees and will have to rely on the licensor to enforce the agreement. It is also arguable that Article 2.1(10), which allows an obligation on the licensor to grant the licensee the benefit of any more favourable terms that he may grant to other licensees, should be sensibly interpreted to require the licensor to impose (and even take reasonable steps in good faith to enforce) matching obligations.

Having said that, there has been at least one example of the Commission objecting in the past (in the context of an exclusive distribution agreement but the principle is the same) to attempts by a distributor to insist that the supplier impose upon its other distributors a restriction on active sales into the distributor's territory. Therefore, given the doubt which must remain and the unacceptable, even if very slight, risk of losing the benefit of the entire exemption, the best solution (by extension from Art 2.1(10)) for those advising a licensee, may be to insert wording as follows:

> "In the event that the licensor should grant a further licence to a licensee which does not contain provisions to the effect of clauses [(*) and (*): those imposing the active and passive sales bans] then the licensor shall immediately inform the licensee of that fact and the licensee shall thereafter cease to be bound by those clauses."

8.7 Restriction VII

An obligation on the licensee to use only the licensor's trade mark or get up to distinguish the product during the term of the agreement, provided that the licensee is not prevented from identifying himself as the manufacturer (Art 1.1(7))

This provision is again fairly straightforward. It also contains some further unnecessary wording (how one wishes the Commission had taken time for one more draft) with the qualification that the restriction applies only "during the term of the agreement". In fact it is clear that all of the restrictions in Article 1 and elsewhere are, unless clearly provided to the contrary, only permitted during the life of the agreement. On the other hand, after termination the licensor would be able to rely on his trade mark rights to prevent infringement, just as he would rely either on his patent rights or on the confidentiality agreement in relation to the know-how, to prevent further manufacture by the licensee (as to which see Art 2.1(3) below).

The main point to bear in mind, is that this restriction is only permitted in the context of a technology transfer agreement and it does not grant an exemption to a simple trade mark licence. There should be no objection to having the trade mark provisions in a separate trade mark licence agreement between the parties, if that is administratively convenient, perhaps for registration or other purposes. A straightforward obligation to apply the trade mark to the licensed products would fall within the definition of "ancillary" restrictions but care does have to be taken to ensure that no other restrictions are added which would not be viewed as ancillary (see discussion in **Commentary Section 8.5**, below).

8.8 Restriction VIII

An obligation on the licensee to limit production to quantities required for manufacture of his own products and to sell the product only as an integral part of, replacement part or accessory to his own products as long as the licensee is free to determine the quantities (Art 1.1(8))

Article 1.1(8) caters for a situation where the licence has only been granted in order to allow the licensee to produce components or accessories for his own products but not to allow him to set himself up as a separate source of supply of the components alone. It should be contrasted with the other permitted restriction in Article 2.1(13) and the prohibition in Article 3(4).

The question that arises is in what circumstances may the licensor limit the quantities that the licensee is able to produce. Article 1.1(8) states that the licensee may be limited to those quantities which he requires as components for the manufacture of his own products but stipulates that the licensee must still be free to determine the quantities. However, Article 2.1(13) allows the licensee to be limited to the supply of "only a limited quantity" of the licensed product to a particular customer where the licence was only granted so as to allow that customer a second source of supply and it goes on to state that "this provision shall also apply where the customer is the licensee". There seems to be a conflict here. Article 1.1(8) is granting an *exemption* subject to a limitation, whereas Article 2.1(13) seems to be saying that the limitation itself may fall within a class of restrictions which do not infringe Article 85.

As it is the exempting provision, one would normally expect Article 1.1(8) to take precedence, so that where the licensee is manufacturing only to provide an input for his own production and is not also purchasing from the licensor (*i.e.* his own production is not a *second* source), then the quantities cannot be limited. On the other hand, where he is purchasing from the licensor (or possibly another licensee) and has been granted the licence only so as to give him a second source of supply, then a ceiling may be placed on the quantities to be produced, without that restriction infringing Article 85 at all or depriving the agreement of the benefit of the exemption in Article 1.1(8).

9. **Duration of restrictions**

As mentioned above, all of the restrictions in Article 1.1 are subject to
limited durations the observance of which is essential (for a rare case on
similar block exemption provisions see *Pilkington,* **Case Note 12**).

9.1 Patent licences

Article 1.2 introduces the general limitation that where the agreement is
a pure patent licence, the restrictions in Article 1.1 may only be
imposed to the extent that and for so long as the licensed product is
protected by parallel patents (see definition in Art 10(13)) in the
territory in which the obligation would be enforced (see *Velcro,* **Case
Note 10**). This is clarified by Recital 12. It also follows from the
definition of the "licensed technology" in Article 10(7) that the patents
relied on must be ones which are "necessary" for proper exploitation of
the licensed process (see **Commentary Section 8.5**).

An exception to the general rule that a restriction may be enforced
for the life of the patent, is that the restriction on passive sales by
licensees (in Art 1.1(6)) is limited under Article 1.2 to five years from
first sale (Art 1.1(6) and Recital 15 refer to "putting on the market") of
the product in the common market by one of the licensees (meaning one
can ignore earlier sales by the licensor or any other party). An interesting
question is whether this means any sale of the product by a licensee even
if he has not manufactured it or whether it refers only to the first sale of
a product which had been manufactured in the common market by a
licensee. There are good arguments for it being the latter, if the intention
is to encourage dissemination of technology within the common market.
Otherwise, if Company A in France has been buying and distributing
the products for a few years from a licensee based outside the EEA and
then manages to persuade the owner of the technology that he should
grant Company A a licence to manufacture, and this is swiftly followed
by a licence to Company B for the Netherlands, both A and B may find
that the permitted duration of the passive sales ban has already expired.
It might therefore make sense to read Article 1.2 as referring to the first
sale by a common market licensee following his appointment as a
licensee. That would still mean that if, having concluded a licence
agreement, he were purchasing and reselling products supplied by the
licensor while gearing up his own production, time would start running
against him but that is at least more under his control.

A final argument in favour of this interpretation, is the Commission's use of the words "is first put" rather than "was first put", which indicates that the Commission is looking forward from the date of the appointment of the licensee. In terms of arguments on interpretation that is clearly scraping the bottom of the barrel. It would also be extremely serious to get the wrong answer, as Article 3.7 black-lists the prolongation of any of the main territorial restrictions beyond the periods expressly exempted. This is another area where clarification is needed and where pending such clarification formal notification may be required.

9.2 Know-how licences

As for patent licences, the Article 1.1(6) restriction on passive sales by licensees of know-how can only run for five years from first sale in the common market by one of the licensees (Art 1.3). All of the other permitted territorial restrictions (those in Art 1.1(1)-(5)) are limited to a period of 10 years from that first sale.

The justification given in Recital 13 for having a shorter protection period for know-how is that it can be difficult to determine when it ceases to be secret. Applying the same logic as argued in relation to patents above, this should mean that the 10-year period could not begin to run until the licensor had appointed a licensee (probably one based within the common market) who was selling the products within the common market. It is possible that a licensor might appoint only one licensee, who was based outside the common market, and wish to reserve the whole of the common market to himself. Assuming that Article 85 could still apply to the ban on selling into the EU, one would get into the interesting argument (if the proposition in Section 9.1, above is correct) that the licensor could not rely on the Technology Regulation to prevent that licensee selling a batch of the products into the common market because the 10- year period would not have begun to run. The better view must be that one reads the duration provision as referring to a continuous period beginning with the date of the first agreement and only ending 10 years after any common market sale by a common market licensee, if such a sale ever takes place, rather than a fixed five or 10-year period which only begins running from such a sale. Until these issues are clarified by the Commission or a court, it will probably be necessary to notify agreements where products manufactured by non-EEA licensees have already found their way onto the common market a significant period before the appointment of the first EEA licensee and where the full period of protection is required.

9.3 Mixed licences

The position for mixed licences is a combination of that which applies for patent and know-how licences as set out above. When relying on the patents, as long as they are "necessary patents" (see **Section 9.1**, above and the discussion in **Commentary Section 8.5**, below) the restrictions will be permitted for the life of the patents. Where it is only the know-how in respect of which restrictions are being enforced, it will be the know-how duration which applies.

For example: if the first licensee were appointed for Spain on 1 January 1999 and began selling the products on that day, the maximum duration of the passive sales restriction for both that licensee and all subsequent licensees within the EU, would be to 1 January 2004. Therefore, if a licensee were appointed for Germany in January 2004 he would find that he had no protection from passive competition from other well established licensees as from day one. The French licensee appointed in January 2009 would, if the agreement were a pure know-how licence, find that he could not benefit from any of the territorial restrictions and would face the risk of active competition from neighbouring licensees. Only by notifying all continuing licence agreements, could the licensor hope to be able to offer some territorial protection to new licensees.

9.4 Improvements

See **Section 12.7**, below for comments regarding the effect upon the permitted durations of any improvements to the licensed technology being added into the licence.

For convenience, the permitted duration of the various restrictions is set out in Table 1.

9.5 Duration generally

It is important to appreciate the significance of the way in which the Regulation limits the permitted duration of the restrictions. Article 1.2, 1.3 and 1.4 state on a number of occasions that "the *exemption* ... is granted for a period not exceeding [ ] years", or words to similar effect. They do not state that the *obligations* must be limited to any particular duration. If, therefore, a patent or know-how licence imposes a

Table 1

Duration of the obligations

	Pure Patent Licence (Article 1.2)	Mixed Licence (Article 1.4)	Pure Know-how licence (Article 1.3)
Article 1.1(1) – Licensor not license others	Life of patents in Licensee's territory	Life of *necessary* patents in the relevant territory *or* (*if no such patents*) as for pure know-how	10 years from first product sale by any licensee in common market
Article 1.1(2) – Licensor not exploit himself	Life of patents in Licensee's territory		
Article 1.1(3) – Licensee not exploit in Licensor's territory	Life of patents in Licensor's territory		
Article 1.1(4) – Licensee not manufacture in other licensees' territories	Life of patents in other licensees' territories		
Article 1.1(5) – Licensee no active selling			
Article 1.1(6) – Licensee no passive selling	5 years from first product sale by any licensee in common market		
Article 1.1(7) – Use of Licensor's trade mark	Life of patents in Licensee's territory	Life of *necessary* patents in licensed territory *or* as for pure know-how	Life of agreement so long as know-how secret and substantial
Article 1.1(8) – Limit Licensee's production			

restriction on passive sales for a period of 10 years, one might have assumed that the agreement would be exempt for the first five years and thereafter would require an individual exemption decision (see Recital 14). However, Article 3(7) states that the exemption "shall not apply" where one of the parties is "required for a period exceeding that referred to ... not to exploit the licensed technology in the territory of the other party or of other licensees". As a consequence, any attempt to impose obligations with a longer duration than specifically permitted by Article 1 will have the consequence that the exemption is disapplied *ab initio* and it will be necessary to notify from the outset in order to seek an individual exemption. That will be so even if it is merely possible that the restrictions might run on too long (see *Pasteur*, **Case Note 27**).

A possible way around this difficulty may be to draft the agreement so that the passive sales restriction applies for only five years, after which it will be automatically renewed for a further five years subject to the parties filing a notification at that point. However, that is not particularly attractive. If it is essential to have a 10-year passive sales ban, the parties will want to know from the outset that an exemption will be granted for that period. It is also easier to justify an exemption for a longer period if one is able to argue convincingly that otherwise the licence agreement will not be entered into at all.

A further qualification is imposed in Article 1.3 and 1.4 in relation to pure know-how licences and mixed licences. The starting point is that the exemption is only available where the know-how has been *identified* and where it remains *secret* and *substantial* (see **Commentary Section 8.4**). These criteria appear as defined terms in Article 10 and essentially the definitions require that the know-how should have some genuine commercial value so that the agreement is not a "sham", just as the patents must be *necessary* (see **Commentary Section 8.5**). It is clear from Article 1.3 that if at any time the know-how ceases to be secret and substantial, the exemption for the territorial restrictions will cease to apply even if this was through no fault of the licensor or resulted from disclosure by the licensee himself (see also comments on Art 2.1(7) and 2.1(15) below).

10. Further permitted restrictions – the White List (Art 2)

Article 2.1 lists a number of restrictions which the parties may wish to include in their agreement and which, although the Commission believes that they are generally not restrictive of competition, are also for the avoidance of doubt covered by the exemption. This is sometimes, though not universally, (some Commission officials use the term to cover the list of exempted provisions in Art 1) referred to as the "**White List**" so as to contrast it with the "**Black List**" in Article 3. For the sake of convenience that terminology is followed here. Recital 18 confirms that such provisions as appear in the White List are commonly found in licences and are not normally anti-competitive. It helpfully adds that this list of restrictions which do not infringe Article 85(1) is not exhaustive. Many of the provisions are uncontentious and require little comment.

10.1 Keeping know-how secret (Art 2.1(1))

The licensee may be subjected to a restriction on divulging "the know-how communicated by the licensor". The inclusion of the words "communicated by the licensor" is yet another example of loose drafting by the Commission, since the know-how could be communicated by a third party on the instructions of the licensor or by a connected undertaking (see Art 6(3) and Recital 9). What the Commission means to say is "the know-how which is the subject of the agreement". One might also argue, given that the list in Article 2.1 is non-exhaustive, that the same principle would apply to any restrictions on the *licensor* concerning disclosure of know-how passed back from the licensee to the licensor, (for instance, relating to improvements). In short, Article 2.1(1) indicates that any restrictions on disclosure of know-how which remains secret should not be viewed as restrictive of competition. It is also clear that in some cases the only way to ensure protection of the know-how will be by prohibiting competing activities, but that would require individual exemption (see *BNP*, **Case Note 30**).

The Commission also confirms that the non-disclosure obligation may continue after expiry of the agreement. This would in fact be true of many of the provisions in Article 2.1. If the Commission is right, at the beginning of Article 2.1 and in Recital 18, to categorise these provisions as ones that generally do not restrict competition (see *Delplanque*, **Case Note 1** and *Jus-rol*, **Case Note 8**), that should be equally true both during and after expiry of the agreement. Recital 20 refers to the post-term use ban in Article 2.1(3) as a normal feature to avoid a perpetual licence and the same must apply to a post-term disclosure ban. Recital 20 also refers to "termination" rather than "expiry" of the agreement and it must be clear that the licensor is able to prevent disclosure whether the agreement has run its natural term or has been terminated early. Finally, one would expect the same approach to be taken to a restriction upon the licensor disclosing the licensee's know-how (see comments above, p 57).

10.2 Sublicensing (Art 2.1(2))

A restriction on sublicensing or assigning is absolutely standard in the vast majority of technology licences and not viewed as anti-competitive (see *Delplanque*, **Case Note 1**). Indeed, given the risk that the proposed assignee might be a competitor for whom the exemption might not apply (see Art 3(4)), such a limitation is desirable for competition law as well as commercial reasons. Given that Article 2.3 allows the exemption to apply to clauses with a more limited scope, it would also be permissible to have a provision which does not absolutely prohibit sub-licences or assignments but makes them subject to prior approval by the licensor of the identity of the sub-licensee or assignee (see *Jus-rol*, **Case Note 8**).

We have discussed above in relation to Article 2.1.1 whether restrictions on the licensee can equally be placed upon the licensor without restricting competition. It is not always the case that such reciprocity is suitable. Any restriction upon the licensor granting licences or sub-licences would have to be tested against the permissible restrictions in Article 1.1. In relation to assignments, the justification for a restriction on the licensee is that it is not really his property to dispose of, whereas a restriction on the licensor could in certain circumstances amount to a restriction of competition and if that could be the case, the parties would have to consider the opposition procedure under Article 4.

10.3 Post-termination restrictions (Art 2.1(3))

The licensee may be prevented after termination of the agreement from exploiting the licensed know-how as long as it still remains secret, even if it no longer qualifies as substantial (see Commission clarification at **Case Note 9**). This has the interesting consequence that unlike Article 1.3 (discussed at **Section 9**, above) which provides that the exemption of the territorial restrictions during the life of the agreement will only apply where the know-how remains both secret and substantial, the post-termination ban on exploiting the know-how at all may be enforced for so long as the know-how remains secret even if its substantiality is in doubt.

The licensee may also be prevented from exploiting the patents for so long as they remain in force, but not thereafter (see *Velcro*, **Case Note 10** and *Ottung*, **Case Note 17**). Recital 20 explains that all of these restrictions are necessary in order to prevent the licence being converted to a perpetual licence. This is not actually true in relation to patents, as the patentee could still sue to enforce any continuing patent rights as long as the agreement had ended and the licensee's contractual rights had expired. On the other hand, any post-termination restriction which goes beyond the scope of the technology and which amounts to a general post-termination non-compete clause would not be permitted and would probably be black-listed under Article 3(2).

10.4 Improvements (Art 2.1(4))

The licensee may be required to grant back licences of any improvements to the licensed technology but only on a non-exclusive basis where such improvements are "severable" from the licensor's technology and only where the licensor also grants licences of his own improvements. An obligation to grant back licences does not turn the agreement into a "reciprocal" arrangement of the type excluded by Article 5.1(3). (See comments on that article at **Section 14.3**, below.)

It is clear that there could be substantial disagreement as to whether an improvement is severable. One may also question whether it was really necessary for the Commission to make this distinction between exclusive and non-exclusive licences of respectively severable and non-severable improvements in this way: if an improvement is not severable then the licensor should be satisfied with a non-exclusive licence since it will not be possible for the licensee to grant a licence of those improvements to any third party (or at least not a licence which is worth having if the improvements cannot be exploited without the licensor's own base technology). The Regulation also causes some small confusion in using the word "exclusive" when presumably it means "sole": the intention is clearly that the licensee should grant a licence only to the licensor and to no other third party but not that the licensee should himself be prevented from exploiting his improvements.

Recital 20 clarifies that obligations to license improvements are not seen as restrictive as long as they are reciprocal (see *Mitchell Cotts*, **Case Note 6**). However, it would be unduly restrictive for the licensee to be obliged to assign outright the rights to his improvements and any attempt to impose such an obligation is specifically prohibited by Article 3(6). Where the improvements lead to a prolongation of the life of the agreement it may become necessary to seek an individual exemption for any extended periods of territorial protection which might be required (see Art 3(7)), unless the arising technology is sufficiently distinct that the parties are able to conclude a new agreement which itself benefits from the block exemption (Recital 14).

Article 2.1(4) does not deal specifically with what happens on termination of the agreement. If the principal licence comes to an end should the licensor still be permitted to benefit from any licence-back of the improvements? A reading of Recital 20 suggests that it is only the continuing co-operation between the parties which justifies inclusion of the right to call for the improvements (see also *Jus-rol*, **Case Note 8** and *Delta Chemie*, **Case Note 11**). Therefore, the licence-back would be expected to terminate at the same time as the principal licence and if the licensor knows from the outset that he will want to continue to benefit from the licensee's improvements after termination, he will need at least to consider notifying the agreement for individual exemption (perhaps making use of the opposition procedure) rather than relying on the Regulation.

On the other hand, the wording of the similar provisions of the Know-how Regulation had suggested that the licence-back could continue where the improvements are not severable from the original technology (notwithstanding the Commission intervention to prevent this in *Delta Chemie*, **Case Note 11**). That would make sense: if the licence has terminated and the improvements are not severable, the licensee would not be able to make use of them so there seems no harm in terms of competition law in allowing at least the licensor to be able to continue to exploit the improved technology, subject perhaps to paying a reasonable royalty. Even if the improvements are severable, one would question why a continuing licence back to the licensor after termination of the principal licence should be objectionable. If it is a non-exclusive licence with no significant restrictions, it would clearly not be an agreement likely to raise Article 85 issues itself and therefore it is not clear why its inclusion in an otherwise exempt agreement should take that agreement outside the scope of the Regulation. As long as the licensee is guaranteed a reasonable royalty for use of his improvements there can be no harmful impact on competition, but this may be yet another case where, pending clarification, the opposition procedure will be appropriate.

Article 2.1(4) also stipulates that the licensor must always agree to license back his improvements if he wants a licence to the licensee's improvements. It also appears that all such further licences of licensor's improvements can be exclusive where the original technology was itself the subject of an exclusive licence to the licensee.

The provision is silent on the question of royalties. The corresponding provision of the Know-how Regulation did provide that either reasonable royalties must be paid by the licensor for the right to use the licensee's improvements after termination of the original licence or the licensor must release the licensee from the post-termination use ban on the base technology. Even though not carried over into the Technology Regulation, that principle may still apply. There is no guidance as to how one might approach the calculation of royalties for improvements contributed by either party during the life of the agreement. Once again the only statement one can make, by reference to Recital 20, is that where there is a significant imbalance, for instance the licensor charges additional royalties for improvements but insists that the licensee's improvements be contributed royalty free, there is a significant risk that this will exceed what is permitted by the Regulation. In the *Boussois* case (**Case Note 7**) the improvements were apparently contributed on the same terms as the original know-how which would imply some royalty payment in most cases. The best suggestion is that the parties stipulate for royalties to be fixed by agreement and, in the absence of agreement, by some other transparently fair method such as expert valuation.

10.5 Quality specifications (Art 2.1(5))

The licensee may be required to comply with certain quality specifications. Such provisions are generally not treated as infringing Article 85 (see *Delplanque*, **Case Note 1**). The licensee may also be obliged to procure certain goods or services from the licensor or an undertaking designated by him. In earlier days such commitments had been thought to require exemption (see *Schlegel*, **Case Note 4**) but there was a growing acceptance that they might not be objectionable in the context of a technology licence (see *Jus-rol*, **Case Note 8** and *Moosehead*, **Case Note 14**). Unfortunately Article 2.1(5) introduces yet another element of uncertainty, in that it recognises that such obligations generally are not anti-competitive but adds the qualification that they are only permitted where the specifications, products or services are "necessary" for a technically proper exploitation of the technology or for ensuring quality.

This further requirement of "necessity" can cause difficulties, particularly where the licensor has structured the agreement so that a significant part of his revenue will come from the margin on products supplied to the licensee, as opposed to a royalty on the licensee's production. In addition, circumstances may change over the life of a long agreement and goods which were initially necessary may become subject to competition from new sources of supply for such components. Although there is a strong argument that the issue of "necessity" should be assessed at the start of the agreement and that it should be irrelevant whether later suitable suppliers emerge for the components, the Regulation itself is not clear on this point. Some support for assessing the situation only at the commencement of the agreement, can be found in Article 4.2(a) which refers to "the time of the agreement". There is also the reference in Article 14, in relation to competitors, to assessing the position at the date of grant of the licence and Recital 21 refers to not needing to protect the parties against foreseeable financial consequences of an agreement freely entered into. Nevertheless, there must remain a risk that a provision not initially seen as restrictive could become so during the life of the agreement.

As a practical point, the licensor would be advised to include in the agreement a specific recognition by the licensee that the goods, services or specifications were necessary at the outset and also require the licensee to serve notice if he wishes to challenge the continued justification for such provisions. The contract should also provide that service of such a notice will give the licensor the right to review the financial terms, to terminate the agreement (just as he can in the event of a challenge to the patents or know-how, under Art 2.1(15)) or to submit a notification to the Commission under the opposition procedure (see comments on Art 4.2 below).

One question which arises from Article 2.1(5)(b), is whether there is any significance in the statement that the obligations must be necessary to ensure conformity with minimum quality specifications which are "*applicable* to the licensor and other licensees". In the Know-how Regulation the similar provision referred to specifications *respected* by the licensor and other licensees. Presumably the change is intended to allow the licensor to enforce the obligation against the licensee without having to show that he has not only inserted it but also enforced it equally rigorously in all of his other licences (although the tailpiece to the provision also allows the licensor to "carry out related checks", which suggests that a degree of supervision is expected). If it was indeed the intention to relax the burden on the licensor this is a welcome change, though it is curious that the corresponding provision in Article 4.2(a), which makes the opposition procedure suitable in circumstances where the goods or licences are not necessary, still refers to the standards being "respected". A prudent licensor would still make sure he is able to demonstrate that he does carry out some checks and take some reasonable steps to behave even-handedly between licensees.

Even with this change from "respected" to "applicable", the position is still not entirely satisfactory. It still suggests that the licensor must himself respect the same minimum quality specifications and must impose them upon all of his licensees. However, while it is likely that the same specifications will be appropriate within the common market that is not absolutely inevitable. Despite increasing harmonisation of laws within the Community, there still remain many areas in which Member State laws or local preferences could require different product standards for domestic production. It is suggested, given that Article 2.1(5) is an example of a provision which normally does not restrict competition, that the common sense view must be that the licensor is entitled to insist on the observance of specifications even if they differ from one Member State to another, as long as the differences are objectively justifiable and as long as the provision is not being used to impose onerous requirements upon one licensee which have no counterpart in agreements with other licensees, or to partition the market artificially (see *Zera*, **Case Note 22**).

10.6 Taking enforcement action (Art 2.1(6))

The duty on the licensee to inform the licensor of third party infringements of the licensed technology and assist in taking legal action, reflects the common interest that the parties should have in protecting the technology. Normally, the agreement itself would go into more detail, such as requiring the licensee to allow the licensor (generally at the licensor's cost) to have conduct of any litigation. Continuing the theme of reciprocity, similar obligations imposed on the licensor in respect of the licensee's improvements (particularly where they are severable) should also be acceptable.

10.7 Duration of royalties (Art 2.1(7))

In relation to know-how, the licensee can be required to continue paying royalties until the end of the agreement, even where the know-

how has come into the public domain as long as that was not "by
action" of the licensor (see *Jus-rol*, **Case Note 8**). The licensee therefore
takes the risk of disclosure by another licensee, unless he can argue that
such disclosure came about through such inexcusable failure of the
licensor to take proper precautions or enforce his contractual rights
that this is tantamount to the "action" of the licensor. An example
could be if the licensor had omitted to insert proper confidentiality
clauses into other licence agreements.

As mentioned above (**Section 9.5**) even if the licensee is himself
responsible for disclosure the territorial restrictions in Article 1 will fall
away. However, the licensee will remain bound to pay royalties and
may be exposed to a further claim in damages for such disclosure.
Where patents are concerned, payments may have been scheduled to
continue beyond the life of the patents in order to make payment easier.
For instance, the licensor may have agreed to defer some royalties until
the last batch of licensed products had been sold and paid for.
Alternatively, the parties might agree on a lower royalty rate which
continues to apply to production for a period after expiry of the patent.
Essentially, the Commission recognises (Recital 21) that it is not its job
to police purely commercial aspects of arrangements or rescue the
licensee from the foreseeable consequences of its own actions (see
Ottung, **Case Note 17**), as long as this does not amount to a disguised
restriction of competition infringing one of the black-listed provisions
in Article 3. National courts can probably be relied on to take a similar
approach (see *Pestre*, **Case Note 26**).

10.8 Field of use (Art 2.1(8))

The licensee may be required to limit his exploitation to one or more
technical fields of application (defined in Recital 22 as a "field of use") or
to one or more product markets. The reference to "product markets" was
in the Know-how Regulation but not in the Patent Regulation and is very
helpful in allowing the licensor to identify clearly exactly which types of
product he is prepared to permit the licensee to manufacture. This is
consistent with the licensor's freedom to choose how far he grants a
licence of his technology where it is capable of a number of distinct uses.
An example might be where a licensor has discovered a technology for
the sealing of packaging and wishes to grant a licence to a manufacturer
of beverage cartons but does not want to permit that licensee to use the
technology for packaging of foodstuffs because he has another licensee
in mind for that product market within the same territory.

Article 2.1(8) is supplemented by Article 3(4) (see below), which confirms that any attempts at "customer sharing" within a particular field of use or product market will not be permitted where the licensor and licensee were already competing manufacturers before the grant of the licence. Recital 23 also points out that customer sharing could be constituted by an explicit prohibition on delivering to certain customers or through some other obligation which had "equivalent effect". In practice it will normally be clear whether the limitation of the licence is genuinely by reference to a certain field of application or product market or whether the description being used is an artificial one, designed merely to prevent the licensee from being able to supply certain customers within the territory who have particular requirements. A conflict between Article 2.1(8) and Article 3(4) can generally be avoided by examining carefully with the clients why they have chosen the particular limitation of their licence and what they intended to achieve by it.

It follows that where the parties were not competing manufacturers before the licence was granted, they will be able to agree that the licensee (or licensor) should only supply certain customers within a particular field of use or product market. They could agree therefore that the licensee would package and deliver a carbonated drink manufactured under a know-how and trade mark licence to the hotel and catering trade but that supplies to supermarkets and other large retailers would be reserved to the licensor. That would be a restriction of competition but not black-listed and could be notified under the opposition procedure of Article 4. On the other hand, if the catering and retail markets had a genuine demand for a different type of product (for instance the catering trade wanted the syrup to which water was then added through dispensing equipment, whereas the supermarkets need the entire made-up product already packaged for retail) these could constitute two separate product markets in which case the licensee can be allocated one without this qualifying as a restriction of competition under Article 2.1(8). Inevitably, this is a matter about which one cannot generalise and which requires careful analysis in each case.

10.9 Minimum royalties/production (Art 2.1(9))

Obligations to pay a minimum royalty or produce a minimum quantity of products are generally perceived as part of the purely commercial balance between the parties and unlikely to have any effect upon competition. Nevertheless, Recital 21 states that the setting of royalty rates so as to achieve one of the restrictions black-listed in Article 3 will render the agreement ineligible for exemption and logically this should apply to the amount of the royalty as well as the period over which it is payable. One example might be if the licensor insisted on being able to increase the royalty rate at short notice and was clearly doing so, or invoking the threat of doing so, in order to deter the licensee from engaging in relatively low pricing (black-listed in Art 3(1)). Another example could be if royalty rates were set on a rising scale so that they became prohibitive above a certain production level and thereby had the effect of limiting production contrary to Article 3(5).

While this might appear unlikely, Article 7(4) confirms that the minimum quantity obligations if imposed upon a competing manufacturer might have the effect of limiting his use of his own or others' competing technologies and would justify withdrawal of the exemption.

10.10 Most favoured nation (Art 2.1(10))

Obligations to grant more favourable terms in the event that they are subsequently offered to other licensees are often referred to as "most favoured nation" or "most favoured customer" clause. The possible implications for achieving equivalence of restrictions between licensees were previously discussed in relation to Article 1.1(6). It is important to point out that Article 2.1(10) does not oblige the licensor to agree to insert such a clause in any of his licences: it merely provides that if he does so that is not normally seen as restrictive of competition. The licensor therefore retains freedom to treat his licensees differently (see discussion of specifications in **Section 10.5**, above) as long as in doing so he does not bring about one of the anti-competitive consequences prohibited elsewhere in the Regulation.

It does also remain possible that a most favoured nation clause may in certain circumstances be anti-competitive if the practical effect is to deter the licensor from granting further licences (see *Neumeyer*, **Case Note 2**). That could conceivably happen if the provision were poorly drafted so that the licensor found himself obliged to grant to his licensee the benefit of a single term contained in another licence even though that other licence were, when viewed as a whole, no more favourable or even less favourable. For example, a licensor might have appointed a first licensee with a royalty rate of 10% but subsequently appointed a second licensee with a 5% royalty rate in exchange for that second licensee agreeing to commit a significant amount for marketing. If the "most favoured nation" clause were poorly drafted the first licensee might be able to claim the benefit of the lower royalty rate without taking on the corresponding financial commitments for marketing. That could lead to a situation where the Commission felt that the agreement deterred other licensing sufficiently to deny effective competition, so that withdrawal were justified under Article 7(1). However, if the licence agreement is drafted so that the licensee is only entitled to insist on an improvement in terms where a second licensee is given an agreement which viewed as a whole is more favourable, it is far less likely that this could be seen as restricting competition.

10.11 Trade marks (Art 2.1(11))

Under Article 1.1(7) an obligation to use the licensor's trade mark or get up is treated as a serious restriction but is exempted as long as the licensee is able to identify himself as manufacturer. Article 2.1(11) allows a further obligation on the licensee to mark the product with an indication of the licensor's name or the licensed patent. However, even if the Article 1.1(7) obligation in relation to the trade mark or get up is not imposed, it would seem reasonable that the licensee must still be free to identify himself as the manufacturer of the product as a quid pro quo for imposition of the Article 2.1(11) obligation.

10.12 Increasing production capacity (Art 2.1(12))

The licensee can be prevented from using the technology to construct facilities for third parties as long as he is free to expand his own production capacity. This is explained by Recital 24 as forming part of the general prohibition of any restriction upon the quantities which the licensee may produce. However, the licensee is not intended to be able to construct facilities for others and thereby give them access to licensor's technology. The licensor is entitled to demand additional royalties for such increased capacity, though these must fall within the definition of "normal commercial terms" and if they were excessive this would be viewed as a restriction on manufacture in breach of Article 3(5). Recital 21 confirms that the setting of royalty rates so as to achieve one of the prohibited aims will make the agreement ineligible for the block exemption (see comments on Art 2.1(9) above). Article 2.1(12) raises some difficult issues which are discussed at more length in **Commentary Section 8.6.**

10.13 Controlling quantities (Art 2.1(13))

This provision introduces an exception to the general prohibition upon limiting the quantities manufactured. The general prohibition in Article 3(5) is qualified in circumstances where the licence has only been granted in order to allow a particular customer a second source of supply, perhaps as an alternative to the licensor or where the customer is located in the territory of a single non-exclusive licensee. One presumes that if the customer were made a party to that agreement the Commission would still be prepared to treat it as an agreement between only two undertakings (see **Section 5**, above) but it would be as well to avoid that where possible. This provision also envisages that the licensee may be manufacturing or subcontracting as his own second source of supply, providing components for his own finished goods, which ties in with the obligation in Article 1(1)(8) discussed above. The reference to giving the customer a second source "inside the licensed territory" is confusing: it is presumably referring to the territory of the licensee who is being appointed as the second source but in reality where a licensee is appointed only to supply to a single named customer the concept of a "territory" is meaningless. The location of the premises from which the licensee manufactures and delivers is irrelevant as long as it does not actually impinge on the rights granted to any other licensee.

It is important to note that this exception can only be relied upon where the licensee represents a "second" source of supply and therefore it would not apply where neither the licensor nor another existing licensee are serving the licensed territory in which the customer is located. This interpretation is reinforced by Recital 23, which in fact refers to a prohibition on a "second licensee" as though the exception were only available for a customer in the territory of an existing licensee, who by definition would have to be a non-exclusive licensee. However, one would suggest that despite the reference to a "licensed territory" such a limited licence should also be permitted for the benefit of customers in territories which the licensor has reserved to himself and not only in territories which are the subject of a licence.

Another feature is that Article 2.1(13) only applies where the licensee is limited to supplying a "particular customer" (see again Recital 23 which refers to a "single customer"). Therefore, if it were intended that the licensee should act under a *single agreement* as a second source for more than one customer, the exception will not apply. It would also appear from Article 3(4) that in such circumstances, as a restriction on supplying to particular customers, it would be black-listed if the parties were already competing manufacturers but otherwise could be notified under the opposition procedure.

It is not at all clear what would happen where a licensee was granted a licence specifically to supply one customer and then later, in a separate licence, were permitted to supply another customer who had also requested a second source of supply. There must come a point where, if that licensee were manufacturing for supply to a number of customers, that would be viewed as the creation of "an independent supplier in the market" going beyond what the Commission intended to permit in Recital 23. Effectively, it would be too easy a way of circumventing the prohibition on limiting supplies to certain customers and would not at least need to be submitted under the opposition procedure (see comment above). It does not appear as though Article 2.1(13) could apply where the "customer" requiring the second source is the licensor himself but in such circumstances it might be possible to rely on the general dispensation for subcontracting agreements (see **Commentary Section 2.1**).

10.14 Reservation of patent rights (Art 2.1(14))

The licensor may reserve the right to enforce his patents so as to oppose "exploitation" of the technology outside the licensed territory. The first point to note is that this is described only as a *reservation* of the licensor's existing patent rights and does not confer any right to do anything which is prohibited elsewhere: the limitations which the licensor may impose by contract within the agreement are already circumscribed by Article 1. Even that reservation must be read as subject to other limitations imposed by the Regulation and by Community law on free movement of goods. It must be clear from looking at earlier provisions of the Regulation that in these circumstances the definition of "exploitation" will be given a narrower meaning than under Article 10(10) and that although the licensor may prevent unlicensed manufacture outside the territory, he would not be able to prevent a passive *sale* of the patented products within the territory of other licensees in the common market after the first five years. Any attempt to exercise intellectual property rights so as to prevent trade in licensed products lawfully put onto the market could lead to withdrawal of the exemption under Article 7.3(b).

10.15 Termination for challenge (Art 2.1(15))

The licensor may terminate the agreement if the licensee disputes either that the know-how is secret and substantial or that any patents within the common market are valid. If the licensor were to go further and seek to prohibit outright the licensee from issuing such a challenge, it is likely (based on case law and earlier block exemption regulations: see *Neumeyer*, **Case Note 2** and *Bayer*, **Case Note 16**) that the Commission would view this as a restriction of competition although it is clearly a suitable candidate for use of the opposition procedure (see Art 4.2(b)). The position in relation to trade marks is far less clear. Article 5(4) states that the Regulation does not apply to provisions relating to intellectual property rights other than patents which are not ancillary and it might be difficult to argue that a prohibition on challenging any trade marks was ancillary to the licensing of the patents or know-how. On the other hand, recent decisions have suggested that a clause prohibiting a challenge to the licensor's trade mark might not be viewed as a restriction on competition. The safest course for a licensor who does not wish to notify under the opposition procedure, would be to avoid an outright trade mark no challenge clause but rely instead on a similar right of termination in the event of challenge.

The Article leaves open the question of a challenge to the validity of patents outside the common market. It is quite conceivable that a single licence may relate to both Community and non-Community patents. If the Commission is prepared in Article 2.1(15) to confirm that a right to terminate for challenge to a Community patent did not breach Article 85, it must follow that a similar right in response to a challenge to a non-Community patent would not be treated as a restriction of competition. However, if it could amount to such a restriction it would not be saved by Article 2.2 or 2.3, so once again the opposition procedure would be necessary and the licensor might just as well include an absolute prohibition on challenge in line with Article 4.2(b).

10.16 Challenge of necessity (Art 2.1(16))

The licensor is given a more limited right to terminate the licence agreement in relation to a specific patent (but apparently not the entire agreement) where the licensee claims that the patent, although valid, is not *necessary*. Such a clause would be advisable where a number of patents are being licensed under a single agreement, since if the licensee succeeds in showing that the patent is not "necessary" and the agreement has not been notified the licensor could find that the entire agreement is invalid and unenforceable. The licensor might also argue that any such challenge is evidence of a breakdown in the relationship and therefore should allow him to terminate the whole of the agreement without that being viewed as a restriction of competition. There is a risk that such action would be viewed as an attempt to coerce the licensee into accepting an unnecessary patent within the licence and therefore should have been submitted under the opposition procedure in line with Article 4.2(a).

10.17 Best endeavours (Art 2.1(17))

An obligation on the licensee to use best endeavours to manufacture and market can amount to an extremely onerous requirement, particularly when combined with a minimum royalty or production target as permitted under Article 2.1(9). This could in particular be used in an agreement with a competitor to deter him from concentrating on exploiting his own technology (a straightforward restriction on competing would be black-listed by Art 3(2)) and is one of the circumstances in which an agreement covered by the block exemption could have that exemption withdrawn by the Commission under Article 7(4).

10.18 Non-compete (Art 2.1(18))

Although the licensee may not be prevented from competing with the licensor or other licensees in respect of developing or distributing competing products (that would be black-listed under Art 3(2)), the licensor is given the right to terminate any exclusivity within the licence and to stop licensing improvements where the licensee does so. This is a new provision, not found in the Patent or Know-how Regulations. There is no suggestion that the royalty rate must fall in order to take account of the fact that the licensee no longer has an exclusive licence.

In relation to improvements, it is not at all clear whether the licensor can continue to insist on a licence-back of the licensee's improvements during the life of the now non-exclusive agreement. As it is the licensee's own decision to commence competing activities which trigger this event, it is suggested that the licensor should be allowed to continue to benefit from the improvements (probably on a non-exclusive basis), even though the exchange of improvements is no longer reciprocal and therefore does not benefit from the presumption contained in Recital 20. Presumably, it is only subsequent improvements which the licensor can refuse to add into the licence: one would expect the licensee to be able to continue to benefit from a (non-exclusive) licence of any improvements discovered before he began competing, since those improvements would have become part of the licensed technology.

Where the licensee does compete in this way, the licensor is entitled to require proof that the licensee is not misusing any of the licensed know-how, although one can foresee significant argument as to how the licensee must prove this. The licensee may well argue that he should not be obliged to disclose the possession of his own or some other third parties' valuable know-how which he is using in place of the licensor's know-how and which may itself be subject to strict confidentiality clauses. As a practical matter it may be necessary to simply prohibit competing activities or make them subject to prior approval, thereby infringing Article 3(2) and requiring a full notification (see *BNP*, **Case Note 30**).

Once again the Article contains an apparently unnecessary qualification, in that the right to terminate only applies where the licensee begins competing "within the common market". A licensor might be equally concerned if his licensee begins competing outside the common market as this could still distract the licensee from fully exploiting the licensed technology or might involve some misuse of that technology. One could argue that *any* clause designed to deter competition outside the common market, even an outright prohibition on such activities, should be capable of being categorised as a provision which will not infringe Article 85. At the very least a right to terminate in such circumstances should not infringe Article 85. Moreover, the withdrawal of exclusivity and even the withholding of improvements may not themselves amount to significant restrictions of competition, but a degree of uncertainty is bound to remain. It would seem excessive to be required to use the opposition procedure on these grounds alone.

11. **Scope of exemption (Art 2.2 and 2.3)**

These provide that for the avoidance of doubt, the exemption shall apply to clauses of the type listed in Article 2.1 where they could infringe Article 85, even if the agreement does not contain any of the obligations exempted by Article 1. The same applies where the clause has a more limited scope than permitted by Article 2.1. Therefore, the clauses identified in Article 2.1 and any restrictions with more limited scope will always benefit from the block exemption. Where the parties are in any doubt as to whether a clause is merely one of more limited scope than permitted by Article 2.1 or is an entirely different type of restriction, they will always be able to rely on the opposition procedure under Article 4.

12.   The Black List (Art 3)

Article 3 lists examples of a number of provisions the presence of any one of which will prevent the block exemption applying at all to the agreement (*i.e.* it disapplies both Arts 1 and 2). The list of prohibited provisions in a block exemption is commonly known as the "Black List". To take them in order:

12.1 Pricing and discounts (Art 3(1))

Although the licensor will be able to give guidance in the form of a recommended retail price, any restrictions as to prices, components of prices (*e.g.* how much to charge for an after-sales warranty) or discounts for the licensed products are prohibited. This would even extend to the imposition upon the licensee of a *maximum* resale price. One would be able to make out a good case that maximum prices are pro-competitive and benefit consumers and therefore would not prevent the agreement benefiting from an individual exemption upon notification. In at least one unpublished case the Commission has been prepared to accept that a standard franchise agreement including a maximum resale clause did not infringe Article 85 because the effects were not significant, even though any price fixing is normally assumed to attract Commission action however trivial the agreement. In any event, significance is not relevant when considering a block exemption. The inclusion of a provision which appears on the Black List would mean that the agreement would require a full notification and the opposition procedure would not be available.

It is self-evident that when Article 3(1) mentions prices and discounts this refers to terms concluded between one of the parties and any third party for the licensed products. It is not intended to prevent the parties agreeing as between themselves the prices or discounts which might apply to goods which they sell to each other, for instance where the licensee is required to source components from the licensor (if such components come within the definition of "licensed products") or where the licensee is required for a period while commencing production to purchase the products themselves from the licensor. Moreover, it is inevitable that any royalty rate charged by the licensor will have some impact upon the price which the licensee can charge. The licensor might express the royalty as a percentage of the licensee's sale price and also impose an obligation to pay an annual minimum level of royalties. If this were to have the effect of unduly restricting the freedom of the licensee in practice to determine his own prices, then Recital 21 confirms that the benefit of the exemption would be lost.

12.2 Competing activities (Art 3(2))

The agreement may not prevent one party from competing with the other or with any third party within the common market in respect of R&D, production or distribution of "competing products". That term is defined in Article 10(17) as products which, "in view of their characteristics, prices and intended use, are considered by users to be interchangeable or substitutable for the licensed products". Article 3(2) must therefore be interpreted as including a prohibition on the licensee being restricted from engaging in competing activities which he was in a position to pursue without the benefit of the licence. This can be contrasted with the restrictions exempted in Article 1, which all relate to the licensed technology and products manufactured therefrom and amount merely to a limitation of the possibilities offered by the licence. The prohibition on restricting competing activities will be one of the most common reasons for not following the Regulation, but is rarely a bar to individual exemption on notification (see *Moosehead*, **Case Note 14**). It may be justified as the only way of guaranteeing that the licensed technology is not being misused (see *BNP*, **Case Note 30**).

There is specific reference to Article 2.1(17) and (18), which still allow imposition of a best endeavours obligation on the licensee in relation to the licensed technology and permit the licensor to terminate the exclusivity of the licensee in the event of such competition. What is worth pointing out, is that Article 3(2) only refers to competing products. It therefore appears that a restriction upon the licensee (or the licensor for that matter) engaging in manufacture or distribution of non-competing products (which could include components for the licensed products) would not be a black-listed clause. It is perfectly conceivable that the licensor might seek to prevent the licensee from competing with him in relation to a quite distinct range of products which the licensor manufactures and this would not be black-listed but would, if it amounted to a significant restriction of competition, still be eligible for the opposition procedure. Having said that, an opposition from the Commission would be almost certain against a blatant non-compete clause unconnected with the licensed products.

Even if the agreement falls short of absolutely restricting competition in relation to competing products, the parties still need to bear in mind Article 7(1) and (4) below which allow withdrawal of the exemption where effective competition is reduced, particularly if the parties were already competing manufacturers.

12.3 Eliminating parallel trade (Art 3(3))

This refers to one of the parties being *required* without any *objectively justified reason* to refuse to meet certain orders or to place difficulties in the way of other users or resellers. The same prohibition applies where the parties do so as the result of a concerted practice and this follows naturally from the definition of "obligation" in Article 10(16). It is clear that if one of the parties unilaterally takes such action which does not arise from any obligation or concerted practice, the Black List will not apply. That is logical, since otherwise one of the parties by unilateral action could take the agreement outside the block exemption which would have potentially serious consequences for the other party. However, any unilateral refusal would give the Commission grounds to withdraw the benefit of the block exemption under Article 7(3). Any action to limit parallel imports within the EU is likely to be viewed as unacceptable save in the most exceptional circumstances (see *Zera*, Case Note 22).

The location of the words "objectively justified reason" is ambiguous. Does it mean that there has to be an objectively justified reason for imposing the requirement in the agreement at all or does it mean that the obligation can be automatically imposed, as long as its observance is objectively justified on each individual occasion and the third party has an opportunity to be informed of (and perhaps challenge) the reason given? The former offers more certainty, if it is only necessary to justify inclusion of the restriction at the outset. However, this clause does present problems, irrespective of how it is interpreted, because of the scope for argument that the restriction was not sufficiently justified, particularly as no further guidance is given. Where such restrictions are thought necessary, it may be advisable to submit them under the opposition procedure with a claim that the provision is reasonable, rather than risk an allegation at some later stage that the provision was unreasonable and that the agreement was void *ab initio* for lack of exemption.

The tailpiece of this Article refers to products which have been lawfully put on the market within the common market by the licensor or with his consent. This will include products manufactured or sold by any other licensees within the common market. However, if licensor or licensee were required to take steps to prevent entry into the common market of products lawfully marketed outside the common market, for instance by the licensor's US licensee, that would not infringe Article 3(3) but would, if it were capable of restricting competition and trade between Member States, be a possible candidate for the opposition procedure.

12.4 Competing manufacturers (Art 3(4))

Article 3(4) is another provision which needs to be read carefully (see also the discussion in relation to Art 1.1(7) above). This provision only applies where the parties were already competing manufacturers before the grant of the licence and "one of them" (which could of course apply equally if it is "both of them") is restricted in his freedom to deal with customers.

The definition of "competing manufacturers" is contained within Article 10(17), being manufacturers of products which compete with the licensed products. It follows, and is clarified in Recital 23, that where the parties were not previously competing manufacturers, the restrictions identified in Article 3(4) are not *automatically* exempted but may be capable of justification under the opposition procedure.

Restrictions as to the customers who may be served are only black-listed where they apply within the same technical field of use or the same product market. The word "same" confirms that this is only directed at restrictions which relate to the subject matter of the licence *i.e.* which authorise a certain activity but then limit the persons to whom the fruits of that activity may be distributed. An example would be a restriction on selling the licensed products to wholesalers or distributing the goods by mail-order. On the other hand, an outright restriction upon using the technology within another field of use or to serve a different product market (in other words for purposes outside the normal scope of the licence) is not black-listed but appears in the list of non-infringing provisions in Article 2.1(8).

Another qualification is that restrictions as to packaging are only prohibited where these were introduced with the aim of sharing customers. Therefore while the other restrictions will be prohibited if they prevent the licensee from delivering to any class of customer, even when the licensor is <u>not</u> motivated by a desire to reserve those customers to himself or another licensee, the packaging restrictions appear only to be black-listed where the licensor or licensee is attempting to make use of them in order to reserve certain customers to himself. An example would be insisting that the licensee only distribute nuts and bolts in small, relatively expensive packages which make them suitable for display in DIY stores but prohibitively expensive to compete in the trade market which the licensor is serving.

Article 3(4) confirms that the licensee may still be required to use the licensor's trade mark or get up (Art 1.1(7) and see also comments on Art 2.1(11)). It is also confirmed that customer restrictions are legitimate where they arise from a second-sourcing agreement, as permitted under Article 2(1)(13).

A final point to make in relation to competing manufacturers is that Article 7(4) allows the Commission to withdraw the benefit of the exemption where minimum quantity or best endeavours obligations, although normally permitted within Article 2, in practice prevent the licensee from using competing technologies.

12.5 Limiting quantities (Art 3(5))

We have already seen that the licensee (or licensor) may not be subject to quantity/production restrictions, save where the components exception applies (Art 1.1(8)) or in the case of second-sourcing (Art 2.1(13): see also Recitals 23 and 24 of the Regulation). It follows that there are <u>no</u> permitted circumstances in which the *licensor* can be limited as to the quantities that he might manufacture.

12.6 Ownership of improvements (Art 3(6))

The restriction on forced assignments appears to be the most straightforward of the black-listed provisions. The Commission has consistently opposed such expropriation by the licensor (see *Neumeyer*, **Case Note 2** and *Velcro*, **Case Note 10**). Clearly Article 3(6) only applies to an *obligation* in the licence and therefore if the licensee freely chooses to assign certain rights the benefit of the exemption will not be lost.

Strictly interpreted the provision relates only to *assignments* and in practice many licence agreements are more complicated. The parties may both have contributed to any improvements and may wish to agree in advance, so as to avoid destructive arguments later on, that ownership of certain types of improvement will vest automatically in one or the other. It will at least be open to them to argue, in such circumstances, for application of the opposition procedure. However, this would be risky without some form of notification, if the view is taken that such a clause does effectively amount to an anticipatory assignment of what would otherwise have vested in one party. Some comfort can be drawn from the fact that in at least one case an agreement that ownership of technology developed by the parents should vest in their joint venture which funded the work was granted negative clearance (see *Odin*, **Case Note 19**).

It is important to bear in mind the provisions of Article 2.1(4), on the continuing applicability of the exemption where improvements are licensed (as opposed to being assigned) and the limitations on duration of the exemption in Article 1 (see **Section 12.7**, below). The importance of the distinction between assignments and licences of improvements is confirmed by Recital 20.

The Regulation, as ever, assumes that it will be the licensor who is insisting on expropriating the improvements of the licensee. It therefore appears that the opposition procedure would be available where it is the licensee who has the upper hand and is insisting on an assignment to him of the licensor's improvements.

12.7 Duration of exemption (Art 3(7))

This provision black-lists any attempts to extend the duration of the territorial restrictions concerning exploitation of the licensed technology (see **Section 9**, above), either through other agreements or through automatic prolongation of the agreement. In relation to know-how licences, the territorial restrictions are always limited to the five or 10-year periods from first sale of products incorporating the "licensed technology" even if it is subsequently improved as long as some of the original technology is still utilised in the process (see definition at Art

10(7)). Therefore, prolongation of these periods within the scope of the block exemption is not possible. Recital 14 confirms that exemption for know-how licences may be granted by individual decision (following notification) for longer periods, although that might mean that the territorial restrictions could relate only to that new technology. How effective that might be, will depend upon whether the improvements are genuinely valuable so that the parties would only wish to manufacture products incorporating them or whether one or more parties would continue to manufacture "unimproved products" which could be subject only to the initial duration restrictions.

Recital 14 also confirms that where an improvement to licensed know-how results in something which is "distinct", that innovation could be the subject of a separate agreement which could benefit from the block exemption. This is bound to lead to argument: does it apply only where the innovatory know-how can be used to manufacture a product or carry out a distinct operation without making use of any of the original know-how? It would be prudent to assume that is the case.

Recital 14 only refers to improvements of know-how. Where any improvements give rise to separate patents, it will be possible (see Recital 12 and Art 1(2)&(4)) to continue to enforce the territorial restrictions in relation to those patents for so long as they remain in force. This is confirmed by the definition of "the licensed technology in Article 10(7) which includes the initial "necessary patents" together with any improvements. See also the comments below in **Section 17.3** on continued applicability of the Regulation as a whole (as opposed to the duration of the exemption) where the agreement is automatically prolonged by improvements.

13. **Opposition procedure (Art 4)**

13.1 The Commission has continued in this Regulation with its practice of including an opposition procedure. The purpose of this procedure is to permit individual exemption for agreements which comply with the spirit of the block exemption but may infringe the letter of certain specific provisions. The criteria for use of the procedure are that:

- the agreement contains restrictions of competition which go beyond those specifically exempted by Articles 1 and 2;
- the agreement does not contain (see **Commentary Section 7**) any restrictions which appear in the Black List in Article 3;

- the parties submit a notification to the Commission;
- the Commission does not object within four months.

13.2 It is important to remember that this is a notification procedure. Therefore, although Article 4 begins by stating that "the exemption provided for in Articles 1 and 2 shall also apply ..." this does not amount to an extension of the block exemption. In other words, any resulting exemption does not apply as from the date of the agreement but only from the date of the notification (see **Section 13.7**, below).

13.3 The notification which is submitted must comply with Commission Regulation 3385/94. This is the regulation which deals in detail with the form and content of notifications to the Commission and it requires a substantial submission of information and legal argument. As mentioned elsewhere, notification can be extremely onerous and represents a significant incentive to fall within the scope of the block exemption. However Recital 25 of the Technology Regulation confirms that the burden under the opposition procedure will in general be far lighter, since the Commission can waive the requirement to supply certain information and will "generally" be satisfied with the text of the agreement, together with an estimate of the market structure and of the market share of the licensee. Unlike the previous Patent and Know-how Regulations there is, curiously, no requirement in the Technology Regulation that the notifying parties must state clearly in the notification that they are applying for the benefit of an opposition procedure and identify the relevant provision in the Regulation (even though such a mention appears in Section A.II of the explanatory document attached to Regulation 3385/94). Nevertheless, it must remain advisable to spell out clearly in any application that the benefit of the opposition procedure is being sought.

13.4 The Commission has four months within which to raise an objection to the notified agreement, failing which it is deemed to benefit from a specific exemption. Generally the four-month time period would not begin running until a full notification had been submitted. Therefore, the parties would be advised to include as much information as is easily available and to request the waiver in respect of the rest. Article 4.3 of the Technology Regulation confirms that the four-month period only begins running when the notification takes effect under Article 4 of Regulation 3385/94 *i.e.* the date on which the notification is received, unless the Commission notifies the parties that it is incomplete in a material respect. The Commission has one month under

Article 4.5 of Regulation 3385/94 to serve such a notice, failing which the notification is deemed to have become effective.

13.5 Article 4.2 gives two specific examples of types of agreement which are thought particularly suitable for the opposition procedure. These are not exhaustive and this Analysis section has already identified other occasions (*e.g.* **Sections 14.2, 14.3** and **14.4**) where the opposition procedure might be used. The two examples given in Article 4.2 are:

1. Where the licensee is made subject to obligations which are not thought necessary for a technically satisfactory exploitation of the technology or for meeting quality standards. This is extremely helpful because it is clear that this is one area where there could be substantial disagreement and where a licensee might later seek to argue, if the agreement was not notified to the Commission, that the block exemption did not apply (see **Section 10.5**, above). If the licensor has structured the arrangement so as to derive most of the benefit from supplying certain products to the licensee, that may be a good reason to consider use of the opposition procedure.

2. Where the licensee is prohibited from contesting the know-how or patents, often referred to in the context of trade marks as a "no challenge" clause. A licensor who is communicating know-how will often want this protection and may not be satisfied with the right to terminate for challenge under Article 2.1(15). However, it seems unlikely that the Commission would raise an objection within the four-month period to an agreement which complied in all other respects with Articles 1 and 2 of the Regulation simply because of the inclusion of a no challenge clause and it is therefore unfortunate that Article 2.1(15) could not have been extended to automatically exempt such agreements. Alternatively, if there were a real concern about such provisions, this could have been added in Article 7 as a ground for withdrawal rather than something which necessitates a notification.

13.6 Article 4.4 provides that where any agreements have previously been notified which could now benefit from the opposition procedure, it will be sufficient to write to the Commission claiming the benefit of the procedure. This may offer some benefit for agreements which previously had to be notified because they contained provisions infringing the (much longer) Black Lists of the Patent and Know-how Regulations.

13.7 Article 4.5 confirms that the Commission only has four months within which to oppose the exemption and this is significantly shorter than the six month period contained in previous block exemptions. This provision also contains a reminder that copies of the notification will have been transmitted to the Member States (even if the notification is in abbreviated form it will still be necessary to send multiple copies – currently 17 are required). The Member States have an opportunity within two months to request the Commission to oppose and one presumes that this obliges the Commission to transmit copies swiftly to allow that time to the Member States before the four-month deadline expires. This illustrates another drawback of notification and of the opposition procedure: that it brings agreements to the attention of national authorities, even though those authorities and the Commission are supposed under Article 9 not to use the information for any other purpose or to disclose it (see **Section 18**, below). Where the Commission does raise an opposition at the request of a Member State, that opposition may only be withdrawn after consulting the Advisory Committee (Art 4.6) although the Commission is never obliged to follow the advice of the Committee and therefore could decide to overrule the objections of the Member State(s).

13.8 Article 4.7 confirms the usual position in relation to notifications, which is that exemption can run from the date of the notification and logically this must be true for all uses of the opposition procedure. Therefore, where there is no opposition or the opposition is withdrawn, the starting point for exemption will be the date of notification unless it turns out that the agreement did comply with the Regulation, in which case the exemption will apply as from the date of the agreement. However, where the parties are required to amend an agreement so as to qualify for exemption, Article 4.8 confirms that the exemption shall only apply from the date of amendment. Depending upon the significance of the agreement and the time which elapses, this could have serious consequences for the parties as they would have been operating an agreement for a period which was not exempted and therefore could be exposed to a claim for damages in a national court from any third party who could show that he had been adversely affected. The parties therefore have every incentive, first to think carefully about whether it is worth submitting under the opposition procedure agreements containing clauses which are bound to be opposed and secondly to be ready to respond as quickly as possible to any opposition which is maintained.

13.9 Article 4.9 confirms that where the opposition is maintained, the notification will be dealt with under the normal Regulation 17 procedure. This is likely to mean that the Commission will request a more complete notification with most of the information required by Regulation 3385/94 and the notification will not be effective until it has been furnished. Moreover, where the opposition is a serious one, it is likely that the Commission will act under Article 15(6) of Regulation 17 to remove any protection from fines which is otherwise conferred by notification.

13.10 Having said so much about the opposition procedure, a word of caution: what evidence is available suggests that in practice it will rarely be of use. The Commission's annual Competition Reports occasionally publish statistics on use of the procedure under the various regulations and consistently refer to its non-use. For instance, in 1992 from the whole of the EU the Commission received only one notification under the opposition procedure of the Know-how Regulation and none under the Patent Regulation. Typically the reason for its non-applicability, where reasons are given, is that the agreement was either clearly outside the scope of a block exemption (see *Odin*, **Case Note 19** and *Quantel*, **Case Note 24**) or contained a black-listed clause. It is not yet known what use is being made of the procedure under the Technology Regulation and it is quite possible that the greater flexibility of that Regulation together with the shorter Black List will mean that Article 4 is of more assistance than its predecessors.

14. Ineligible agreements (Art 5)

- patent or know-how pools
- licences between competitors in joint venture
- reciprocal agreements between competitors
- licences of non-ancillary non-patent rights
- pure sales agreements

Certain categories of agreements are viewed as unsuitable for automatic exemption, generally because of their complexity or the fact that they are likely to lead to unacceptable co-ordination of behaviour between actual or potential competitors. Some of them such as patent and know-how pooling, certain joint venture agreements and certain reciprocal arrangements may be saved if they comply with the additional conditions in Article 5.2.

14.1 Technology pools (Art 5.1(1))

The first category is know-how or patent pools. There is no attempt to define these terms. A commonly accepted definition of a pool would be where two or more rights owners agree to share their intellectual property rights to a particular technology, so that each member of the pool can use all of the pooled rights.

Recital 8 merely states that technology pools pose "different problems" which cannot be dealt with in a single regulation (repeating the wording from Recital 5 of the Know-how Regulation). Nevertheless, they have often passed through the Commission with little difficulty on an individual notification (see *Philips*, Case Note 23). It is clear that a multi-partite patent pool or know-how pool which included significant restrictions of competition could not itself be exempted by the Regulation, since Article 1.1 expressly limits the scope of the Regulation to agreements between no more than two undertakings. The effect of Article 5.1(1) is that where two or more parties do agree to place their rights into a pool, they will not be able to benefit from the block exemption for any otherwise exempt agreements that any two of them might enter into relating to any of the pooled technology which they are still permitted, under the terms of the pooling arrangement, to license. They might instead wish to consider whether they could benefit from the block exemption for research and development agreements in Regulation 418/85 (see *KSB*, Case Note 20) which moreover could cover an agreement between more than two parties.

One exception to this prohibition is contained in Article 5.2(2), which states that the Regulation may nevertheless apply to licences between members of a patent pool as long as the parties are not subject to any territorial restriction on manufacture, use or sale within the common market. By way of example, an agreement between two members of a patent pool in relation to pooled technology could still qualify for the block exemption if it were granted to allow the licensee to manufacture components for his own products in line with Article 1.1(8) as long as the licence were non exclusive and the territory were at least as large as the EEA.

14.2 Joint ventures (Art 5.1(2))

Also excluded are licensing agreements between competitors where they are also parties to a joint venture (or between one parent and the joint venture) where the agreement relates to the activities of the joint venture. Article 5.2(1) introduces an exception to this exclusion in the case of an agreement between one of the parent companies and the joint venture, as long as the "participating undertakings" (*i.e.* the parents and the joint venture together) do not in aggregate exceed certain market share thresholds, which are 20% of the relevant market where the licence involves production only and 10% where the joint venture is also engaged in distribution. For a case which fell between these thresholds but involved both manufacture and distribution see *Fiat*, Case Note 21.

The market share thresholds of Article 5.2 are relaxed under Article 5.3 to allow them to be exceeded during two consecutive financial years by not more than one-tenth in each year. Where the increased threshold is exceeded, the exemption still continues for a period of a further six months from the end of the year in question, in order to allow the parties to assess the situation and submit an individual notification if required.

Agreements involving joint ventures are discussed in more detail at **Commentary Section 9.**

14.3 Reciprocal agreements (Art 5.1(3))

Reciprocal licences are traditionally excluded from block exemptions, even if they are contained in separate agreements. The prohibition also extends to the grant back of a trade mark licence or of exclusive sales rights. This provision is not very clear. It does not specify whether the parties must be competitors in relation to the products covered by both agreements or just one of them. Probably the only sensible way to interpret this clause, is to assume that the Commission would only be concerned if the reciprocal licences both relate to products in respect of which both of the parties would be competitors and that therefore:

- Company A and Company B are both biscuit manufacturers
- Company B also manufactures soap powder
- Company A does not manufacture soap powder or any similar products
- Company A grants to Company B a patent licence to manufacture a certain type of biscuit
- Company B grants to Company A under an entirely separate agreement a trade mark licence to sell the soap powder of Company B

- Conclusion – this does not amount to reciprocal licensing for products in respect of which both parties are competing manufacturers
- The patent licence could come within the block exemption and would not be excluded by Article 5.1(3) (though if the two agreements were connected they would be excluded by Art 5.1(4) below)
- However, the trade mark licence would not be covered by any block exemption regulation and might need to be notified if it were restrictive

The prohibition also applies where, in return for a technology licence, one party grants back to the other exclusive sales rights for products in relation to which they are both competitors. However, where the licensor grants to the licensee a patent licence which the licensee genuinely requires in order to produce the goods with the intention that those goods are then sold back exclusively to the licensor for distribution, then even if the parties were competitors the agreement could escape Article 85 entirely as a subcontracting agreement (see Commission Notice on Subcontracting discussed in **Commentary Section 2.1**, p 101-102).

The prohibition on reciprocal licences does not of course include a situation where one party grants a patent or know-how licence but insists on a licence back of improvements to the extent permitted by Article 2.1(4). This is confirmed (in rather abbreviated form) by Recital 8 where it refers to the prohibition as applying only where licences are granted in exchange for other licences "not related to improvements to or new applications of the licensed technology".

The exception in Article 5.2(2) also applies so that reciprocal licences may still be exempted where the parties are not subject to any territorial restriction on manufacture, use or sale of the licensed products within the common market (see comments at **Section 14.1**, above).

14.4 Non-ancillary restrictions (Art 5.1(4))

Also excluded from the exemption are agreements which contain "provisions relating to intellectual property rights other than patents which are not ancillary". Article 5.1(4) is the counterpart to Article 1.1, which extends the exemption to such provisions which are ancillary. To understand this provision it is necessary to consider Recital 6 and the definition of "ancillary provisions" in Article 10(15). It can then be seen that the intention is to exclude the application of the Regulation to agreements which contain restrictions on other intellectual property rights, such as trade marks or copyright, which have a scope wider than the permitted restrictions attaching to the licensed know-how or patents. The licensor is not to be allowed to impose restrictions relating to the trade marks which go further in limiting competition than he could have achieved through legitimate use of his patent or know-how rights (see **Commentary Section 8.5**).

14.5 Distribution agreements (Art 5.1(5))

Article 5.1(5) is extremely brief. Some clarification can be found in Recital 8. It is essential that the licensee is actually taking responsibility for working the patent or exploiting the know-how and this is because the exemption has only been granted in order to encourage dissemination of technology. Recital 8 does clarify that the licensee could be having the products manufactured for him, perhaps under a subcontracting agreement which would not itself infringe Article 85 or require exemption (see **Section 14.3**, above). However, a mere licence to sell patented goods produced by the licensor would not qualify. In such circumstances the parties should consider making use of the block exemption Regulation 1983/83 for exclusive distribution agreements or possibly Regulation 1984/83 on exclusive purchasing agreements. Conversely, those Regulations cannot be used where there is a substantial element of manufacture (see *Delta Chemie*, **Case Note 11**).

14.6 Opposition procedure not available

It is important to note that Article 5 states that *this Regulation shall not apply* in the circumstances identified. This has the effect that the opposition procedure is also not available in those circumstances and therefore it will be necessary to submit a full notification in accordance with Regulation 3385/94.

14.7 Saving provisions (Art 5.2)

The exceptions to the prohibitions in Article 5.1, which allow certain parent-joint venture licences below market share thresholds and which "save" technology pool licences or reciprocal agreements without territorial restrictions, are dealt with at the relevant points of **Sections 14.1-14.3**, above.

14.8 Turnover increases (Art 5.3)

As mentioned at **Section 14.2** this allows for small increases in the Article 5.2(1) turnover thresholds for parent-joint venture licences.

15. **Article 6**

Essentially, Article 6 simply clarifies a few points where there might have been some doubt whether the Regulation applies.

15.1 Extension to sublicences (Art 6(1))

Article 6(1) confirms that is not necessary for the licensor to own the technology as long as he is entitled to grant the licence. It is therefore possible that the licensor will already hold the technology under a licence covered by the Regulation and that he will then grant further licences which are also block exempt. However, the head licensor will be unable to exercise much in the way of direct control over the sublicensee without risking the creation of a tripartite agreement which would infringe Article 1.1 (see comments at **Section 5**).

15.2 Extension to assignments (Art 6(2))

Article 6(2) is to a certain extent the converse of Article 5.1(5). Just as it is not permitted to dress up a sale agreement as a licence, Article 6(2) confirms that where the technology is apparently assigned but in fact the assignor still carries the risk of exploitation, such as where the assignee is paying for the technology according to his usage of it, then the assignment will be treated as being akin to a licence (see **Commentary Section 4**). This provision may have limited use since most genuine assignments, even if the consideration is calculated to some extent according to usage, are unlikely to contain other significant restrictions of competition. Where that could occur, Recital 9 reflects the Commission view that there is a "danger" that parties might be attempting to evade the provisions of the Regulation but that nevertheless the block exemption should apply.

It is not really clear why parties who wanted to impose restrictions of the type found in technology licences would want to try to dress up their agreement as an assignment which, if any of the provisions did restrict competition, might not be covered by any block exemption. The Commission refers to the parties attempting to evade the "requirements of this Regulation", which slightly misses the point that the Regulation is not in any sense compulsory but is supposed to offer a benefit to the parties. Nevertheless, even if one disagrees with the underlying assumption, it is certainly helpful to have the confirmation that the Regulation can still apply to such assignments.

15.3 Connected undertakings (Art 6(3))

Finally, Article 6(3) extends the scope of the exemption to agreements where "connected undertakings" accept certain rights or obligations. The definition in Article 10(14) covers companies within the same corporate group, which are traditionally treated as forming part of a single entity so that the agreement is still a bipartite one and Article 1.1 may still apply (see comments at **Section 5**).

16. Withdrawal (Art 7)

Despite the strict conditions for application of the block exemption and the numerous qualifications and reservations, the Commission retains the power to withdraw the benefit of the exemption where an exempted agreement has unforeseen restrictive effects upon competition which still make it unsuitable for exemption. This is not a procedure which the Commission would expect to invoke regularly. To date there has only been one case of actual withdrawal and a few threatened under other block exemption regulations (discussed in **Commentary Section 5.5**, below), none of which involves the Technology Regulation. If the benefit of the exemption were withdrawn, that would only apply from the date on which the withdrawal decision were taken.

A senior Commission official has commented that the Commission would adopt a minimalist approach and would normally not seek to withdraw the benefit of the entire exemption but would instead grant a specific exemption for the future, subject to satisfaction of a number of conditions designed to bring the agreement back into line with the general exemption criteria of Article 85(3).

The Commission gives specific examples of suitable cases for withdrawal as follows:

Table 2

The following Table summarises the categories of agreement covered by the Regulation.

Scope of the Regulation

Patent Licence		
a) including: (Recital 4)		
▪ Member State national patents	√	
▪ Community patents	√	
▪ European patents	√	
b) including: (Art 8.1)		
▪ patent application	√	
▪ utility model	√	
▪ application for registration of utility model	√	
▪ topography of semiconductor product	√	
▪ certificat d'utilité and certificat d'addition	√	
▪ application for certificat d'utilité or certificat d'addition	√	
▪ supplementary protection certificate for medicinal or other product	√	
▪ plant breeder's certificate	√	
c) including: (Art 8.2)		
▪ any of the above applications made after agreement concluded but within statutory time limits	√	
Know-how Licence	√	
Technology Assignment (Art 6(2))		×
▪ unless risk of exploitation remains with the assignor (Art 6(2))	√	
Patent or Know-how Pool (Art 5.1(1))		×
▪ unless no territorial restrictions within EU (Art 5.2(2))	√	
Technology Licence between joint venture parents who are competitors where the licence relates to the activities of the JV company (Art 5.1(2))		×
Technology Licence between a joint venture parent and the JV Company where the licence relates to activities of the JV (Art 5.1(2)) – unless licence limited to production and JV and parents combined have less than 20%* market share (Art 5.2(1))	√	×
– unless licence covers production and distribution and JV and parents combined have less than 10%* market share (Art 5.2(1)) [*may be exceeded by 10% in any one but not two consecutive financial years and exemption continues for 6 months from end of second year (Art 5.3)]	√	
Reciprocal Technology Licence or exclusive sales agreement between competitors (Art 5.1(3))		×
– unless no territorial restrictions within EU (Art 5.2(2))	√	
Technology Licence including provisions relating to non-ancillary unpatented intellectual property rights (Art 5.1(4))		×
Technology Licence for the purpose solely of sale rather than production (Art 5.1(5))		×
Technology Licence where the licensor has been authorised by a third party to grant licences (Art 6(1))	√	
Technology Licence where the obligations of the parties are assumed by connected undertakings (Art 6(3))	√	

16.1 Market share threshold (Art 7(1))

This reflects the fact that the block exemption does not include any assessment of the market share of the parties and therefore grants exemption to agreements which may lead to high concentrations of market share. Therefore, the exemption may be withdrawn in particular where the licensee has, or at any point achieves, a market share exceeding 40%.

At one stage during drafting of the Regulation it had been proposed to limit application of the entire Regulation by reference to market shares but this was dropped very late in the day following opposition and lobbying, particularly from industry. The principal objections were first that it would place an intolerable burden upon companies to work out with certainty their market shares so as to determine whether they were covered by the exemption and second that the resulting uncertainty would mean that a large number of agreements which should be block exempt would instead have to be individually notified. The last remnant of this proposal appears here, giving the Commission grounds to withdraw the exemption where competition is significantly limited and *in particular* where the licensee has a market share exceeding 40%. Recitals 26 and 27 confirm that the Commission will pay "special attention" to cases where the licensee has a market share exceeding 40% and invites the parties to consider notifying such agreements for individual exemption.

The definition in Article 10(9) confirms that the "licensee's market share" means the proportion of the relevant market held by the licensed products and any other goods or services provided by the licensee which users might consider interchangeable or substitutable. The relevant geographic market for these purposes could be the common market or a substantial part of it and not just the licensed territory, though if the licensee has been granted as his territory one or more Member States it has to remain likely that they will be treated as the relevant market. Recital 26 confirms that the Commission is only concerned about a lack of "real competition in the licensed territory". Therefore, there may be circumstances where the Commission is happy to allow an agreement to be covered by the block exemption where market shares far exceed 40% but there could equally be other cases where exemption might be withdrawn even though that threshold is not exceeded. In any event the burden of proof will fall on the Commission to establish the market share and to show a harmful effect on competition.

16.2 Refusal to supply (Art 7(2))

The exemption may also be withdrawn where the licensee unilaterally and without any objectively justified reason refuses to meet unsolicited orders from customers in the territory of other licensees. This is without prejudice to Article 1.1(6) which allows a contractual restriction on such "passive" sales for an initial five-year period. The inclusion here of the reference to the reason being "objectively justified" does not raise the same difficulties as in the case of Article 3(3), since it only constitutes grounds for withdrawal and the licensee will have an opportunity to explain his behaviour to the Commission, whereas in the case of Article 3(3) a later determination that the reason was not justified will have the effect of depriving the parties of the benefit of the exemption *ab initio*.

16.3 Blocking parallel trade (Art 7(3))

Although this refers to "the parties", it must in fact refer to unilateral action where one or more of the parties independently take steps designed to frustrate parallel trade. This supplements Article 3(3) (see **Section 12.3**, above) under which the benefit of the exemption is automatically lost where one party requires the other to take such steps, or where there is a concerted practice to do so. Once again (see comments in **Section 16.2**, above) the parties would have an opportunity to explain their conduct and reasons.

16.4 Competing manufacturers (Art 7(4))

The Commission recognises that the obligations to produce minimum quantities or use best endeavours to manufacture and market the licensed products (included in the list of approved restrictions at Art 2.1(9) and (17)) could have unforeseen effects on competition where the parties were already competing manufacturers. This is only likely to become an issue if the licensee is complaining to the Commission. It would therefore be a practical step for the licensor to insert a provision in the agreement reciting the parties' common view that the agreement complies with the Regulation but reserving to the licensor a right to terminate the agreement as a whole if the Commission withdraws the benefit of the block exemption in these circumstances, or perhaps for any other reason.

17. **Scope of the Regulation (Art 8)**

17.1 Definition of patents (Art 8.1)

Even before considering the interpretation given in Article 8.1, it is necessary to refer to Recital 4 to the Regulation which confirms that all references to "patents" include national patents of the Member States, "Community patents" and "European patents". None of these is defined in Article 10 of the Regulation (but see the footnote to **Section 4.3**, above).

Article 8.1 extends the definition of "patent" to include patent applications, utility models and similar matters. Most of these categories were already identified in the Patent Regulation. However, three new additions are topographies of semi conductor products, supplementary protection certificates for medicinal products and plant breeders' certificates. There is no explanation either in the Recitals or elsewhere for this extension, or any recognition of the particular issues which might arise.

For instance, plant breeders' certificates had previously been specifically excluded from the exemption in Article 5 of the Patent Regulation, on the basis that experience at that time was inadequate to allow block exemption. Plant breeders' rights are different from ordinary patents (though not different enough to escape Art 85: see *Nungesser*, **Case Note 3**) because the first generation of propagating material may be capable of producing further generations in breach of the breeder's rights and therefore it may be necessary to control the persons to whom that material is sold and the conditions under which those persons may themselves be granted a licence for further exploitation. For this reason, despite the extension in Article 8, it is possible that many plant breeders' agreements will need to include additional restrictions beyond those permitted by this Regulation and therefore will continue to be notified.

17.2 Patent applications (Art 8.2)

Article 8.2 extends the Regulation to agreements where patent applications are made within the appropriate time limit (under the Patent Regulation it was necessary to submit applications within one year of invention). This increased flexibility is helpful. One minor difficulty which remains is that Article 1.2 only allows the territorial restrictions for so long as the products are actually protected in other territories by "parallel patents". The common sense view must be that as long as it is intended to apply for a patent in those territories and as long as that application has a reasonable prospect of success, the territorial restrictions will be viewed as enforceable (extending the notion of "parallel patents" to include "parallel applications" by combining Article 8.1 with the definition in Article 10(13)) but any parties who wish to rely upon the Regulation would be advised to submit their applications as soon as practicable.

17.3 Improvements (Art 8.3)

This provides that the Regulation shall apply where the agreements are automatically prolonged by inclusion of new improvements *communicated by the licensor*, as long as the licensee is entitled to refuse those improvements or each party must be able to terminate on expiry of the initial term and at least every three years thereafter. There is no explanation as to why communication of the licensee's improvements should not have the same consequences and one could say that there is nothing in the Regulation to prevent this. Certainly, the definition of the "licensed technology" in Article 10(7) refers to improvements without any distinction as to who discovered them. In addition it is important to note that it is only the Regulation and not the entirety of the exemption which is stated to apply in such circumstances. Article 3(7) (see **Section 12.7**, above) continues to prevent the territorial restrictions from being extended except where approved by individual decision.

18. Confidentiality (Art 9)

Article 9 is an interesting provision in that it seeks to limit the use which the Commission, and the Member States, may make of information submitted in order to claim the benefit of the Article 4 opposition procedure. There is a certain logic here, since this concerns agreements which arguably came very close to being covered by the block exemption and therefore would not have been brought to the attention of the authorities. However, some doubts have been expressed as to whether the Commission has power to give such assurances of confidentiality or to bind the Member States. The practical points to be made are as follows:

- if the Commission does oppose exemption the parties will effectively have the option of treating the notification as made under Regulation 17 or of abandoning the notification and risking the consequences;
- if the Commission becomes aware of matters in which it decides to take an interest, it can always initiate separate proceedings under Regulation 17 and compel the information to be provided. The same applies to Member States under their national competition laws;
- parties who do notify under the opposition procedure would be advised to take advantage of the concession in Recital 25 to provide as little information as is necessary.

19. Definitions (Art 10)

Those definitions which are significant have already been treated in relation to the key provisions to which they relate.

20. Transitional provisions (Art 11)

20.1 Article 11.1

This Article repeals the Know-how Regulation as of 1 April 1996. That Regulation would otherwise have remained in force until 31 September 1999.

20.2 Article 11.2

This Article recognises that the Patent Regulation had originally been due to expire on 31 December 1994 and had been extended in stages until 31 December 1995. Article 13 attempts to close the gap by effecting a further renewal as from 1 January 1996, until 31 March 1996.

20.3 Article 11.3

This Article completes the coverage by providing that agreements already in force on 31 March 1996 which complied with the Patent or Know-how Regulations shall continue to be exempt under the

Technology Regulation. There is some logic for this approach in relation to the Know-how Regulation, since parties had a legitimate expectation that agreements which complied with the Know-how Regulation would continue to be exempt at least until the natural expiry of that Regulation in 1999. Parties had no such expectations in relation to patent licences since the Patent Regulation was, as mentioned, due to expire at the end of 1994 and any extensions were only likely to be temporary until the Commission finalised the Technology Regulation. In any event, given that the Technology Regulation is more generous than its predecessors, the extension is not unreasonable.

Article 11.3 does not state for how long that exemption will endure but logically it must be for the life of the new Regulation and therefore parties who had agreements in force on 31 March 1996 will effectively be able to argue for application of any of the Patent, Know-how or Technology Regulations as appropriate.

22.   **Review (Art 12)**

Article 12 is self-explanatory. The Commission is to review progress of the Regulation and draw up a report at around the turn of the century and it is anticipated by Commission officials that the Commission may move towards further relaxation and a more generous regulation.

23.   **Duration (Art 13)**

Finally, the Commission confirms the entry into force of the Regulation on 1 April 1996, to apply until 31 March 2006. The interrelationship between Article 13 and Article 11.3 means that parties can rely upon the Technology Regulation for all agreements currently in force even if they came into force before 1 April 1996. It follows that if agreements were signed before 1 April 1996 but did not take effect until afterwards, it is only the Technology Regulation which can be relied upon. It also confirms the retrospective revival of the Patent Regulation. It was possible that there might have been some legal challenges, on the basis that agreements previously exempted by the Patent Regulation fell out of exemption during the first three months of 1996 and were therefore void under Article 85(2) without the possibility of being saved retrospectively. This does not seem to have happened yet and will have less significance with the passage of time. At the very least, there must be a question mark as to the ability of the Commission to grant retrospective exemption for agreements which cannot satisfy Article 3 of Regulation 19/65 because they do not fall within the class of agreement permitted retrospective exemption by individual decision under Article 4.2(2) of Regulation 17. It is unfortunate that the Commission did not adopt a further extension of the Patent Regulation in late 1995 to avoid this issue and one hopes that if such points do arise, the Commission will feel itself compelled (or at least morally obliged) to do what it can to plug the gap.

Part 4

· **Commentary** ·

1. **Introduction**

Any consideration of the Technology Regulation needs to begin with a clear understanding of what a block exemption regulation is and what it is not.

The Regulation offers an exemption for agreements which comply strictly with its terms. The justification for granting this automatic exemption is that an agreement which does fit within the framework of the Regulation is deemed to meet the criteria for exemption contained in Article 85(3) of the Treaty. As a result, the agreement is granted an automatic exemption from the prohibition in Article 85(2). It does not need to be notified to the Commission and the parties can implement the agreement without facing the possibility of fines or a challenge to its enforceability in court. The Regulation therefore can be seen as a device provided for the administrative convenience of the Commission which offers a degree of certainty and cost savings to the parties.

As to what it is not, the Regulation is not mandatory. Despite the impression that is sometimes, given it is not a "blueprint" for technology licensing which the parties are bound to follow. Nor does it prevent the parties from entering into more complex or more restrictive arrangements. Finally, the mere fact that the Commission has drafted a Regulation for such agreements should not lead to the presumption that all technology transfer agreements are caught by Article 85 or need exemption. Unfortunately, one does have to accept that the existence of the Regulation does add to the tendency for competition authorities to assume that technology licences are restrictive of competition, even where the licence is enabling the licensee to engage in an activity which would otherwise have been entirely closed to him. Moreover, there is an even stronger presumption that the Regulation in general terms places a limit on the type of restrictions which can be imposed and that any agreement which contains more restrictive provisions will need to be backed up by special circumstances if it is to receive an exemption. Practical experience shows the Commission often responding to a notification by directing the parties to redraw their agreements so as to bring them into line with one or other provision of the Regulation. The parties often need to be sure of their ground and extremely determined if they are to withstand that pressure.

In this section a number of the fundamental questions surrounding the Regulation its scope, purpose and usefulness are discussed. Taking them in order:

- does Article 85(1) apply at all to the agreement in question and therefore is there any need to consider the Regulation?
- exactly what types of agreement can benefit from the Regulation?
- what are the benefits of the Regulation?
- what are the drawbacks of the Regulation?
- when should the opposition procedure be used?
- when would one want to go beyond what the Regulation permits?
- some of the difficult areas within the Regulation;
- issues which arise on joint ventures and concentrations;
- contrasts with the earlier Patent and Know-how Regulations.

2. Could Article 85(1) apply?

It is important to remember that the Regulation is only relevant if the agreement requires an exemption. That means that it must infringe Article 85(1) on the basis that it is capable of having an appreciable effect on competition and on trade between Member States. Many agreements do not produce such effects, either because of the size and market share of the parties or the limited area within which they operate. The advantage of the Regulation is that it absolves the parties from the need to enquire into such matters, which may prove impossible to resolve with certainty even if detailed market analysis is available. Instead the parties know that if they comply with the Regulation they will have an exemption if it later turns out that they needed it. However, before deciding that they need to rely upon the Regulation, the parties should spend some time considering the following:

2.1 Are there two or more undertakings?

Case law has confirmed that Article 85 only applies to agreements between two independent "undertakings". Consequently, a number of bilateral agreements may, on closer inspection, escape Article 85. Some issues to examine are:

Are the parties to the agreement members of a single group of companies who would be categorised as forming a single "undertaking" under Article 85? Within large corporate groups it is quite common to conclude technology transfer agreements between parent and subsidiary or between two subsidiaries of a common parent, if only so as to formalise the arrangement and make clear the duties and responsibilities of each. It may be necessary to have a formal agreement in order to justify payments of royalties and other transfers of funds between affiliates in different countries. Nevertheless, if the companies are under common control Article 85 will not apply. There is a theoretical exception that where a company enjoys a degree of genuine autonomy it could be said to be independent of its parent for Article 85 purposes and therefore constitute a separate undertaking but though this possibility has been recognised we are not aware of any ruling in which it has been applied. If there were any risk that the wording of a licence could suggest a degree of independence and later give rise to competition problems, it would be worth considering a recital in the agreement spelling out that the entities have been directed by their parent to conclude this agreement. The position would of course have to be reviewed again if one of the companies were subsequently sold outside the group and that would be part of standard due diligence where the licence is an important asset of the target company.

Even if independent, is the other party an "undertaking" at all? To be classified as an undertaking the party needs to engage in economic activity. Therefore, an individual who comes up with a patentable invention or builds up valuable licensable know-how may not necessarily be treated as an undertaking for Article 85 purposes. It would be necessary to investigate whether this inventive activity provides his livelihood or whether it is just a fringe activity. There have been a couple of cases where individuals have been treated as undertakings but these were quite exceptional. Where the individual is the *licensor* it may be easier to argue that he should not be treated as an undertaking. On the other hand, if a corporate licensor grants a licence to an individual *licensee* in his sole capacity but where he is clearly intended to work the licence and pay royalties, then the fact that he is a sole trader rather than a small company is not likely to alter the finding that he is for economic and competition law purposes an undertaking within the meaning of Article 85.

Even if legally independent, is the licensee genuinely independent for competition law purposes? One example of a relationship where European competition law recognises that the requisite independence may be lacking is where the other party is an agent of the first. Agency arrangements are common in relation to distribution of goods but are less likely to apply in technology licensing, since it is far less likely that the owner of technology would appoint somebody else to exploit that technology as his "agent".

The Commission has had great difficulty with the concept of agency. It has for many years been working on a new notice which will confirm the circumstances in which an independent entity who acts as an agent is treated as an integral part of the organisation of the principal, so that any agreements between them are not really capable of eliminating any competition which would otherwise have existed. In the meantime one has to look at the old agency notice (Commission Notice on exclusive dealing contracts with commercial agents, OJ 1962 No 139 of 24.12.62) and the case law for the key principles. From this it can be seen that the main criteria for determining whether the agency exemption applies, are whether the agent performs activities for other parties as well as the principal and whether he undertakes significant risk. If the agent is acting as an agent for others or has other business activities or if he is expected to assume a significant degree of risk, he will normally be treated as sufficiently independent from his principal and Article 85 could apply. Given that one of the main reasons for appointing a licensee of technology is to place the risk of success or failure on him, or at least to spread the risk, one would not normally expect the licensee to be appointed as an agent but it is not impossible.

More likely than agency, is that the owner of the technology might appoint a subcontractor to exploit some part of the technology on his behalf. The Commission recognised some time ago that subcontracting agreements were capable of escaping Article 85. That could be the case if the owner of technology allows a subcontractor to exploit that technology under strict conditions and where it can be shown that the subcontractor could not have engaged in the activity without the licence. The Commission's Notice on subcontracting dates back to 1979 (OJ 1979 C1 of 3.1.79). It should be studied carefully but essentially allows the owner of the technology to limit its use to the purposes of the subcontracting agreement. The subcontractor may also be required to supply the goods produced only to the owner or to perform the services only on behalf of the owner. Finally, the subcontractor may be required to license back on an exclusive basis any improvements which are not severable from the original technology. The Notice supplements, in relation to subcontracting, a more general notice on co-operation between enterprises published in 1968 (OJ 1968 C75 of 29.7.68).

The requirement to pass back non-severable improvements is also recognised as not infringing competition in Article 2.1(4) of the Technology Regulation, though the Subcontracting Notice is actually less demanding than the Regulation and does not require a reciprocal licence back by the licensor of his own improvements.

The permitted obligation in the Subcontracting Notice to supply the goods back to the contractor may also go further than Article 2.1(13) of the Regulation (see **Analysis Section 10.13**), which allows the licensee to be limited to supplying the licensed products to a particular customer who could in certain circumstances be the licensee himself, but which does not apparently envisage that the customer might be the *licensor*. It might be interesting to test, perhaps using the opposition procedure, whether Article 2.1(13) could in fact cover a situation where the licensor is manufacturing for his own use and wishes to appoint a licensee to provide him with a second source of supply. In any event it is clear that the Subcontracting Notice will only be of use for a limited class of technology licences and will not be appropriate where the licensee is being assigned a territory in which to manufacture and to develop the market or where there are any significant restrictions imposed on the licensor. Moreover, as with the Minor Agreements Notice (see **Section 3.1,** below) it is expressly stated to be without prejudice to any view that might be taken by the European Court. Curiously, unlike other such Commission notices, there is no reference to the views of national courts but it would be sensible to read it as if the reference were included.

2.2 Open or closed licences

Not all exclusive technology licences infringe Article 85. There is considerable jurisprudence on the question of whether an "open exclusive licence" is caught by Article 85(1). The reference to an "open" licence is generally accepted as describing a licence where the licensor grants to the licensee an exclusive territory and agrees not to appoint other licensees within that territory or himself exploit the technology within that territory, but where no restrictions are placed upon the sales activity of the licensee or of any other licensees in other territories. In other words, the licensee is not guaranteed absolute "territorial protection" but neither is he confined to his allotted territory. He has to accept that he might face competition from licensees appointed in neighbouring territories who might decide to target customers within his territory but he is also free to offer similar competition to those licensees if he wishes.

This is a difficult area because the European case law is inconsistent as to whether particular provisions infringe Article 85(1) or require exemption under Article 85(3). The principal cases (*e.g. Nungesser*, **Case Note 3**) suggest that an open licence may escape Article 85(1), at least where the technology is new and a reasonable period of exclusivity is thought necessary to justify investment by the licensee (but not where it merely involves extended exploitation of established technology: *Velcro*, **Case Note 10**). Recital 10 of the Regulation recognises this when it notes that certain agreements may not be incompatible with Article 85(1) if justified by the scale of the research and the resultant increase in the level of competition. The licence is accordingly treated as essentially permissive: it is opening the door to allow the licensee to engage in activities in which, but for the licence, he could not have been a competitor in the market.

However, this debate, although still of considerable academic interest, is inevitably of less relevance today for licensors and licensees. First, statements such as those in Recital 10 are extremely vague and subjective: they fall short of giving the certainty which investing parties may require since they cannot risk the Commission later concluding that the market was not sufficiently competitive for them to escape Article 85. Secondly, if they wish to include further restrictions (such as limitations on sales activities) it is likely that they will require an exemption, whether individual or block exemption. Finally, given that the Regulation certainly covers for the avoidance of doubt such simple open exclusive licences, the parties may not be concerned whether they require an exemption or not. One exception might be if a simple exclusive know-how licence were granted in which the licensor agreed not to compete with the licensee for a period exceeding 10 years from first marketing of the product by a licensee. In those circumstances the parties would note the limitation in Article 1.3 of the Regulation upon territorial restrictions exceeding 10 years in know-how licences. They would have to consider whether the level of investment in a new product justified such a period of protection in an "open exclusive" licence and whether the agreement was in reality likely to have appreciable effects on competition so as to require notification.

Another point to bear in mind, is that elsewhere the Regulation demonstrates the Commission's ambivalence about exclusive licences where the licensee has a significant market share. Article 7 and Recital 26 confirm the possibility of withdrawal of the block exemption where the licensee's market share exceeds 40% (see also **Section 5.5**, below). The Regulation goes further in Recital 27, inviting the parties to notify even agreements covered by the block exemption if the licensor agrees not to grant other licences in the territory and the licensee's market share exceeds or is likely to exceed 40%. Therefore, the Commission is saying that even open exclusive licences may not only require exemption in some circumstances but may go further than is contemplated by the block exemption.

3.   If Article 85(1) could on its face apply are there any options?

3.1 De minimis

Agreements which are likely only to have an insignificant effect on competition or trade will not infringe Article 85(1). It will depend in each case upon the circumstances, the size of the parties, market structure etc whether the agreement will produce effects that are "appreciable" (see *Delplanque*, **Case Note 1**). The Commission has given some assistance in its Notice on Agreements of Minor Importance, which was amended quite significantly in December 1997 (OJ 1997 C372 of 9.12.97). Essentially, the Notice takes the approach that where the parties to the licence have between them only a small share of the market, then any agreements between them are unlikely to infringe Article 85. Even where there remains a risk of infringement, the Commission will normally not take action itself but will leave enforcement to the Member States. In the case of those Member States which have not given their competition authorities the power to apply Article 85 and Article 86 (and at the time of the amendment to the Notice, the UK was one such Member State and likely to remain so – see **Section 12**, below) the Commission has said it will at least expect them to apply their own domestic competition law to achieve similar effects to those which would have been obtained by applying Articles 85 and 86. If a Member State could not take effective action and if the Commission considered that the agreement was harming the operation of the internal market, it could still act.

The Notice introduces two market share tests.

1. Where an agreement is a "horizontal" one between parties at the same level in the market (*e.g.* both are manufacturers or both are distributors) the Commission is concerned that any agreement between them is very likely to restrict competition and therefore it has set the market share threshold at 5%.

2. On the other hand where the agreement is a "vertical agreement" (*i.e.* between parties at different levels such as a producer of a bulk pharmaceutical compound and his licensee who is applying the licensed technology to produce the finished product) the market share threshold is set at a more generous 10% level.

In calculating these market shares, it is necessary to take account not only of the shares of the licensor and licensee but also those of any parties with whom licensor and/or licensee have concluded similar agreements.

There are two difficulties in seeking to apply the Notice to technology transfer agreements. The first is that if the licensor is also himself making use of the licensed technology for the same purposes as the licensee, even though in a different territory, the agreement could be viewed as a horizontal agreement between two competing manufacturers and therefore subject to the 5% level. The fact that prior to entering into the agreement the licensee was not an actual or potential competing manufacturer would not appear to allow the parties to rely on the Notice during the life of the agreement. The Notice does say (in para 9) that where the agreement is a "mixed horizontal/vertical agreement" or is difficult to classify then the 5% threshold will always apply.

The second difficulty is more fundamental. The previous version of the Notice had applied a 5% level to all agreements. While the Commission was ready to extend the threshold to 10% for some vertical agreements, it was clearly nervous at opening the door too widely to agreements which could still be significantly restrictive. Therefore, very late in the legislative process, it introduced a significant qualification in paragraph 11. This provides that where the purpose of a horizontal agreement is to fix prices or limit production or to share markets or sources of supply, then Article 85 might still be infringed however small the market shares. In relation to vertical agreements the qualification provides that where the aim of the agreement is to fix resale prices or where it confers territorial protection on the undertakings or third parties, then once again the Notice cannot be relied on at all. Therefore, whether a technology transfer agreement is treated as horizontal or vertical, if there are any provisions relating to allocation of exclusive or partially exclusive territories then the revised Notice will not offer any protection. The jeopardy is increased further by the fact that paragraph 5 of the Notice says that the Commission will not impose fines where parties have assumed "in good faith" that they could rely upon the Notice. That was intended to offer comfort to parties who were not sure whether they were above or below the market share thresholds but it clearly means that if the agreement includes any territorial provisions the parties could not assert their good faith belief and will therefore be at risk of fines. Effectively, the Commission through these late amendments has managed to render the Minor Agreements Notice inapplicable to the vast majority of technology transfer agreements and this a regrettably retrograde step at a time when the application of competition law generally is becoming more relaxed.

It does not follow that parties who conclude technology transfer agreements should entirely ignore the Notice. What the Notice does still represent, is helpful confirmation of the accepted principle that restrictive agreements whose effects are *de minimis* can escape the prohibition in Article 85 and this can be true even if the parties have large shares of the market. Market share is one indicator but it is also necessary to look at the agreement itself and the types of restrictions which it contains. It is also necessary to look at the structure of the market. Even where the parties do have a market share exceeding 5% or 10% it is quite possible, if one or two other competitors have significantly larger market shares, that the agreement will not be capable of affecting competition or trade to any significant degree.

Market definition is not yet an exact science in European competition law, although at the same time as issuing the latest Minor Agreements Notice the Commission published a new notice on market definition (OJ 1997 C372/5 of 9.12.97). The latter is helpful and the Commission, in Article 16 of the Minor Agreements Notice, directs parties to make use of it. It is also important to bear in mind that ultimately the burden of proof is on the Commission to establish what is the appropriate market and to demonstrate that an agreement does have the object or effect of harming competition. Once again, it is for the parties to the agreement to stand their ground and force the Commission to discharge the burden of proof of defining the market and demonstrating the effects.

The position can of course change as the agreement progresses. If the product is genuinely novel the parties may theoretically have 10% of a non-existent market but there would initially be no impact on trade between Member States. On the other hand, if entering a mature market the parties may initially have a very low market share and therefore the agreement may be incapable of having an appreciable impact upon competition but that could change if the licensee is successful. It is therefore necessary periodically to review whether reliance on the Notice or on the general *de minimis* concept is still appropriate and, if the agreement appears to have grown into something more significant, to reconsider whether either block or individual exemption is required. In brief, a "wait and see" approach is reasonable as long as it is thought through and periodically revisited.

There is the further caveat that the Notice, even if it represents a commitment by the Commission to take no action, is expressly stated not to bind the European Court or national courts. It does not amount to a "block negative clearance" in the same way that the Technology Regulation represents a block exemption. Therefore, the parties still run the risk that competition law will be raised in national courts even in respect of minor agreements and particularly where one party is seeking to evade its contractual obligations: there has been a significant growth in the use of such "Euro defences". Perhaps the picture will become clearer when the Commission completes its reviews of its approach to vertical and horizontal restraints (see **Section 11,** below) and may then be prepared to take a wider ranging and more generous approach.

3.2 Article 4.2 of Regulation 17

The Technology Regulation grants an exemption without the need for notification and that exemption applies automatically from the commencement of the agreement. On the other hand, if it turns out that an agreement needs to be notified for individual exemption, Article 6.1 of Regulation 17 provides that an exemption can only be backdated to the date of notification. A number of exceptions to this principle are contained in Article 4.2 of Regulation 17.

Article 4.2(1) provides for the possibility of exemption for an unnotified agreement where the parties are undertakings based in a single Member State and where the agreement does not "relate either to imports or to exports between Member States". Logically, Article 4.2(1) does not require that the agreement should not have an "effect" on imports or exports, since if that were the case Article 85(1) would not apply in any event. The precise meaning of the provision is not clear and Article 4.2(1) has rarely been invoked successfully (one of the few successful cases having concerned beer supply agreements between breweries and tied houses in the UK). However, it must be possible that a licence between two parties based in a single Member State, granting a licence to work a patent in that state but being silent as to any restrictions on imports or exports, could benefit from the exception and could contain a range of restrictions (even going beyond those permitted in the Technology Regulation) without needing to be notified. If it were later argued that the agreement infringed Article 85(1) and required exemption, it would be open to the parties to the agreement to ask the Commission to take an individual decision confirming exemption as from the date of the agreement.

Article 4.2(2)(b) of Regulation 17 provides that notification is not necessary where an agreement involves no more than two parties and only imposes restrictions on the exercise of the rights of an assignee or user of industrial property rights, referring specifically *inter alia* to patents and trade marks. It could apply to a non-exclusive licence *i.e.* one involving the acceptance of no restrictions by the licensor but imposing a range of restrictions upon the licensee, as long as those restrictions relate only to use of the licensed rights.

An important point to remember is that Article 4.2 only relates to circumstances in which an early notification is not necessary in order to allow the possibility of backdating any eventual exemption. Nevertheless, if it is subsequently determined that Article 85(1) does apply to the agreement, the Commission will only grant an exemption where the criteria of Article 85(3) are met. It follows that an agreement which is significantly more restrictive than would have been permitted by the Technology Regulation must run a significant risk of being declared ineligible for a back-dated exemption. There would also be the possible further risk of Commission fines and of national court action by affected third parties claiming damages.

As part of its vertical restraints review (see **Section 11**, below) the Commission is considering radically amending Article 4.2 so as to permit backdated exemptions in a wide range of cases, with a view to reducing the flood of protective notifications. If this approach is adopted it could save the parties from going through the notification process until it is absolutely necessary and also absolve the Commission from having to study a large number of agreements which do not really give rise to any difficulties. However, it will probably not do much to improve the position of agreements which already have a dedicated block exemption regulation, such as technology transfer agreements. If the agreement departs significantly from the provisions permitted by the Technology Regulation, the parties will have no certainty from the outset that the Commission will ultimately accept that the agreement should benefit from an exemption without being heavily amended. If the Commission does insist on amendments it is very likely that it will not be prepared to backdate the exemption in respect of those provisions which do require amendment (and indeed it could not legitimately do so, since the reason the Commission would be asking for the amendments would be because it felt that those provisions could not meet the criteria for exemption in Art 85(3)). As a result, parties who wanted to exceed the block exemption and argue for exemption would still need to file a notification at the point that they conclude the agreement and hope that they could persuade the Commission or at least achieve some early certainty. One would not therefore expect any changes to Article 4.2 to result in a lessening of the incidence of notification of technology transfer agreements.

3.3 Other regulations

Space does not permit a discussion here, but the parties should consider whether any of the other block exemption regulations might be more suitable, such as Regulation 1983/83 on exclusive distribution; Regulation 1984/83 on exclusive purchasing; the Franchising Regulation 4087/88; the Specialisation Regulation 417/85 or the Research and Development Regulation 418/85[1] (the limitations of which are demonstrated by *KSB*, **Case Note 20**). Perhaps the key point to bear in mind, is that only one block exemption can be relied upon with respect to any agreement or arrangement. Therefore, parties need to identify the single block exemption which is most appropriate and most generous for their circumstances but it is not possible to take an à la carte approach and rely on a combination of provisions from more than one Regulation. Having said that, it is quite possible that parties might negotiate first a patent licensing agreement covered by the Technology Regulation and very shortly thereafter conclude quite independently an exclusive distribution agreement which could be covered by Regulation 1983/83. If they do so they would need to be able to convince the Commission and/or any court that the two agreements were in no sense

---

1 These are all likely to be replaced by the "super block exemption" discussed at Section 11 below.

interdependent and if they were insufficiently persuasive might find that the two agreements were treated as a single arrangement which did not benefit from either of the block exemptions.

3.4 Choosing the Technology Regulation

Having analysed the provisions of the Regulation and some of the alternatives considered above, the parties may find themselves forced to decide whether to opt for use of the Technology Regulation or to submit an individual notification for exemption. The third possibility of course is to ignore the issue altogether and risk the application of Article 85 without seeking individual or block exemption. Whether that course should be followed will depend upon the parties' own assessment of:

- the real significance of the agreement, taking account of the sums invested, its scope and likely duration;
- the risk of litigation by the parties: does one have far more to lose than another if the agreement is declared unenforceable?
- the likelihood of the agreement coming to the attention of the Commission and of the Commission deciding that it merits the resources for an investigation and prohibition decision;
- the possibility of actions for damages by third parties.

In practice, it is litigation which is generally the greater risk and which prompts one or other party to argue in favour of exemption. Most litigation has involved licensees challenging enforcement of restrictions but it is not unknown for a *licensor* to claim at a later stage that his licence was invalid (see *Velcro*, **Case Note 10**). The threat of Commission fines is always a deterrent but in reality the Commission only adopts between 10 and 20 prohibition decisions a year (see Table 3 in **Section 7**), so it is unlikely that it would devote the resources to prosecuting a relatively unexceptional technology transfer agreement. Nevertheless, any risk, however small, of the Commission imposing fines of up to 10% of total group annual turnover might make the odds look too unattractive. Similarly, although so far it appears that no person has yet succeeded in getting a UK national court to award damages for breach of European competition law, the day cannot be far off when a plaintiff will be successful.

Ultimately, however, the decision on seeking exemption will be prompted mostly by considering the issues of significance and enforceability. A licensor who has handed over his technology will have to assess how important it is that he should be able to enforce the restrictions upon the licensee, such as those preventing him using the technology for unauthorised purposes or insisting that he continue to acquire his raw materials from the licensor and not compete outside the licensed territory. Traditionally UK national courts (and others, see *Pestre*, **Case Note 26**) have taken a consistently "robust" approach to attempts by defendants to avoid contractual obligations by pleading breaches of competition law. However, if any provision were clearly excessively restrictive the national court would have to take account of Article 85(1) and (2) and declare the prohibition void. It would then be a question of English law whether the provision could be severed and whether the agreement then stood or fell entirely (see **Section 8.1,** below). Similarly, if one of the parties argues that the agreement is covered by the Technology Regulation, the UK court would have to carry out that assessment and if it found that the agreement contained one of the clauses in the Black List would then have to declare all of the anti-competitive restrictions void, even if some of them individually would have been covered by the Regulation.

Essentially, the decision always comes down to a number of questions. If the parties are determined for whatever reason not to notify, they should be asked whether it is essential that they include restrictions going beyond the Regulation. If they cannot be certain of being able to enforce those restrictions, they must at least take that possibility into account when negotiating the other commercial terms. If advising the licensor, one should seek to provide that he retains a right to terminate without cause on relatively short notice so that, should competition issues arise, he always has the possibility of bringing the entire relationship to an end rather than finding himself locked into an agreement which leaves the licensee with too much freedom. Alternatively, the licensor could consider reserving a right to terminate if certain of the restrictive provisions are subsequently held to be unenforceable. The only (rather remote) risk here is that it will be argued that the inclusion of such a clause is a "penalty" designed to deter the licensee from challenging the anti-competitive nature of the agreement and that the termination clause should also be struck down as unenforceable. Although one would not expect most English courts to take that approach, it is not unknown for the Commission to do so and it has to be possible that the Commission might try, through its coercive or fining powers, to prevent reliance on such clauses.

4. **What types of agreement are covered by the Technology Regulation?**

To some extent the title of the Regulation is slightly misleading. It would be more accurate to describe its subject as "technology licensing" rather than "technology transfer" as it appears in the English version. That is because if there were an outright transfer of a patent or body of know-how, the Regulation would be unlikely to apply. Recital 1 of the Regulation acknowledges that the Commission had power (under Reg 19/65) to exempt certain categories of agreements which would have included contracts for the assignment of a package of industrial knowledge. However, the Commission, both in the Patent and Know-how Regulations and now in the Technology Regulation, has chosen to limit the scope of its block exemptions to circumstances in which the relationship is closer to that of licensor and licensee.

The Regulation is designed to apply wherever the "assignor" retains the risk associated with exploitation *i.e.* where the level of revenue which he receives from the assignee/licensee is dependent upon the use which the assignee/licensee makes of the technology. Article 6(2) and Recital 9 of the Regulation make it clear that where a licence is for some reason disguised as a transfer or assignment, it will still be treated as an agreement potentially exempted by the Regulation provided that the "assignor" is paid according to the extent to which the technology is exploited by the assignee/licensee. If the owner of the technology is making a decision to sell his technology outright, he will have to make an assessment from the outset of the value of that technology. If he wants to hedge his bets and retain some right to a share in the success which the licensee makes of his subsequent exploitation, then he has to accept that the agreement may be categorised as a "technology transfer agreement" within the meaning of the Regulation and that any other restrictions which are imposed, such as an obligation to source raw materials or other inputs from the "assignor", will also be subjected to the Regulation.

In practice this is probably as much a benefit as it is a burden: if any restrictive agreements are concluded in conjunction with a purported transfer of intellectual property (such as an obligation to continue to source raw materials from the transferor), those agreements will themselves be subject to the possible application of Article 85 and could require exemption. The parties do at least have the opportunity in such circumstances of arguing for application of the block exemption granted by the Regulation.

There may still be circumstances where it will be uncertain whether the agreement should be treated as an outright transfer of intellectual property/know-how or whether it might be classified as an agreement falling within the Regulation. For instance, an inventor might assign one or more patents outright with no possibility of recovering them and impose no restrictions on exploitation or any minimum production obligations but might (being unable to predict the possible success of the invention and hence unable to calculate a fair selling price) want a production based royalty. If he has assigned all of his patents then it is unlikely that there could be any infringement of Article 85 and the applicability of the block exemption would not be relevant. However, if he has assigned only patents for some countries within the EU and if he also wants a contractual restriction on any form of exploitation in the countries where he has retained patent rights, he may find that he is then able to continue to rely on the Regulation. This does create a situation where applicability of the Regulation is dependent upon something which does not in itself have any impact on competition (*i.e.* the manner in which the royalty/remuneration is calculated) but one just has to accept that block exemption regulations are often of necessity limited and there can be some arbitrary results around the fringes.

In addition, it is important to remember that the Regulation does not extend only to simple licences for patents and know-how. There is a wide range of variations on patent rights such as patent applications, utility models and plant breeders certificates which are brought within the Regulation's definition of "patents". There are also numerous exceptions where the Regulation limits it application depending upon the relationship between the parties, whether they are already competitors concluding reciprocal agreements and whether they are joint venture parents. For convenience the various permutations are set out in Table 2 at **Analysis Section 15.3**.

5. **Benefits and drawbacks of the Regulation**

The major benefits and possible pitfalls of seeking to comply with the provisions of the Regulation are the following:

5.1 A significant degree of legal certainty

As discussed in the Introduction, the block exemption gives legal certainty without the need for notification. This certainty was the outstanding feature of the earlier block exemption regulations such as the exclusive distribution block exemption granted by Regulation 1983/83, which is an extremely short and simple regulation. However, as block exemptions have become more complex a degree of vagueness or subjectivity has inevitably crept in and this is particularly illustrated by the Technology Regulation. In an understandable desire to cater for the needs of commercial parties without providing a charter for anti-competitive agreements, the Commission has introduced a number of value judgements such as whether certain provisions are "necessary". An example is Article 2.1(5) where the licensee can be required to procure goods or services from the licensor where those are "necessary" for technical or quality reasons. To some extent this undermines the potential for achieving certainty and can throw the parties back on notification, even if only under the truncated opposition procedure (see **Section 6**, below).

The use of such vague wording, or at least of wording susceptible to more than one interpretation, places significant responsibility on the draftsman of an agreement which the parties wish to benefit from the block exemption. The shortage of case law concerning block exemptions is another major handicap. Where possible it would be highly advisable to track the wording of the Regulation. For instance, if dealing with a know-how licence it would be worth considering incorporating the relevant definitions from Article 10 and include Recitals confirming that both parties acknowledge that the information meets the various criteria of secrecy, substantiality and identification. This is particularly important because notwithstanding what has been said earlier (see Introduction) about the European purposive approach to interpretation, it is likely that such questions will be decided by national courts, some of whom may still take a very literal approach. Similarly, when framing the territorial restrictions it would be advisable, where dealing with both patents and know-how, to set out the restrictions separately in terms which correspond in both scope and duration to Article 1.2, 1.3 and 1.4 (see the consequence of not doing so in *Quantel*, **Case Note 24**).

5.2 Avoiding the costs and management time of notification to the Commission

Notification using the Form A/B can generate a significant amount of work and legal costs. A full notification of a complex technology licence may involve weeks or even months of work. Describing the market within which the licence operates and assessing the likely effects of the licence upon competition in that market will often involve the gathering of information which is not readily available. The simple logistical effort of putting together the information and preparing and binding the 17 copies which the Commission requires should not be underestimated.

Notification itself is not the end of the story. The Commission has significantly speeded up its handling of cases. A preliminary examination would normally be conducted and some written reaction, generally with a request for further information, might be expected within up to six months. That could then lead to a protracted and costly dialogue resulting ultimately in some negotiated changes to the agreements before the file was informally closed some two years or more after notification.

It is therefore not surprising that parties are often attracted by the thought of avoiding this process and may seek to comply with the Regulation, in which case the existence of the agreement will in all likelihood never come to the attention of the Commission. However, when considering these cost savings, one must also recognise that it can be equally costly in terms of time and legal fees to verify that an agreement complies with the Regulation and therefore the notional savings from avoiding notification may be partly illusory. For instance, a significant amount of time could be spent debating whether certain other intellectual property rights are "ancillary" or not and whether there is a risk that at some stage in the future one of the parties might seek to argue that they were not. It is also necessary to count the costs of the commercial concessions that may have be made in order to ensure compliance.

5.3 Avoiding the need to disclose significant information to the Commission

The information which has to be disclosed is not only bulky: much of it might be confidential. At the very least it can include information in a format which would be difficult or expensive for competitors to compile. Where technology licences are concerned and in particular where the agreement relates to valuable know-how, there is an additional reservation about providing it to the Commission or to any agency. As discussed below (in **Section 8.4**) the Regulation already complicates matters in requiring that the know-how be identified in written form. If relying on notification rather than the Regulation, it will still be necessary to identify so far as possible the know-how which is the subject of the licence, so that the Commission can assess whether it appears to be sufficiently valuable to justify the restrictions contained in the agreements.

The Commission does have a duty to protect all confidential information. This is a general duty in Regulation 17 (and is in fact also reflected in Art 9 of the Regulation). Generally, this confidentiality is well respected. However there is a natural tension between the Commission's duty to protect the confidentiality of notifying parties and its overriding duty to ensure proper enforcement of competition law. Ensuring the latter may involve publishing a Notice in the *Official Journal* informing the world at large that a notification has been received and inviting comments. In order to invite comments it is necessary to publish a short summary of the notification which may itself go further than the parties would wish. Should the proceedings develop along more formal lines it is possible that interested third parties will at some stage have a right of access to the Commission's file. Although genuinely sensitive and confidential material can be withheld from such inspection, the Commission will press the parties to limit to the bare minimum the information in respect of which they claim confidentiality. Many commercial undertakings find it culturally extremely difficult to accept this degree of openness and it can be another factor which militates in favour of compliance with the Regulation.

Finally, in relation to confidentiality it is important to revert to the 17 copies of the notification mentioned above. The reason for this large number of copies is that one set is passed to the competent authority in each Member State. That authority will also be under a general duty to respect confidentiality as part of its commitment to co-operate with the Commission and assist proper enforcement of competition law. However, it has to be recognised that allowing the notification to be so widely disseminated inevitably increases the risk of leaks. There is always a concern that some authorities may be prompted by the notification to begin their own investigations into activities within their territory. Some may also have wide-ranging freedom of information laws. In order to minimise the risks, notifying parties often confine the most sensitive information to confidential annexes of which they only enclose three copies which do not circulate outside the Commission. The parties might also ensure where possible that such sensitive information itself be copied onto extremely dark paper which is itself difficult or impossible to photocopy and that it be heavily marked on each page as "Business Secrets – Confidential" in a separate tightly bound volume. Despite all of these precautions, mistakes are sometimes made by the authorities. The person responsible for compiling the notification always faces a difficult decision between seeking to hold back from the Commission information which is not "necessary" to its assessment and running the risk that sensitive information might leak. The best advice must be to seek early in the proceedings to develop a co-operative relationship with the Commission officials and agree with them that certain information (particularly technical information or pure commercial know-how) need not be supplied.

5.4 The relative generosity of the Regulation

The Regulation sets out to identify most of the types of restriction which are found in technology licences and would normally be eligible for exemption under Article 85(3). Therefore, if one is dealing with a relatively straightforward bipartite technology licence, one might reasonably conclude that the Regulation offers in most cases the greatest latitude which is likely to be available from the Commission. Persuading the Commission to accept a "black-listed" clause in a notified agreement will be difficult and may not be worth the time and money as well as the lingering uncertainty. Many parties may decide to settle for the Regulation, supplemented by the possibility of using the opposition procedure (discussed in **Section 7**, below).

5.5 Possibility of withdrawal

Even if an agreement clearly complies in every respect with the block exemption, the Commission has inserted its own get-out clause in case a particular agreement still has undesirable anti-competitive effects. Article 7 introduces a number of possible instances of withdrawal of the block exemption. The first is where the licensed products face insufficient competition in the licensed territory. The Commission asserts that this could be likely where the licensee has a market share in excess of 40%. The history of this provision is that originally the Commission wanted to make applicability of the entire block exemption dependent upon market thresholds of this type. During the public consultation the objections from industry were so widespread that the Commission was persuaded to change its mind (and should certainly be congratulated for doing so). The remnant of that proposal now appears in Article 7 as a possible justification for the Commission taking a decision to withdraw the benefit of the block exemption in a particular case.

The withdrawal power is still criticised for perpetuating an unacceptable level of potential uncertainty. However, the reality is that withdrawal involves the Commission devoting substantial resources to taking a full decision. That is only likely in major cases affecting a large number of agreements and so far has only occurred or been threatened on a handful of occasions. Any withdrawal is not retrospective and so only takes effect from the date of the decision, which greatly reduces the uncertainty. Moreover, the 40% market share applies to the licensee rather than the licensor and at levels above 40% the licensee already risks being found to be dominant (see discussion of Art 86 and *Tetra Pak* at **Section 8.2**, below). On balance, those who criticise this provision are being unrealistic in their insistence on "certainty" at all costs. The other grounds for withdrawal have been dealt with adequately in **Analysis Section 16**. It is important always to bear in mind that the list is non-exhaustive and that the Commission can take a decision to deprive the parties of the benefit of the exemption on any occasion where the agreement appears to be incompatible with the criteria of Article 85(3). The parties would of course, as with any other Commission decision, have the right to a hearing and be able to appeal it to the European Court of First Instance.

6.   **Opposition procedure**

As explained in **Analysis Section 13**, the "opposition procedure" in Article 4 of the Regulation is one where the Commission invites notifications of agreements which do not squarely fit within the block exemption but which do not contain any black-listed clauses (*i.e.* any of the clauses identified in Art 3 of the Regulation). Where such an agreement is notified and the Commission does not object within a fixed period, the agreement is automatically exempted.

Given the difficulties of balancing the benefits and drawbacks of the Regulation, the revised opposition procedure represents a significant improvement in two respects. First, the waiting period has been reduced to four months (it was six months in each of the Patent and Know-how Regulations). Any shortening of the response time is helpful where time might be of the essence and where both parties may be contemplating significant investment.

The major improvement, however, is in the lessening of the administrative burden of notification under the opposition procedure. Article 4.1 refers to the need for a notification. However, this is heavily qualified by Recital 25 which recognises that the Commission may waive the requirement for certain specific information and states that the Commission will generally be content to receive only the text of the agreement together with an estimate of the market structure and of the market share of the licensee. In the case of new technology the licensee's market share may well be nil. It is likely that the Commission will also insist, in view of the four-month deadline, that the parties point out all of the clauses which exceed the exemption and which have prompted them to use the opposition procedure.

Article 4.2 goes on to identify two particular circumstances in which the opposition procedure may be useful.

1. Where the licensor obliges the licensee to accept goods or services which may not meet the test of "necessity".

2. Where there is an absolute no-challenge clause.

One can envisage other examples, such as where the licensor feels that he does have an objectively justified reason for insisting that the licensee refuses to accept orders from certain resellers. That is a clause which would, in the absence of an objective justification, be black-listed under Article 3(3). Having said that, the justification would have to be extremely compelling if the Commission were to be persuaded to accept it within the four-month period.

The opposition procedure has its limitations. It can still only be used in respect of agreements which meet the basic criteria of Article 1 of the Regulation. In other words, the agreements concerned must qualify as technology licences in respect of qualifying patents or know-how and if it is the latter, the know-how must be sufficiently secret, substantial and identified.

It will be interesting to see how much the opposition procedure is used. Experience of similar procedures under other block exemptions has not been encouraging but in many cases where the Commission did raise an opposition this was because of the inclusion of a black-listed clause. This underlines the point that it is not possible to use the opposition procedure to "sneak through" a black-listed clause. It is clear from the wording of Article 4 that if an agreement did contain a clause falling within Article 3 which the Commission failed to identify or object to, the automatic exemption would not apply. The duty to verify the absence of a black-listed clause remains with the parties. Nevertheless, the Technology Regulation, with its shortened Black List, may give rise to more frequent and more successful uses of the procedure.

7.　**Going beyond the Regulation**

Notwithstanding the more flexible opposition procedure, there are a number of occasions where the parties commonly find that the Regulation is not wide enough for their requirements:

- there are more than two parties (Art 1.1) or the agreement involves a joint venture or pooled technology (Art 5): see Table 2 at **Analysis Section 15.3**;
- the licensor insists on his right to ownership of any jointly developed technology or any licensee's improvements (Art 3(6));
- the licensor needs to be able to exercise some control over the licensee's pricing policy, for instance, by imposing a maximum price or preventing the licensee from "dumping" the products by selling below cost either in his territory or that of other licences (Art 3(1));
- the licensor wants to prevent the licensee engaging in competing activities (Art 3(2));
- the parties wish to agree upon automatic prolongation of the agreement by the inclusion of new patents or improvements, to be covered also by the territorial restrictions (Art 3(7)) or simply to have agreements of longer duration;
- the investment involved deters the parties from risking the application of some of the more uncertain provisions in the Regulation (*e.g.* "objectively justified reason": Art 3(3)).

If any of the above or similar bars apply, so that the parties will not be able to rely upon the opposition procedure, they are forced to choose between significantly amending their agreement or notifying to the Commission. In these circumstances it is likely to be the task of the legal advisor to demystify the notification process.

It is certainly true that notification can be an onerous procedure (see **Section 5**, above). It involves preparation of a memorandum which provides background on the parties, identifies their position in any relevant product and geographic markets, explains the agreement and then puts forward a case for negative clearance or exemption.

Nevertheless it is important to acknowledge that there can be significant benefits to bypassing the Regulation and submitting an individual notification. The Regulation is an administrative measure which has been introduced to reduce the workload of DG IV. The restrictions which it permits are those which in the vast majority of cases will satisfy the criteria for exemption on individual notification. The parties therefore have an opportunity in an individual notification to justify more wide-ranging and commercially valuable restrictions and particularly to get an exemption of longer duration (15 and 20 years respectively for know-how licences in *BBC*, **Case Note 13** and *Delta Chemie*, **Case Note 11**). For a relatively small investment they may be able to obtain a significant commercial advantage. In addition, notwithstanding the number and purported scope of the block exemption regulations, the Commission still receives a growing number of individual notifications and does not have the resources to subject all of them to rigorous scrutiny. (See statistics from 1997 Commission Competition Report at Table 3, below.) A clear, well laid out and persuasively argued notification may succeed in obtaining a comfort letter or at least a closing of the file without further action.

Table 3

1997 Commission Competition Report
Article 85 and Article 86 statistics

New cases

Year	1993	1994	1995	1996	1997
Cases opened on Commission's own initiative	26	21	47	82	101
Complaints	110	170	114	159	177
Notifications	264	235	360	206	221
Total	*400*	*426*	*521*	*447*	*499*

Cases closed

Year	1993	1994	1995	1996	1997
Formal decisions[2]	14	33	14	21	27
Informal procedure	792	495	403	367	490
Total	*806*	*528*	*417*	*388*	*517*

2 No breakdown is given in the 1997 report but on average the Commission will not adopt many more than 15 prohibition decisions in a year: the remainder would be exemption decisions.

Yet another benefit is that even agreements which are arguably covered by the Regulation always run the risk, however remote, of withdrawal of the exemption under Article 7 (see **Section 5.5**, above). It may suit the licensee to argue at some later stage that an agreement has more restrictive effects than might appear at first glance. In practical terms a licensor will derive significant comfort from a joint notification, in which the licensee has also joined in a declaration that the agreement is pro-competitive and that all of the restrictions have been freely accepted.

Finally, there is always the option of simply running the risk of non-compliance with the Regulation and not notifying. This option is always open to a licensor who is not too concerned about having many enforceable restrictions in his agreement. He may not be very worried about enforcement at all if he has reserved the right to terminate without cause on short notice. He may reasonably take the view that unless there is anything particularly novel or interesting about his agreement, the Commission would never be likely to devote the resources to establishing a breach of Article 85 and imposing fines. This may appear an extremely risky course of action but if one looks at the small number of notifications and at the criteria necessary to satisfy the Regulation, there must be a very large number of licensors and licensees who either deliberately or inadvertently are taking precisely this risk.

8.   Difficulties with the Regulation

8.1 All or nothing

The Regulation exempts agreements rather than clauses of agreements. An agreement will only benefit from the exemption if it falls squarely within the terms of the Regulation. The following situations may arise:

- the agreement contains a clause restrictive of competition which does not fall within Article 1 or Article 2 of the Regulation and is not categorised as a similar obligation of more limited scope under Article 1.5 or Article 2.3. The agreement may then be notified under the opposition procedure of Article 4 but if it is not furnished the block exemption does not apply; or
- the agreement contains a provision of the type black-listed by Article 3. It is ineligible for the opposition procedure and a full blown individual notification will be necessary.

In both situations, the consequence of adding a single further restriction will be to take the entire agreement outside the automatic protection of the Regulation. This seems reasonable where parties include a clause which they could see would be black-listed. However, such consequences appear extreme where parties have simply inserted a restriction which in its terms or scope goes further than is exempted by Article 1 or Article 2 but could still have been a strong candidate for exemption on individual notification. It had been thought that the Commission's "all or nothing" approach to drafting block exemption regulations was dictated by the structure of Article 85(3) and of the enabling Council Regulation 19/65, which gives the Commission power to enact block exemptions. The view seemed to be that it was not open to the Commission to allow the exemption to apply to those parts of an agreement which complied with a block exemption but to deny the exemption to certain provisions which were subsequently held (perhaps by a court ruling) not to fall within the block exemption.

Nevertheless, the Commission itself seemed to have overcome such doubts in an earlier draft of the Regulation. The draft published in 1994 (preliminary draft regulation, OJ 1994 C178/3 of 30/06/94) had omitted the opposition procedure and instead contained the following Article 4:

> "If a pure or mixed licensing agreement includes obligations within the scope of Articles 1 and 2 and obligations which restrict competition but which do not fall within the scope either of Articles 1 and 2 or of Article 3, the presence of those restrictive obligations shall not prevent this Regulation from applying to the obligations which do fall within the scope of Articles 1 and 2. The obligations which are not thus exempted shall continue to be governed by Articles 85(1) and (2) of the Treaty".

The consequence of this amendment would have been that including a black-listed clause would continue to make the exemption entirely inapplicable but that inclusion of any non black-listed restriction would simply leave that clause non-exempt and unenforceable. The effect upon the rest of the agreement would then depend upon whether that clause was "severable" under the law applicable to the agreement: whether it was possible to draw a line through that clause without rendering the agreement so different from what the parties had intended that it would be wrong to leave them bound by a contract not containing that clause. In the vast majority of cases it is unlikely that the deletion of such a restriction would have led automatically to termination of the entire agreement.

In the event, the Commission decided not to go down this route and instead reinstated the opposition procedure. Presumably, it was argued that the Commission should not use block exemption regulations to grant "partial" exemptions for agreements and that any block exemption is a major concession which should only be granted to those who comply strictly with its terms. But assuming that it had earlier received advice that such a severability provision was permissible in a block exemption, it is unfortunate that the Commission did not feel able to keep both the severability provision and the opposition procedure. After all, the purpose of the Black List is to identify clearly those types of provision which cannot benefit from either the automatic exemption or the accelerated opposition procedure and which in many cases will not be thought suitable for individual exemption. At the same time, the Regulation contains a number of provisions of uncertain effect, such as whether certain products might turn out to be necessary for a technically proper exploitation of the technology (Art 2.1(5)). The parties might each have concluded in good faith at the outset that the goods were necessary and it may only be at some stage in the future that a court determines that they were not necessary so that the agreement was never exempt. Having failed to notify, the parties will be entirely deprived for the whole life of the agreement of the benefit of the exemption, even for other provisions such as exclusive territory which fall clearly within the Regulation. On those occasions where the licensor would not have concluded the agreement without being able to oblige the licensee to purchase products for him, he would be able to argue that the clause was not severable and the entire agreement should fall. The Commission's decision not to introduce a severability provision is likely to lead to a number of precautionary notifications, which could otherwise have been avoided without any appreciable threat to competition.

Given all this, it is curious that in relation to Article 1.1(3) (see **Analysis Section 8.3**) the Commission states in Recital 7 that the inclusion of restrictions applying outside the licensed territory, even where they could amount to restrictions of competition which by implication were not specifically exempted, would not prevent the exemption from applying to the restrictions which affected territories within the common market. If correct it is difficult to reconcile with the overriding principle that restrictions can only be exempt either by falling squarely within a block exemption or through individual notification, whether through full notification or the opposition procedure. There may be some scope for exploring the extent to which Recital 7 suggests a more flexible approach but the Commission's retreat from the severability principles indicates that it would be unwise to place too much reliance on Recital 7.

8.2 Competition or fairness?

The Commission's duty in its enforcement of Article 85 is to ensure that competition and trade between Member States are not appreciably distorted. Unlike the UK's Office of Fair Trading, it does not have a parallel role of tackling unfair commercial behaviour. In fact, Recital 21 of the Regulation acknowledges that it is not the Commission's role to protect parties from the "foreseeable financial consequences of an agreement freely entered into". One respect in which its competition enforcement role begins to take into account notions of "fairness" such as discrimination, is where an undertaking has a dominant position which it abuses contrary to Article 86.

The distinction was recognised in the *Tetra Pak* case (**Case Note 18**). There, Tetra Pak acquired a company which was the beneficiary of an exclusive licence falling within the Patent Regulation. Notwithstanding that the agreement was therefore exempt from the consequences of Article 85(3), the Commission ruled (and the Court of First Instance agreed) that the enhancement of market power through the acquisition of the exclusive licensee amounted in the circumstances to an abuse of a dominant position. The Commission also threatened if it should prove necessary to remove the benefit of the exemption from the agreement.

This case illustrated quite starkly the different bases on which Articles 85 and 86 operate and the difficulties caused by the fact that no exemption procedure, whether individual or by block exemption, exists for conduct which infringes Article 86. One would argue that where a *licensor* occupies a dominant position, then it is extremely difficult to see how it could abuse this dominant position by entering into an agreement which complies with both the letter and spirit of a block exemption regulation. Under the Technology Regulation the licensor will not legitimately be able to prevent the licensee from exploiting the licensee's own technology and therefore no significant restriction of potential competition is likely where the licensor is merely placing limitations on use of the licensor's own technology. On the other hand, in rare circumstances where the *licensee* is the dominant party and, through acquiring an exclusive licence, enhances that dominant position and blocks other possible competitors, there may exceptionally (as in *Tetra Pak*) be a case for application of Article 86 and/or the removal of the block exemption.

In the vast majority of cases concerning technology licensing agreements, neither the licensor nor the licensee will occupy a dominant position. Therefore, the Commission's only concern in drafting the block exemption should be to focus solely on Article 85 and ensure that terms are not agreed between the parties which could appreciably distort competition. It is inappropriate and unfortunate that the Commission so often takes the opportunity, as it sees it, to redress the balance of bargaining strength between the parties. In doing so it also, despite *Tetra Pak*, makes a generalised assumption that in most cases it is the licensor who has the market power. As a result the Regulation is littered with provisions which appear to be designed to prevent the licensor from bullying the licensee. An example is that an obligation by the licensee to assign rights to improvements back to the licensor is black-listed in Article 3(6) but a corresponding obligation on the licensor would not be black-listed and could be submitted for approval under the opposition procedure. Similarly, the requirement (discussed elsewhere) in Article 2.1(5) that any goods supplied by the licensor should be "necessary" seems to assume, or at least invite the licensee later to argue, that the licensor has leveraged the licensee into accepting such goods.

Only the Commission has power to grant exemptions under Article 85(3). When it does so by individual decision, it often takes advantage of the opportunity to insist on other modifications which it believes are either in the general interest or are for the protection of one of the parties. Notifying parties may argue that the Commission is exceeding its remit but often feel they have little choice but to accept. Such interference with commercial relations is even more objectionable in a block exemption. The court pointed out in a case involving Volkswagen (*VAG France* v *Etablissements Magne* Case 10/86 [1988] 4 CMLR 98) that Commission block exemptions are not supposed to be blueprints for commercial agreements and the Commission should resist the temptation to get into this degree of detail.

8.3 Limited duration

Know-how – the poor relation

Article 1.2 imposes an upper limit for most of the restrictions in pure patent licensing agreements, which is fixed at the life of any parallel patents: meaning the corresponding patents in the territories in which the restrictions are to be enforced. The main exception relates to the restrictions on passive sales activity which in all cases are limited to five years. The reference to the patent life is a reasonable limitation, since it amounts to the term of the natural monopoly conferred upon the licensor by his patent rights.

On the other hand, the Commission has always been reluctant to allow a similar duration in relation to know-how. When the Know-how Regulation was first proposed, the original intention was to allow the restrictions to run for a period of seven years but after consultation this was increased to 10 years and that limitation has been carried over into those provisions of the Regulation relating to pure know-how licences and mixed agreements.

Insofar as pure know-how agreements are concerned, the limitation to 10 years is now generally accepted. Many do still argue that there is no logic in imposing any temporal limitation and that the restrictions should be enforceable for so long as, to use the words of the Regulation, the know-how "remains secret and substantial". The argument goes that since the licensee can be prevented under the confidentiality clauses from using the know-how after termination of the agreement so long as the know-how remains secret (Art 2.1(3)) there is no reason why the agreement itself should not be allowed to endure for that period together with the territorial restrictions. Greater security could have been introduced by allowing the licensee to terminate the agreement upon reasonable notice at any time after the 10th anniversary and one could then have done away with the black-listed provision in Article 3(7).

However, all of these arguments have been rehearsed before and the Commission is clearly not prepared to block exempt a know-how licence containing territorial restrictions which automatically endure for more than 10 years. Instead, parties who wish to conclude an agreement for more than 10 years will have to accept that all of the territorial restrictions fall away at that point if they wish to benefit from the Regulation. Alternatively, they can limit the entire agreement to 10 years, followed by a right of first refusal to renegotiate the agreement, and will have to notify the agreement at the point of renegotiation for individual exemption, similar to the situation envisaged in Recital 14. In practice, this limitation is as likely to work against the interests of licensees as it is to harm licensors, since it will prevent the licensee negotiating a longer period at the outset unless he wishes to run the risk that the investment which he has made may be rendered worthless by an adverse Commission decision. This could be a typical example of where individual notification would be the preferred route. Unfortunately, the parties are still likely to run into difficulties, given the reluctance of the Commission to grant individual exemptions for any period significantly in excess of 10 years, though there are some exceptions noted in Section 7, above. The parties will often still find that they are told to come back for a renewal of the exemption (or, more likely, an extended comfort letter) after five or 10 years.

More difficulties arise in relation to mixed agreements. Where an agreement involves both patents and know-how, the restrictions relating to the patents may endure for the life of the necessary patents but those relating to the know-how may only endure for a maximum of 10 years from first marketing of the licensed products within the common market. Many agreements are likely to be mixed agreements and it may be equally important to the parties, if they wish to license the patents for their full life, that the know-how is also protected during that period. It cannot be satisfactory that the exemption falls away for the know-how after 10 years when the patents, even if the product took some time to introduce after the grant of the patent, could still have another five years or more of life.

Article 1.4 recognises that such situations could arise but only allows the territorial restrictions in mixed agreements to be enforced beyond the 10-year period "in Member States in which the licensed technology is protected by necessary patents for as long as the licensed product is protected in those Member States by such patents" (*NB* with respect to the significance of "necessary" see **Section 8.5**, below.) Consequently, if within a range of licensed products there is one product which is produced using only the know-how and which is not protected by any patents, then the absolute 10-year limitation will continue to apply and the parties will need to consider the issues which are raised above in relation to pure know-how licences. On the other hand, if another product in the range also requires use of a patent, the restrictions can be maintained for significantly longer. The result is that despite combining the Patent and Know-how Regulations, there still remains a substantial distinction between the treatment of patent licences, know-how licences and mixed licences. It could mean the parties will have to think carefully when drafting the agreement so as to ensure that the temporal restrictions distinguish between different products according to what technology is required in their manufacture.

It is even more important to draft carefully where the licensor does not have patent protection in every Member State of the EU (or EEA). In those circumstances he will be relying on his patents in some territories but will have to rely on know-how and confidentiality in others. He cannot rely upon his patent rights in territories where he does not have patent protection since that would not satisfy the definition of a territory in respect of which the product is protected by "parallel patents" under Article 1.2. If he has included know-how, leading to a "mixed agreement", he will be able to rely on the know-how restrictions in those countries but only subject to the more limited duration under Article 1.3. If the drafting is not sufficiently precise and gives rise to confusion over what duration of restriction applies to which territory, there is a serious risk that the agreement will be held to be more restrictive than permitted and therefore black-listed so that the entire agreement will lose the benefit of the block exemption.

Improvements

Another issue of duration arises in relation to improvements. The definition of the "licensed technology" in Article 10(7) includes the initial know-how or patents as well as "improvements subsequently made". Article 8.3 makes it clear that the Regulation continues to apply where the initial duration of an agreement is automatically prolonged by the inclusion of any new improvements whether patented or not. Although it only refers specifically to those improvements communicated by the licensor, it must be arguable that the same principle would apply where the prolongation occurs through communication of the licensee's improvements (see comments in **Analysis Section 17.3**). Logically, one would expect the same principle to apply in relation to the right of the licensee to terminate the agreement every three years where duration is prolonged by inclusion of such improvements, so that the licensor were also given that right.

The problem arises from Article 3(7), which prevents any extension of the territorial restrictions for a period beyond that laid down in Article 1, even where the agreement is legitimately extended in line with Article 8.3.

Here once again, there is a clear distinction in the treatment of patent and know-how licences. In relation to patent licences, Article 1.2 provides that the restrictions in Article 1.1 (apart from the five-year passive selling restriction in Art 1.1 (6)) can apply "for as long as the licensed product is protected by parallel patents". It does not stipulate (and neither does the definition of "parallel patents" in Art 10(13)) that this refers only to patents which were in force at the date of the original licence and therefore it would appear to extend also to any improvement patents which have been added under Article 8.3. Support for this view can be drawn from the wording of Article 3(2) of the earlier Patent Regulation which had referred to the duration of the agreement being extended "beyond the expiry of the licensed patents existing at the time the agreement was entered into" whereas that qualification no longer appears in the Technology Regulation and the definition of the "licensed technology" in Article 10(7) specifically includes improvements to the patents. It therefore appears that there is a strong case for saying that where improvement patents are added then as long as the licensee (and arguably the licensor: see comments above) are given the right to terminate every three years, one can have a perpetual licence with perpetual territorial restrictions for so long as those restrictions could legitimately be enforced in reliance upon any patents which are added into the licence.

The Commission is not prepared to extend the same latitude to know-how licences. Even if genuinely valuable know-how is added which dramatically improves the products, Article 1.3 ties the duration of all the permitted restrictions to a point from the placing on the market within the common market of the licensed products. Therefore, it is only if the improvements lead to the production of a new product that the period could begin again, with a new agreement benefiting from a new exemption as permitted in Recital 14.

This would appear to mean that any parties who provide in their know-how or mixed agreements for the possibility of automatically adding improvements which could have the contractual effect of extending the duration of the territorial restrictions, will have to consider whether to notify their agreement from the outset. They might argue that they can at least benefit from the Regulation until such time as any improvements do arise which then have the effect of extending the duration in breach of Article 3(7). However, to remain fully protected that would mean notifying the agreement to the Commission as soon as any improvements are contributed. If it is foreseeable that this will occur it may make sense to notify early at a point when it can more convincingly be argued that without this provision the technology would not be licensed at all.

Perhaps the best advice to the parties is to consider carefully whether they really want to have *automatic* addition of improvements. If an improvement does constitute either separately patentable technology or new valuable know-how, the parties might reasonably expect that they would need to negotiate separately what would be the appropriate royalty rate and other conditions attaching to such technology. Although they may want some commitment in the earlier agreement that new licences will be offered on reasonable terms, it could clearly operate against the interests of one or other party (without being able to determine from the outset of the agreement who that disadvantaged party might be) for the technology simply to be added to a schedule of the original licence without any account being taken of particular problems or inequities to which this might give rise. Quite aside from these commercial objections, there are good reasons in competition law for making this new technology the subject of a separate licence agreement.

8.4 Justifying and identifying the know-how

The Commission appears concerned that parties might enter into sham agreements, which are not genuine technology licences but are disguised as such to benefit from the block exemption. An example might be where a company grants a know-how licence to a competitor where the know-how is worthless and does nothing to improve the competitor's production but the parties seek to rely on it to justify mutual territorial non-compete provisions. The Regulation already provides (Art 5.1(3)) that the block exemption will not apply where licences between competitors are reciprocal. It also black-lists any attempt at customer sharing (Art 3(4)) and allows for removal of the exemption where a licence has the effect of preventing the licensee from exploiting its own technology (Art 7(4)).

The problem of sham agreements is dealt with in relation to patents in some instances by the stipulation that the patents be "necessary" (see **Section 8.5**, below). With know-how, which has not been tested through an independent verification process, the situation may be less clear. The Regulation therefore insists (through Art 1(3) and the definition in Art 10) that the know-how must be secret, substantial and identified and states in Recital 5 that this is necessary to ensure that the licence "justifies" the automatic exemption.

These additional stipulations throw up certain problems for both licensors and licensees and it remains questionable whether there was any need for the Commission to continue to insist on them. This qualification appeared in the earlier Know-how Regulation but it would be interesting to press the Commission on whether it has any examples of parties concluding agreements for worthless "know-how" solely in order to benefit from the Regulation. Even if that could happen, it is to some extent an occupational hazard of having any block exemption regulations. It would always be possible for businesses and their lawyers to bring anti competitive agreements within the letter of a block exemption regulation while failing to comply with the spirit of that regulation. In each of the regulations the Commission takes power to withdraw the benefit of the exemption where that occurs. It is therefore unnecessary and ultimately self-defeating of the main purpose of the regulations (simplicity and certainty) to introduce, as a fundamental criterion for eligibility, such uncertain and at times subjective tests.

Secret

The Commission sticks by its established definition of "secret" as meaning a bundle of know-how which in that precise configuration is not generally known or easily accessible. Information which has been published anywhere in the world, as for example in an overseas patent, would probably not satisfy that definition. A further example of know-how which would not be considered secret is any technical information contained in a patent application which, following publication, was either rejected or withdrawn. Parties must therefore bear this in mind when considering whether to file an application for a patent and risk being unable subsequently to license the published technical information as know-how instead (or finding themselves unable to continue to rely on the Regulation where the licence had already been concluded prior to publication). If the claim is successful the statutory monopoly granted by the patent is certainly the best protection against any infringement but if the prospects of success are doubtful the owner of the technology may be better off relying on contractually enforceable restrictions based on disclosure and confidentiality clauses.

The definition of secrecy in the Regulation is quite generous. Even published information could, if presented in a different configuration which represents a significant work product, satisfy the definition. Nevertheless, the consequences of the know-how ceasing to be classified as "secret" for any reason, including the deliberate disclosure by the licensee, are extremely serious since the exemption of the restrictions in Article 1 continues only for long as it does remain secret. If the licensee were guilty of deliberate disclosure he could still be required to pay the royalties for the life of the agreement (Art 2.1(7)(a)) and even be exposed to an action for damages under Article 2.1(1). It would not therefore seem unreasonable to stipulate that the licensee should also remain subject to the other restrictions imposed upon him for the full five or 10 years as appropriate. It might be worth considering the inclusion of a clause specifying this consequence of disclosure and arguing later for a specific exemption if in the circumstances it could be justified.

Another problem which used to arise in relation to the secrecy criterion but which will shortly disappear, is the relationship with the

Restrictive Trade Practices Act 1976 ("RTPA") where the agreement is between two parties engaged in business in the United Kingdom. Essentially, the RTPA provides that where two parties accept relevant restrictions under an agreement so that it is "registrable", a copy of the agreement will be filed by the OFT on a public register. There was scope under the RTPA for getting certain provisions withheld from the displayed copy and placed instead on the special section of the register, on the basis that they were commercially valuable and it was in the public interest to do so, but it was not possible to be <u>certain</u> of maintaining confidentiality. If parts of what constituted the know-how were put on display in this way they would immediately cease to qualify as "secret" within the meaning of the Regulation, since any third party would be able to obtain copies for payment of a small fee to the OFT.

Recent changes to the RTPA had significantly, though not entirely, eliminated this problem. In 1996 the Secretary of State made the Restrictive Trade Practices (Non-Notifiable Agreements) (EC Block Exemptions) Order 1996 (SI 1996 No 349) providing that agreements which are covered by Community block exemption regulations no longer need to be filed with the OFT. Therefore, if an agreement were clearly within the Regulation the problem was solved. However, if the parties were unsure for other reasons whether their agreement complied with the Regulation and they needed to rely on the opposition procedure, they might not have known for four months whether their agreement qualified. Under the RTPA they have to send in particulars within three months. They could therefore still have been at risk that the agreement would be placed on the register, with the consequences mentioned above. The OFT had made the practical suggestion that parties could ask the OFT for an extension of the three-month period while they waited to see whether the Commission either confirmed that the agreement was covered by the Regulation or let the four-month period elapse without comment, in which case the agreement was again presumed to comply with the Regulation and therefore could be treated as non-notifiable under the RTPA. On the other hand, if the Commission responded that the agreement did not benefit from the opposition procedure (for instance because it contained a clause similar to one of the black-listed clauses) the agreement would no longer be non-notifiable and the parties would find themselves arguing about what would appear on the public register. This issue will disappear when the UK's new competition legislation is enacted since that will do away with the RTPA and replace it with a structure based on Article 85, together with block exemptions mirroring the European regulations (see **Section 11**, below).

Substantial

With respect to whether the know-how is sufficiently substantial, there is no evidence that parties are dressing up agreements as know-how licences in order to gain the benefit of a block exemption in circumstances where the know-how was without commercial value and was a front for market sharing or similar activity. The Regulation already black-lists in Article 3(4) any field of use or product market restrictions where the parties were already competing manufacturers. Where they are not already competing, they may use the opposition procedure but that will simply bring the agreement to the attention of the Commission and guarantee that it is looked at quickly. In any other circumstances, how likely is it that a licensee will accept a licence of valueless know-how and in return agree not to exploit it in a defined territory? Even where he does so, the restriction can only be enforced in relation to "the licensed products" manufactured with the "licensed technology" and only, by virtue of Article 1.3, for so long as it remains secret. It therefore seems entirely unnecessary to add the criterion of substantiality, which ought to remain a matter for the parties to determine themselves, on the assumption that the licensee would not pay for something which is insubstantial. As mentioned earlier (see **Section 8.2**, above), if the concern is that the licensor is abusing his market power to force the licensee to take a licence of valueless technology, that is something which ought to be tackled under Article 86.

Identified

Matters are complicated by the insistence that the know-how should have been "identified". Even though the RTPA problem may largely have been dealt with (see above) there does not appear to be any significant benefit in competition terms from imposing this further requirement. A less technical objection is that the insistence on identification ignores commercial reality. If one accepts that restrictions can only be enforced in relation to the "licensed technology" as defined, it must be clear that it is in the interests of the parties to identify so far as they can the know-how which is the subject of the licence. Failure to do so will make it more difficult for them to enforce any contractual rights against infringement or disclosure of the know-how.

It should be left to the parties to determine whether to run that risk. It is one thing to accept that failure properly to identify the know-how may mean that it will be incapable of protection in an infringement action. However, it is quite another (and, to use popular EU jargon, entirely "disproportionate"), for the Commission to introduce the further consequence that failure properly to identify the know-how in a manner acceptable to the Commission will lead to loss of the entire exemption.

Although one may criticise this requirement it is clearly not advisable to ignore it. The definition at Article 10(4) stipulates that the know-how must be set out or recorded in some form, at the latest when it is transferred or shortly thereafter. It does not specify that the document or record must have been passed to the licensee but the document does have to be made available in the event of a dispute. From the point of view of the licensor it would be advisable to ensure that the licensee signs some acknowledgement identifying the document or record as comprising the valuable know-how for which he accepts a need to pay royalties, even if it should later come into the public domain other than through the fault of the licensor (see **Analysis Section 10.7**). If there is likely to be continuing co-operation with further disclosures of know-how during the agreement, the parties will have to maintain the discipline of regularly recording what has been exchanged if they wish to continue to be able to enforce any territorial restrictions in respect of its use.

Consequences

Despite the principled objections to these requirements, the parties have to be advised not to ignore them and to make every effort so far as possible to substantiate a claim that the know-how meets the criteria of the Regulation. The key point to bear in mind, is that as long as there is some original know-how which remains secret, substantial and has been identified then the main restrictions within the block exemption will be allowed. What the parties might consider is adopting within their agreement word for word the same definitions as those used in the Regulation. In other words they would provide that the definition of the "know-how" in respect of which any contractual restrictions could be enforced should be that know-how which fulfils the criteria of the Regulation, thereby ensuring that they cannot be said to have inserted any restrictions which go beyond the Regulation and which deprive them of the benefit of the entire exemption. This could be backed up by a provision asserting that both parties intend that the agreement should be covered by the Regulation and, having carefully considered their agreement, sincerely believe that it does so. There is every benefit, if you are (or are advising) the party most likely to be seeking to enforce the restrictions, in getting the other party to sign up to such a statement long before any dispute arises.

8.5 Problem of "necessary" patents and "ancillary" other intellectual property rights

Necessary

Recital 12 to the Regulation refers to certain restrictions being permitted in respect of territories where the licensed product is protected by patents as long as they remain in force. An earlier draft of that Recital had referred to "necessary patents". That qualification was dropped in the adopted version of the Recital but it remains in the definition of the "licensed technology" in Article 10(7) and therefore any restrictions in Article 1 which refer to the "licensed technology" or the "licensed products" (the latter being defined in Article 10(8) as products manufactured using the licensed technology) involve an analysis of whether the patents are genuinely "necessary". Article 1.4 which introduces the limitations on permitted duration of the restrictions, adds the qualification specifically in relation to mixed patent and know-how agreements that the patents should be "necessary". The words "by a mixed agreement" were added late in the drafting stage (and rather clumsily) into Recital 5 to reinforce the requirement of "necessity" when patents and know-how are combined in a single agreement. The consequence of these provisions is that where the parties to a pure patent licence or a mixed agreement wish to rely on any patent rights they will need in addition show that the patent is "necessary". Perhaps rather inconsistently, there is no requirement that any know-how should be "necessary", in addition to being secret, substantial and identified (as to which see **Section 8.4**, above).

   One looks without success for some assistance as to the definition of "necessary". The definition in Article 10(5) is rather circular: stating merely that "necessary patents" are:

> "patents where a licence under the patent is necessary for the putting into effect of the licensed technology insofar as in the absence of such a licence, the realisation of the licensed technology would not be possible or would only be possible to a lesser extent or in more difficult or costly conditions. Such patents must therefore be of technical, legal or economic interest to the licensee."

There is no avoiding the Commission's suspicion that parties might be using a sham agreement in order to obtain periods of protection longer than, for example, the 10 years allowed in a know-how agreement for restrictions between licensor and licensee. Since, in the absence of a notification, it will only be the parties themselves who are in a position to scrutinise the agreement, what this effectively amounts to is an invitation to the licensee to challenge the necessity of a particular patent in a pure or mixed licence. If he should do so, the licensor will be entitled, as long as he has reserved the right to do so contractually, to terminate the agreement in conformity with the white-listed provision in Article 2.1(16). It would also be prudent for the parties to consider, as for the procurement obligations white-listed under Article 2.1(5), the insertion of a recital that both parties acknowledge that the patent is valuable and necessary. In reality, it would have been better for the Commission to have left this as a ground for withdrawal under Article 7 rather than give rise to uncertainty as to whether an agreement falls outside the scope of the exemption.

Ancillary

Article 5(4) of the Regulation identifies a class of agreements to which the Regulation *will not* apply, being licensing agreements which contain provisions relating to intellectual property rights other than patents which are not ancillary. The effect of this exception to an exception is to open the door to the possibility of exemption for agreements containing restrictions on other intellectual property rights, not just patents and know-how. The definition of "ancillary provisions" in Article 10(15) confirms that a provision in relation to a non-patented intellectual property right will be regarded as ancillary if it imposes obligations no more restrictive than those which attach to the know-how or patents and which comply with the Regulation.

This is an interesting development. The corresponding provisions in the Know-how Regulation had referred to intellectual property rights other than patents (and referred specifically to trade marks, copyrights and design rights as well as software) where these are "of assistance" in achieving the object of the licensed technology. Article 5(4) of the Technology Regulation does not contain this wording. However, Recital 6 offers some clarification by providing that the extension of the exemption to licensing of other intellectual property rights is only appropriate where such "licensing contributes to the achievement of the objects of the licensed technology". Since the technology does not by definition have any "objects" (or at least any which go beyond the technology itself) the only way to make sense of this recital is to take it as referring to the legitimate objects of the technology licence. For example, a licence to affix the licensor's logo to a product such as a fizzy drink does not in any way contribute to the achievement of the bottling technology which allowed production of the drink but it certainly will assist with sale of the product and therefore, as long as the restrictions in relation to the logo do not restrict competition or trade in a way which could not have been achieved by the permitted restrictions in relation to the licensed technology, the Regulation should apply. On the other hand, if they are used to impose limitations that could not have been achieved by enforcement of the "core" rights, that will not be permitted (see *Velcro*, **Case Note 10**). It would clearly make sense to insert recitals in the licence explaining the "objects" of the licence so as to tie in and justify the logo/trade mark clauses.

Some have questioned whether the effect of Article 5(4) is to open up the scope of the Technology Regulation to cover any intellectual property or similar agreements as long as they contain an element of know-how or some patents and as long as the wording of the restrictions is within the same terms as the patent or know-how restrictions. It must be clear that this is not the case but how far the door has been opened is a question of degree. For the exemption to apply, an agreement will still have to satisfy the definition of a technology transfer agreement from one of the categories identified in Article 1.1 and the word "ancillary" in this context must include a notion of the other rights being subordinate. This also comes across from Article 5(4) which refers to "licensing agreements" which is defined in Article 10(6) as referring to pure patent licensing agreements, pure know-how licensing agreements and mixed agreements. An agreement which is predominantly a trade mark licence with some know-how attached will not qualify (see *Moosehead*, **Case Note 14**).

There are bound to be border-line cases where it is not absolutely clear whether it is the patents or know-how, on the one hand, or the trade marks or copyrights, on the other, which are seen as being more valuable and which give the essential "character" of the agreement. To some extent proper drafting will help in making clear that the agreement is primarily a patent or know-how licensing agreement. Where genuine doubt remains but the parties believe it is necessary to deal also with the other intellectual property rights in a single agreement, this would appear a good case for use of the opposition procedure by reference to Article 4.2(a), arguing that it was necessary for the licensee to take the other licences in order to achieve a "technically satisfactory exploitation of the licensed technology" in the broadest sense.

Another helpful change which ties in with the extension of the exemption to include ancillary rights, is the removal of the prohibition (previously found in the Black Lists for both the Patent Regulation and the Know-how Regulation) on charging royalties on products not wholly or partially manufactured making use of the licensed patents or know-how (an issue dealt with in *Windsurfing*, **Case Note** 5). For instance, it is possible that a patent or know-how licence to manufacture a complex electrical product might be accompanied by a copyright licence to reproduce the user manual. That manual might have an actual or nominal sales price upon which a royalty would be charged but it would often not be a product which was itself manufactured using patents or know-how (it might of course contain or disclose know-how but not necessarily). Previously, it would have been prohibited to charge a royalty if relying on the block exemption. Now under the Technology Regulation the question will be rather whether the licensing of the manual is genuinely "ancillary" to the manufacture of the product. Since the Commission would presumably continue to view the charging of a royalty on a product which was manufactured under a licence for rights other than "licensed technology" (which in Art 10(7) is defined only to include the patents and know-how) as a restriction of competition, it would probably be prudent to make use of the opposition procedure.

8.6 Site licences

A new and potentially extremely serious pitfall has recently been identified in relation to Article 2.1(12). This is the apparently innocuous white-listed provision which states that a restriction on the licensee constructing facilities for third parties does not normally infringe Article 85 but for the avoidance of doubt is also exempted. Unfortunately, it goes on to say that this is "without prejudice to the right of the licensee to increase the capacity of his own facilities or to set up additional facilities for his own use on normal commercial terms ..."

In the past this provision has not been given much attention. As an exception to an approved clause it was not viewed as necessarily mandatory. Moreover, the "or" was read as allowing the licensor the option to permit the licensee only to increase his capacity at his licensed plant – if he could – but not to establish other facilities at other addresses. In other words, it was assumed that it still permitted "site licences" of the type common in many large manufacturing industries, where the permission given to the licensee is determined by reference to a particular plant or facility which, by implication, has a physical capacity limitation.

A current case shows the Commission taking a quite different approach. The Commission reads Article 2.1(12) in conjunction with the black-listed provision of Article 3(5). From this it concludes that *any* provision which may restrict the licensee (explicitly or by implication) from increasing his output is prohibited and that therefore the licensee must always and expressly be permitted to open additional facilities at other sites.

The case, including a complaint to the Commission, arose out of a dispute between ARCO and Repsol which has since been settled with Repsol withdrawing the complaint. Nevertheless, the Commission is considering adopting a decision to confirm its position on a number of issues (a salutary warning that complaining to the Commission can be rather like opening Pandora's box and sets in train a procedure which is outside the control of the parties). The proposed decision may involve a confirmation of the Commission's views that any restriction on the licensee building new plant is an infringement of Article 85(1), in which case it would require an exemption and would not be covered by the block exemption because of the Commission's reading of Article 2.1(12) – a reading which the Commission claims is clear and should already have been widely understood.

If the Commission is right, it will leave open the further question of who determines what are the "normal commercial terms" that would govern the extra capacity. It is understood that the Commission is not planning to advance a definition but leans in favour of maximum freedom being given to the licensee so as to avoid any hidden deterrent to his expansion plans. It is clear that he could not be subject to any restrictions going beyond those applying in the original licence. In addition, the Commission takes the view that any licence which satisfies the block exemption must expressly point out the freedom of the licensee to expand capacity in this manner and a failure to do so will be interpreted as a prohibition on expansion which will deprive the agreement of the benefit of the exemption.

Whether or not the Commission is dissuaded from adopting the proposed decision, it has raised an issue which cannot be ignored. Parties who wish to avoid the risk of granting an unlimited licence and who want to be able to rely on the Regulation, need to proceed carefully. It is not clear whether the Commission takes the view that the freedom to build other sites would extend to the whole of the EU or only within the territory allocated to the licensee. There have been suggestions that it is the former but this view must be resisted and if necessary the question will have to be taken to the ECJ. In the meantime, licensors should consider adopting a narrow definition of the manufacturing "territory" which would be confined to the site address and introducing a more relaxed territory in which active and passive sales could be permitted. However, the Commission might now interpret it, such a formulation would comply with the wording of the Regulation and if in doubt one could always consider falling back on the opposition procedure, arguing that the agreement contains no specifically black-listed clauses.

9. Joint ventures and concentrations

Particular problems arise in relation to technology transfer agreements which are either concluded as part of a joint venture arrangement or need to be reviewed as part of a notified merger (often described in Community jargon as a "concentration").

As already briefly discussed (**Analysis Section 14.2**) Article 5.1(2) provides that the Regulation will not apply where competing undertakings who hold interests in a joint venture conclude between themselves a licensing agreement which relates to the activities of the joint venture. Therefore, if Company A and Company B are both motor manufacturers who establish a jointly owned company to provide them with components and if Company A grants to Company B a patent or know-how licence for some manufacturing process to allow Company B to incorporate the components into Company B's vehicles, that could be viewed as relating to the activities of the joint venture and therefore would be prohibited.

The mere fact that Company A and Company B are competitors will not itself be enough to rule out the applicability of the Regulation if they are not also linked by a joint venture: it is only where they introduce further restrictions of the type prohibited by Article 3(4) that such an arrangement would be black-listed. The Commission's concern in Article 5.1(2) relates to the combination of a licence between competitors, which must already be approached with caution, together with the fact that if they share an interest in a joint venture they may have an even greater disincentive to competing with one another. For the same reason, if they are not parents in a joint venture company but conclude reciprocal licences, the application of the Regulation will be excluded by Article 5.1(3).

Licensing agreements between one of the parents and the joint venture company itself are treated somewhat more leniently under the

Regulation. Even though the parents are competitors, the Regulation recognises that the joint venture may depend upon them for certain licences and therefore Article 5.2 introduces the market share thresholds of 20% for production joint ventures and 10% for combined production and distribution ventures. This exemption may be useful in a large and fragmented commodity market where there is no doubt that the products of many producers compete with each other and where the parties are able with some certainty to assess their market shares. In calculating the market share it will be necessary to take the combined shares of both the parents and the joint venture. This could easily mean that a venture which starts off below the thresholds will in time come to exceed those thresholds. The slight relaxation in Article 5.3 to allow the thresholds to be exceeded by a further 10% for two consecutive years does not add much, since there will be very few cases where the parties can calculate their shares with such precision.

Even where a licence agreement is concluded only between one of the parents and the joint venture company, it is likely that the other parent will also be in some way a party to that arrangement, either because he was involved in negotiating it during the establishment of the venture or because he has some right of veto over contracts with parent companies. Normally, that would have the effect of turning the licence agreement into a tripartite agreement. Most other block exemption regulations, including the Patent Regulation, allow one to treat a subsidiary company as a "connected undertaking" with its parent company and therefore to count them as only one party when assessing whether an agreement is a bipartite agreement or not. This gave rise to the problem that where the joint venture was a 50/50 deadlocked company it would not count as a "connected undertaking" with either of its parents and the exemption could not apply. The Know-how Regulation added a further test for a "connected undertaking" as one which was jointly controlled by the parties to the agreement in question. Therefore, if Company A and Company B each owns 50% of their joint venture Company C and if, at the time of setting up Company C, they agree that it will benefit from a know-how licence from Company A, that will still be treated as a bipartite agreement because Company C will be treated as a connected undertaking with both Company A and Company B.

There is one curiosity of the drafting of Article 5.1(2) which deserves a brief mention. It only excludes application of the Regulation to licensing agreements between a parent company and the joint venture where those agreements "relate to the activities of the joint venture".

This therefore means that the Regulation could continue to apply in the unlikely event that one of the parents decided to grant to the joint venture a licence which did not relate to the activities of the venture. Without wanting to be too artificial, one could imagine a situation where Company A and Company B are competing motor manufacturers who set up their joint venture Company C to produce components. Company B is extremely active in Germany and wishes to keep Company A out of that territory and therefore procures that Company A grants to the joint venture an exclusive licence to manufacture and distribute Company A's vehicles in Germany. Company C does not in fact exploit that licence and therefore motor manufacture could not be said to be one of its "activities" but because this is a territory entrusted to Company C as the licensee, Company A can be prevented itself from manufacturing or distributing in that territory. Company B is thereby protected from competition. If this does indeed fit within the wording of the Regulation it clearly does not comply with the spirit of the Regulation and would be a clear case for withdrawal if discovered by the Commission.

When the agreement is entered into in connection with the establishment of the joint venture, it is also necessary to consider the possible application of the Merger Regulation 4064/89. The Merger Regulation, as most recently amended, on 1 March 1998, applies to all joint ventures which are entrusted on a lasting basis with the functions of an autonomous economic entity (often known as "full function" joint ventures). Where such a venture is concluded between parent companies who between them have worldwide turnover exceeding ECU 5 billion and where both of the parents (if there were more than two parents it is unlikely the Technology Regulation would be considered) have EU-wide turnover exceeding ECU 250 million the Merger Regulation would apply to the formation of that joint venture. The amendments of 1 March also introduced more complicated turnover rules so that the Merger Regulation could also apply where the combined worldwide turnover was more than ECU 2.5 billion and where the parties had significant turnover both aggregate and individually in at least three Member States: these other thresholds having been introduced to try to reduce the number of multiple national merger filings.

The point of mentioning the Merger Regulation is that where the joint venture is a qualifying "concentration" then both the formation of the venture and any agreements which are "ancillary" to that venture can benefit from a lasting exemption (for the life of the joint venture at least). A Commission explanatory notice from August 1990 (OJ 1990 C203) concerning such ancillary agreements confirms that intellectual property licences can be exclusive and do not need to be limited in duration. The Commission might also be prepared to accept that certain territorial limitations on exploitation of the licence, so as to confine the joint venture to its stated purpose, are permissible. However, if any licence goes substantially beyond what would be permitted by the block exemption the Commission is unlikely to accept that it is essential for the joint venture and therefore the parties will find themselves having to amend it before the venture as a whole can be cleared. Alternatively, the merger filing will be treated as a Regulation 17 notification (*i.e.* a standard notification on Form A/B) for the licence agreement, which will then be subjected to a separate analysis of its suitability for exemption. For an illustration of the different conclusions which the Commission might reach as to whether a licence should be cleared as ancillary, see *Securicor*, **Case Note 28** and *Voest*, **Case Note 29**.

 A final point to make in relation to joint ventures, is that whether or not they form part of a qualifying "concentration", they generally receive quite favourable treatment from the Commission on notification where they genuinely facilitate the introduction or dissemination of new products or technology. Their complexity means that often a notification will be necessary and the Commission can be expected to seek some changes before giving an exemption. For examples of the Commission's approach see *BBC*, **Case Note 13**, *Cekacan*, **Case Note 15**, *Ford*, **Case Note 25** and *Pasteur*, **Case Note 27**. It is also possible that even an extremely complex joint venture with reciprocal technology licences and joint R&D could be given negative clearance (see *Odin*, **Case Note 19**).

10. Contrast with the earlier Regulations

The Regulation came into force on 1 April 1996 and replaces the Patent Regulation and the Know-how Regulation with respect to agreements entered into after that date. However, as previously mentioned (**Analysis Sections 20 and 23**) the Patent Regulation had been further extended until 31 March 1996 and by virtue of Article 11.3 the Patent Regulation and Know-how Regulation will continue to apply in relation to agreements which fell within those Regulations and which were in force as at 31 March 1996. There is no specific reference to duration but one assumes that the prolongation of those exemptions will last for the duration of the Technology Regulation.

Nevertheless, there will be many who are familiar with the Patent Regulation and Know-how Regulation and who might be concerned to establish what are the differences introduced by the Regulation. This Section therefore seeks to summarise the key changes.

10.1 End of the dilemma

One of the main criticisms of the existence of the Patent Regulation and the Know-how Regulation was that it gave rise to circumstances in which parties were not clear whether their agreement properly fell within one or the other. That small dilemma in relation to mixed agreements is now resolved. An added benefit is that the Commission took the opportunity to extend to pure patent licences a number of the refinements which it had introduced in the Know-how Regulation. For example, the Regulation in Article 2.1(12) and (13) permits restrictions on constructing production facilities for third parties and the second source limited licences. The Regulation in this respect represents a continuing trend in relaxation by the Commission as it grows in experience and confidence with respect to technology licensing.

10.2 Certainty and duration

As the Patent Regulation and Know-how Regulation neared the end of their lives there was understandable concern as to whether they would be renewed. The Technology Regulation will remain in force until 2006 and there have been many hints that any further changes in the future are likely to be in the direction of further relaxation. However, it does not appear that the Commission is contemplating any changes to such a recent regulation in the context of its review of vertical restraints (see **Section 11**, below).

10.3 Amended White List and Black List

In most respects the White List in the Regulation is carried across wholesale from the Know-how Regulation. However, it has been extended by the addition of some new provisions and the inclusion of provisions covering matters previously contained in the Black List of Article 3.

Where a provision was previously black-listed, its inclusion in an agreement entirely ruled out the application of the Regulation including the opposition procedure. The effect of transferring certain matters to the White List, is that where a provision goes further than permitted under the White List it is not automatically exempt but neither is it black-listed and therefore it is possible to use the opposition procedure. For those familiar with the earlier regulations, the main changes to note are the following.

1. Article 2.1(3) acknowledges that it is not anti-competitive to oblige the licensee not to exploit the know-how or patents after termination where the patents are still in force or the know-how is still secret. In the past a restriction on using know-how after termination where it was no longer secret had been black-listed whereas now, if such a restriction were seen as anti-competitive (which it normally would) it would still be possible to seek to justify it under the opposition procedure.

2. Article 2.1(4) allows a grant back of improvements by the licensee save that the licence may not be exclusive where the improvements are severable. The Patent Regulation (Art 2.1(10)) had been better in some respects in that it white-listed obligations by both parties but it did not distinguish between severable and non-severable improvements in insisting upon non exclusivity. The Know-how Regulation (Art 2.1(4)) dealt with severability and reciprocity but was unnecessarily complicated.

3. Article 2.1(5) allows the licensee to be required to observe specifications and procure goods or services where they are necessary. Previously, an obligation to do so where they were not "necessary" would have been black-listed. Now, if there is any debate over necessity, it is possible to use the opposition procedure and Article 4.2(a) identifies that as a specific candidate for the opposition procedure. Even where such stipulations are necessary the Commission still has power, as in all cases, to withdraw the benefit of the exemption under Article 7.

4. Article 2.1(7) of the Regulation confirms that the parties are free to extend payments beyond the life of the licensed patents or the disclosure of the know-how, save where that disclosure occurs through the fault of the licensor. This is a subtle change from the

Patent Regulation where lengthier duration to facilitate payment appeared only as an exception to the Black List (Art 3(4)) rather than in the White List but is essentially unchanged from Article 2.1(7) of the Know-how Regulation. What is worth noting, is that an obligation to pay royalties for use of the know-how where it is the licensor who was responsible for it coming into the public domain, is no longer black-listed although it is not easy to see how one could justify such a provision under the opposition procedure. Similarly, an obligation to pay royalties for products which do not involve the complete or partial use of the licensed technology is no longer black-listed. It is possible to conceive of circumstances where the licensor might want to impose a royalty on every unit of production of a certain category of goods, without having to prove that the licensed know-how was essential in every case. The risk remains that in such circumstances there would be likely to be some doubt about the "substantiality" of the know-how, so that some form of notification might be necessary.

5. The second-sourcing exception in Article 2.1(13) was not previously found in the Patent Regulation and existed only as an identified candidate for use of the opposition procedure in the Know-how Regulation. It is highly significant that it is now a white-listed clause. It is extremely useful in permitting the licensor to grant a licence (or perhaps more than one – see comments in **Analysis Section 10.13**) where the sole purpose of the licence is to allow the licensee to supply the second-sourcing needs of one of the licensor's customers. This can also apply where the licensee is one of those customers who is producing his own components.

6. Article 2.1(15) of the Regulation giving the licensor the right to terminate the agreement in the event of a challenge to the know-how or patents was previously an exception to the black-listed provisions in Article 3(1) of the Patent Regulation and Article 3.4 of the Know-how Regulation. This is complemented by Article 2.1(16) which also white-lists a right to terminate where the licensee claims that a patent is not "necessary". It is helpful to have confirmation that this variation on the no-challenge clause is no longer seen as anti-competitive. In addition, an outright prohibition on challenging during the life of the agreement has been removed from the black-list and is instead identified in Article 4.2(b) as a suitable candidate for use of the opposition procedure.

7. The best endeavours obligation in Article 2.1(17) previously appeared as an exception to a black-listed provision *e.g.* Article 3.9 of the Know-how Regulation. It is now clear that an obligation to use best endeavours is not anti-competitive, although where the parties were already competing manufacturers the Commission may specifically withdraw the benefit of the block exemption under Article 7(4) where that has the effect of deterring use by the licensee of other technologies.

8. Another provision which is entirely new is the reservation in Article 2.1(18) of the licensor's right to terminate exclusivity where the licensee enters into competing research and development, production, use or distribution. This is another example, similar to the right to terminate for challenge, which is welcome in permitting the licensor to make a reasonable response to competition without being able contractually to prevent such competition. Indeed, for the licensor to attempt to do so would remain black-listed under Article 3(2) of the Regulation.

9. As mentioned earlier (in **Section 8.5**) a significant deletion from the Black List, as compared to the preceding Regulations, is the removal of the prohibition upon charging royalties for products manufactured without at least partial use of the licensed technology.

10. Finally, the Black List no longer prohibits a restriction within the same technical field of use or product market as to customers who may be served by the parties, except where the parties were already competing manufacturers (Art 3(4)). If they were not already competitors it may be possible to justify such restrictions under the opposition procedure.

11. **Future developments**

11.1 **European Union**

Section 3 contained brief references to an ongoing review by the Commission on its policy towards vertical restraints, which was launched in 1997. The Commission has been canvassing views and gradually developing its thinking on how it should treat restrictions in vertical agreements *i.e.* agreements where the parties are not at the same level in the supply or technology chain and are not direct competitors. This review is driven largely by the acceptance that far too many agreements which do not in fact lead to an elimination of competition are required to be examined under Article 85, leading to significant compliance costs without any real consumer benefit. The Commission has therefore been reviewing whether some of the block exemptions for vertical agreements could be relaxed and is proposing to replace a number of those block exemptions with a "super block exemption". The current timetable points to such an exemption being finalised, at the earliest, around the end of 1999.

The vertical restraints review is unlikely to have much of a direct impact on technology licensing agreements. First, the Commission recognises (see **Section 3.1**, above) that technology licences can often be clarified as horizontal rather than vertical agreements and therefore are not necessarily suitable for the more lenient approach. In addition, the Technology Regulation is relatively new and the Commission has expressed itself satisfied with the Regulation and unwilling to amend or replace it for some time. Commission officials believe the Regulation is already quite sophisticated and generous. Any changes will probably have to await the Commission's separate initiative, reviewing its approach to horizontal agreements, which is unlikely to lead to any new legislation before at least the year 2000.

Nevertheless, the vertical restraints review could still be of some interest to parties engaging in technology licensing. It seems likely that the new super block exemption will grant a fairly broad exemption for agreements where the parties are below certain market share thresholds, similar to the approach originally proposed for the Technology Regulation itself. What is helpful is that even if not strictly applicable to technology licensing agreements, the introduction of such a relaxation will lend support to any arguments on individual notification that there should be a presumption in favour of exemption.

11.2 United Kingdom

Parties to technology transfer agreements which may affect trade and competition in the United Kingdom will also have to consider the application of the UK Competition Bill. At the time of writing, it is envisaged that the Bill will receive Royal Assent in the Autumn of 1998 and that its substantive provisions will be brought into force a year later. Certain agreements will also benefit from a transitional period before the new provisions become applicable.

The new Act will introduce two new prohibitions modelled on Articles 85 and 86 of the EC Treaty. The Government's intention is that the new domestic prohibitions will be interpreted and applied to ensure consistency with EU competition law, as indeed they are required to under EU law (see comments at **Section 3.1**, above). Nevertheless, the Government was not ready to give the OFT the power it had requested, to enforce Articles 85 and 86 directly by administrative action. The Government was apparently concerned that the OFT might use such power to attack certain areas such as professional rules which are excluded from the domestic prohibitions. Notwithstanding this refusal, the general principle behind the Bill remains that whether the agreement comes within the jurisdiction of UK or EU competition law or both, the agreement should be subject to the same competition law test. The drafting of the Bill, however, does not provide a guarantee of complete consistency with the EU system.

Agreements which comply with the Technology Regulation will be automatically exempt from the UK equivalent of Article 85(1). An agreement which benefits from an individual exemption following notification will also benefit from automatic exemption from the UK prohibition. However, the Bill confers a power on the Director General of Fair Trading ("DGFT") to revoke or impose conditions on such automatic exemption from the UK prohibition. The DGFT has indicated that the power would be used in rare circumstances, for example where an agreement raises particular concerns for the UK market. In any event, there remains serious doubts whether EU law would permit a national competition authority to impose stricter domestic competition law requirements on an agreement benefiting from a Commission exemption.

Commission comfort letters will also be relevant for the application of the new Act. If an agreement does not benefit from a block exemption but has the benefit of a comfort letter stating that it merits an exemption, there is no automatic exemption from the UK prohibition. There is therefore no automatic protection from action by the DGFT or challenge to the agreement in court. However, the DGFT has indicated in draft guidelines which he has issued on the practical operation of the Bill, that he would not expect to depart from the Commission's competition law assessment of such an agreement.

Therefore, as a general rule, technology transfer agreements which affect trade between Member States and which benefit from the Regulation or have been given an exemption or comfort letter should receive similarly favourable treatment under the Competition Bill. However, the Act will not confer complete immunity from the domestic prohibition and an assessment of its application will have to be made in cases where the agreement may raise particular concerns for the United Kingdom, particularly in the early days of the legislation while practice is developing.

In assessing the potential application of the Bill to technology transfer agreements, it should also be noted that the Government has made it clear that it intends to provide by secondary legislation special treatment for vertical agreements under the UK equivalent of Article 85. The Government has not yet confirmed the definition of vertical agreements which will qualify for the special treatment. It indicated during the Commons stages of the Bill that pure intellectual property agreements would not qualify. However, even if technology transfer agreements do qualify within the definition of vertical agreements, an assessment of the application of the Bill to such agreements is still advisable. The Government has emphasised that any general dispensation for vertical agreements can be terminated by the Director General in individual cases and examined under the prohibition in the normal way. The risk of such action by the Director General should be assessed at the outset of an agreement, especially for long term agreements.

12. Conclusion

It can be seen from the foregoing that the Regulation while a significant improvement on its predecessors still leaves a number of questions unresolved. The opportunities to obtain clarification will be few because it is in the nature of things that there are very few Commission decisions or court judgments which deal with interpretation of block exemption regulations. It is generally left to the parties and their advisors to reach their own conclusions on whether an agreement complies with the Regulation and to weigh the risk of sailing too close to the wind on particular points.

The Technology Regulation represents a trend towards more generous treatment of intellectual property licences. The shortened Black List may make possible greater use of the opposition procedure. Whether the Regulation will lead to a significant drop in the number of individual cases handled by the Commission using either the truncated or full length notification process, is more doubtful. Indeed, there must be a risk that by clarifying the application of Article 85 to a range of agreements, practices and restrictions while making the Regulation more "flexible", it will have the opposite effect of encouraging even more notifications.

Appendix

· Case Summaries ·

These summaries are provided for convenience and with a view to bringing out the practical elements which have influenced the decision on suitability for exemption. Every effort has been made to check their accuracy but summarising inevitably involves some distortion and it would be advisable to refer to the full texts.

References used are to:

- **CMLR*** *Common Market Law Reports* published by Sweet & Maxwell
- **EMCR** *European Merger Control Reporter* published by Kluwer (of which the author is joint editor)

Cases summarised

1. Re the Agreement of Burroughs AG and Etablissements L Delplanque et Fils

2. Re the Agreement between Kabel-und Metallwerke Neumeyer AG and les Etablissements Luchaire SA

3. L C Nungesser and Kurt Eisele v EC Commission

4. Re the Agreements between Schlegel Corporation and Compagnie des Produits Industriels de l'Ouest SA

5. Windsurfing International Inc v EC Commission

6. Re Mitchell Cotts Air Filtration Ltd

7. Re the Agreement between Boussois SA and Interpane-Entwicklungs-und Beratungsgesellschaft mbH & Co KG

8. Re the Agreement between Jus-rol Ltd and Rich Products Corporation

9. Commission Press Release of 12 October 1988

10. Velcro SA v Aplix SA

11. Re the Agreement between DDD Ltd and Delta Chemie

---

*Note – some would maintain that only the *European Court Reports* are authoritative, particularly if pleading before the ECJ, but the author finds the CMLR more accessible, more clearly presented and more up to date.

1. Re the Agreement of Burroughs AG and Etablissements L Delplanque et Fils [1972] CMLR D67

Main facts

Burroughs, a Swiss company, concluded an agreement with the French company Delplanque regarding a licensing contract for special plasticised carbon paper: a relatively new product which, due to its high cost price and its characteristics, was sold on the market at a higher price than traditional multi-use carbon paper.

The agreement, dated December 1972, granted to Delplanque an exclusive licence to manufacture certain patented carbon paper products in France and a non-exclusive licence to manufacture certain other patented carbon paper products in the EC, Great Britain (not at that time part of a Member State) and Africa. It also granted to Delplanque a non-exclusive licence to use trade marks belonging to Burroughs in the same territory. Delplanque was prohibited from granting sub-licences.

Burroughs agreed to lend all necessary technical assistance to Delplanque regarding designs, specifications etc and Delplanque undertook to manufacture in sufficient quantity to satisfy demand and to comply with the technical instructions of Burroughs in the manufacture of the products, to which it was only allowed to make modifications to improve quality. Delplanque agreed to keep secret the technical information supplied to it for the duration of the agreement, which was 10 years, plus a further period of 10 years.

The manufacture of the products in question constituted only a minor part of the activities of both companies. The agreement was notified by the parties for negative clearance.

Main conclusions

The exclusive nature of the manufacturing licence granted to Delplanque could potentially have the effect of restricting competition. However, in this case the Commission considered that any such restriction would be negligible as Delplanque held such a small share of the French market in multi-use carbon papers.

The Commission held that the obligations on Delplanque to manufacture a sufficient quantity and to comply with the technical instructions of Burroughs did not constitute a restriction on competition, as they had no other purpose than to permit the sufficient and technically adequate exploitation of the patented technology. The obligation of secrecy was a necessary precondition for the disclosure of technical know-how. The prohibition on the granting of sub-licences was also a necessary pre-condition, given that the holder of a patent is the only one able to permit the utilisation of his right in the invention and that the secrecy of the know-how can only be guaranteed if the owner of the know-how is able to determine to whom it can be communicated.

The Commission held that the agreement did not fall within Article 85(1).

Referred to at Analysis Sections 10.1, 10.2, 10.5, Commentary Section 3.1

2.   Re the Agreement between Kabel-und Metallwerke Neumeyer AG and les Etablissements Luchaire SA [1975] 2 CMLR D40

Main facts

In February 1963 Neumeyer notified to the Commission an agreement concluded in 1958 with Luchaire. Neumeyer developed a whole range of special techniques for the machining of steel parts using a cold-extrusion process. The manufacturing techniques were based on secret processes and on a large number of patents in various EC countries.

In a licensing and technical assistance agreement Neumeyer granted Luchaire an exclusive licence for the manufacture in France of the products using Neumeyer's secret and patented manufacturing techniques, an exclusive right to sell the products in certain non-EC countries (Spain and Portugal – not Member States at the time) and a non-exclusive licence to sell the products in all countries of the EC.

The parties agreed to exchange all relevant information concerning the application of the licensed techniques. Neumeyer undertook to give Luchaire all necessary technical assistance for the 20-year duration of the agreement. Luchaire undertook to grant Neumeyer a non-exclusive licence in respect of any patent relating to any improvements to the processes which Luchaire might discover/develop, so that Neumeyer could use such improvements for its own production and also authorise any other licensee to use them. Luchaire also undertook to keep Neumeyer's know-how secret. Finally, Neumeyer undertook not to grant to any third party any licence in respect of the know-how on terms which were more favourable than those applying to Luchaire.

Main conclusions

The Commission considered that Neumeyer's undertaking not to grant any licence in respect of its techniques to any firm on more favourable terms than those applying to Luchaire was not caught by Article 85(1) as it would not in general dissuade the licensor from granting further licences to third parties. It did say, however, that in specific cases, where the market situation was such that the only way to find other licensees was to grant them more favourable terms than the first licensee, this obligation could be an obstacle to the granting of further licences and would restrict competition. The Commission did not give any examples of such a specific case in its decision.

The exclusive manufacturing licence granted to Luchaire restricted Neumeyer's ability to make agreements with other applicants for licences on French territory. Given Luchaire and Neumeyer's substantial market share in such products the exclusive licence also appreciably restricted competition within the EC. The agreement, therefore, fell within the scope of Article 85(1).

However, Neumeyer's undertaking to grant Luchaire exclusive rights contributed to economic progress by guaranteeing Luchaire a sufficient return on its investments by virtue of the territorial advantages it derived from the exclusion of any other firm which might have been interested in manufacturing within the territory. This exclusivity enabled an additional manufacturer within the EC (Luchaire) to use the improved techniques which resulted in considerable savings in raw materials and the production of more high-quality finished products. The agreement also permitted Luchaire to ask for Neumeyer's technical assistance, for example, in designing new parts and equipment, and this encouraged joint improvement of the licensed techniques.

In addition, users of the machine-steel products would have obtained a fair share of the benefits of the economic and technical progress, as they would have had at their disposal high quality goods tailored to their needs together with technical assistance. Also competition between rival products was sufficient to guarantee users a share in such benefits.

The Commission considered that Luchaire's exclusive licence was indispensable to the attainment of these desirable objectives, given the investments required to apply Neumeyer's techniques and to promote sales of products manufactured by the extrusion process. At the time the agreement was entered into, the extrusion process was not widely used and had to compete with many other processes to which users were already accustomed. Although Luchaire occupied an important position in the EC market, the agreement did not give it power to eliminate competition in a large part of the relevant product market. The Commission therefore held that the agreement satisfied all the tests for a decision granting exemption under Article 85(3).

As originally drafted, the licensing agreement had not satisfied the tests of Article 85(3) because it contained a general obligation on Luchaire not to export the products to other EC countries (except certain specified Member States). It also contained an obligation on Luchaire to transfer to Neumeyer ownership of such improvements, whether patentable or not, as Luchaire might make in conjunction with Neumeyer and an obligation not to contest the validity of Neumeyer's patented processes. These obligations constituted substantial restrictions of competition which could not be regarded as being of the essence of the licensed patent rights or as contributing to the improvement of production or distribution of goods or to promoting technical and economic progress. At the Commission's request, the parties deleted these obligations from the agreement in March 1974.

The Commission granted an exemption which was effective from the date the agreement was amended in 1974 until its termination in December 1977.

Referred to at Analysis Sections 10.10, 10.15, 12.6

3.   L C Nungesser KG and Kurt Eisele v EC Commission (Case 258/78) [1983] 1 CMLR 278

Main facts

INRA, a French research institute, was successful in developing new varieties of maize seed which could be grown in the colder climate of Northern Europe. Mr Eisele was the sole partner and majority shareholder in Nungesser, a supplier of seeds in Germany.

In December 1960 Eisele and INRA entered into an agreement under which Eisele agreed to represent INRA for the purpose of securing registration of the maize varieties developed by INRA. In February 1961 INRA discovered that under German legislation in force at the time an owner of breeders' rights established outside Germany was not able to have those rights registered with the relevant German authorities. To overcome that difficulty, INRA assigned to Eisele breeders' rights in Germany for four varieties of maize seed and Eisele became the registered owner of these rights in Germany.

In 1965 INRA and Eisele entered into a further agreement relating to six varieties of maize seed. Eisele was granted an exclusive right to organise sales of these maize varieties in Germany. He undertook to refrain from organising the sale of maize varieties other than those of INRA. Eisele agreed to supply seeds to every German undertaking and co-operative which offered the necessary technical assurances, with the prices to be fixed in agreement with INRA. Eisele also agreed to import at least two-thirds of the German market's seed requirements from France through the French organisation responsible for co-ordinating INRA maize exports. Eisele was then entitled, on payment of a royalty, to produce the remaining third of the seeds necessary to satisfy the German market. He was authorised to use the INRA trade mark which was internationally protected. In addition, Eisele undertook to enforce INRA's proprietary rights in its varieties, in particular against passing off. INRA undertook to ensure that the necessary steps were taken to prevent INRA maize varieties from being exported into Germany other than through Eisele.

Eisele subsequently assigned his exclusive rights to distribute INRA varieties in Germany to Nungesser.

In February 1974 the Commission received a complaint from a French undertaking following a threat of legal proceedings by Nungesser after the Complainant had offered INRA seed, lawfully acquired in France, for sale on the German market.

In its decision of September 1978, the Commission found that the exclusive grant of the licence and the attempts of INRA and Eisele to restrain parallel imports restricted competition contrary to Article 85(1). In considering the application of Article 85(3) the Commission considered that the test for exemption of the exclusive selling rights and the accompanying export prohibitions was not satisfied. This was because no new market was penetrated or new product launched, and the exclusive distribution system established by INRA precluded consumers from obtaining a fair share of any benefits.

Eisele and Nungesser applied to the ECJ for a declaration that the Commission's decision was void.

Main conclusions

The ECJ dealt first with the applicants' submission that the principles which had been developed by the ECJ in relation to patent and trade mark law could not apply to breeders' rights on account of the specific characteristics of those rights. In particular, the applicants argued that the reproduction procedure for maize seeds was more complicated than the reproduction of products protected by trade mark or patent rights because it depended to a marked degree on the hazards of climate and soil. The ECJ held that this line of argument failed to take into account the many products capable of forming the subject-matter of trade marks and patents and was not sufficient to justify special treatment for breeders' rights.

In relation to Article 85(1), the ECJ considered that, taking the agreements of 1960, 1961 and 1965 as a whole, Eisele's position on the German market was that of an exclusive licensee. The ECJ distinguished between (i) a "so-called open exclusive licence or assignment" where the exclusivity relates solely to the contractual relationship between the parties, whereby the owner merely undertakes not to grant other licences in respect of the same territory and not himself to compete with the licensee on that territory, and (ii) an exclusive licence with absolute territorial protection under which the parties propose to eliminate all competition from third parties.

The ECJ considered that the grant of an open exclusive licence would not in itself have been incompatible with Article 85(1) if justified as an incentive to investment. However, in this case it was clear from the documents that the parties did intend to restrict competition from third parties on the German market and the Court had consistently held that such absolute territorial protection granted to a licensee was contrary to Article 85(1).

The ECJ then went on to consider the Commission's refusal to grant exemption under Article 85(3). It found that the absolute territorial protection granted to Eisele manifestly went beyond what was indispensable for the improvement of production or the promotion of technical progress, as demonstrated in particular by the prohibition, agreed to by both parties, of any parallel imports of INRA maize seeds into Germany even if those seeds were bred by INRA itself and marketed in France. This in itself constituted a sufficient reason for refusing to grant an exemption under Article 85(3) and the ECJ did not examine the other grounds set out in the decision for refusing to grant such an exemption.

Referred to at Analysis Section 17.1, Commentary Section 2.2

4. **Re the Agreements between Schlegel Corporation and Compagnie des Produits Industriels de l'Ouest SA (CPIO) [1984] 2 CMLR 179**

Main facts

In February 1983 Schlegel of New York and CPIO of France applied to the European Commission for negative clearance of a Know-how Communication Agreement pursuant to Article 2 of Regulation 17. By that agreement Schlegel granted CPIO a non-exclusive right to use its methods and industrial processes for the manufacture of automotive weatherseals in consideration of payment of periodic royalties. CPIO had the right to manufacture in all EC countries (but not outside the EC) and to sell weatherseals incorporating Schlegel's know-how world-wide. The Schlegel know-how for the production of weatherseals was a new technology for CPIO, to which it could not have had access without Schlegel's co-operation.

The parties also notified an agreement concerning the purchase and use of an upstream product (a wire carrier) supplied by Schlegel for the manufacture of weatherseals for motor vehicles. CPIO was required to purchase from Schlegel all its requirements for wire carrier to be used in the production of weatherseals for motor vehicles. Schlegel was free to sell the wire carrier to any other customers in France or elsewhere and CPIO was free to resell the wire carrier to third parties within the EC.

The demand for the wire carrier depended directly on the demand for weatherseals which in turn depended on the planned production of vehicles. In the EC there were a large number of producers of weatherseals who supplied the vehicle manufacturers and the whole rubber industry was considered as potential suppliers in the market.

The parties agreed that the Know-how Agreement did not depend on the legal validity of the Purchase Agreement for the wire carrier.

Main conclusions

As regards the Know-how Agreement, it contained no provisions which had as their effect the prevention, restriction or distortion of competition within the EC. The agreement on the use of Schlegel's methods and industrial processes for the manufacture of automotive weatherseals was non-exclusive and left CPIO free to manufacture the weatherseals in any country in the EC and to sell them world-wide. The prohibition on CPIO manufacturing weatherseals outside the EC would not restrict competition within the EC appreciably.

There were no grounds for believing that Schlegel or CPIO might abuse a dominant position within the EC or a substantial part of it.

The Commission found that the Purchase Agreement did fall under Article 85(1) and was liable to affect trade between Member States. The securing of exclusive purchase and use obligations so that the possibility of changing suppliers was postponed for the duration of the agreement (which was five years) went beyond a normal long-term sales agreement. The agreement also had the effect of reserving an appreciable part of the wire carrier demand for Schlegel.

The Commission considered, however, that the agreement fulfilled the requirements laid down in Article 85(3). It contributed to improving production and distribution and to promoting technical and economic progress.

In the automobile industry, where it is necessary to plan production in advance, long-term agreements for the supply of components were indispensable and were normal practice for both car manufacturers and suppliers. In cases such as this where production planning was secured by exclusive purchase and use obligations, it rationalised the production of the supplier and of the car manufacturer, and further rationalised the continuing process for delivery and reception of goods. Greater production quantities permitted continuous improvement of the product concerned and its manufacturing process, because a sufficient return was only possible with certain minimum quantities.

The Commission considered that the expected advantages of the agreement outweighed the anti-competitive effects of the exclusive obligations to purchase the wire carrier from Schlegel and that the restrictions were indispensable within the meaning of Article 85(3). The five-year duration of the agreement did not exceed what was necessary to achieve these advantages. The agreement also allowed consumers a fair share of the resulting benefit, due to the fact that in the market effective competition for supply existed, which the Commission assumed would be reflected in the purchase price for the wire carrier. The benefits resulting from the rationalisation of the parties' production would also benefit car manufacturers and final consumers, because CPIO was in a very competitive market for weatherseals which the Commission assumed would be reflected in CPIO's sales prices for weatherseals.

The agreement did not allow the parties the possibility of eliminating competition in respect of a substantial part of the products in question. There was substantial demand for supply of weatherseals in the EC and the secret technical processes did not constitute a barrier to entry of competitors in the market. It was not considered that the market share tied up by the agreement between Schlegel and CPIO would be a significant part of the total market of the products concerned within the EC.

The Commission granted negative clearance in respect of the Know-how Agreement and exemption of the Purchase Agreement for the five-year duration of the agreements.

Referred to at Analysis Sections 8.3, 10.5

5. Windsurfing International Inc v EC Commission (Case 193/83) [1986] 3 CMLR 489

Main facts

Windsurfing, an American manufacturer of sailboards and sailboard components, applied to the ECJ for a declaration that the Commission's decision of July 1983 was void in so far as it contained a finding that a number of clauses in the licensing agreements concluded between Windsurfing and German undertakings constituted an infringement of Article 85(1).

One of the clauses at issue related to the obligation on the licensees to sell components covered by a German patent (which was deemed to be confined to rigs) only in conjunction with boards approved by the licensor: in other words, to sell the products only as part of a complete surfboard package.

The Commission held that this obligation to sell the patented product in conjunction with a product outside the scope of the patent was not indispensable to the exploitation of the patent.

A further issue concerned the obligation on the licensees to pay royalties on the sales of components calculated on the basis of the net selling price of the complete package. Windsurfing argued that that the clause could not be interpreted as meaning that the royalty on sales of components was based on the net selling price of the whole sailboard. However, the Commission noted that the definition of the product contained in the agreements did not treat the rig as an item for separate sale and there was, therefore, no means of calculating royalty for sales of rigs alone. It seems from the Commission's arguments, that such a method of calculation might be justified where "the number of items manufactured or consumed or their value are difficult to establish separately in a complex production process, or ... there is for the patented item on its own no separate demand ...".

Main conclusions

The Court agreed with the Commission that the above exception did not apply in this case, but nonetheless held that the royalty provision did not infringe Article 85(1) as the actual royalty levied on the basis of the final product, combining the patented and non-patented elements, was no higher than would have been charged on the basis of the patented element alone. This was evidenced by the fact that, in a series of new licensing agreements, the royalties calculated on the basis of the rigs alone were no lower because the licensees acknowledged that it was equitable to accept a higher percentage royalty rate once the licensor's remuneration was to be calculated on the "price" of the rig alone.

Referred to at Commentary Section 8.5

6. Re Mitchell Cotts Air Filtration Ltd [1988] 4 CMLR 111

Main facts

In September 1984 Mitchell Cotts & Co (Engineering) Ltd, a UK company, and Sofiltra Poelman SA, a French Company, submitted to the European Commission a notification of various agreements and an application for negative clearance concerning the creation of a joint venture company called Mitchell Cotts Air Filtration Ltd ("the Joint Venture Company").

The agreements related to the manufacture and sale of high-efficiency air filters utilising microfine glass fibre for the nuclear, biological, chemical and computer markets.

Sofiltra manufactured high-efficiency particulate air filters from small pleated paper media composed of submicronic glass fibres in France. Mitchell Cotts had been involved for eight years in the manufacture and marketing of air filtration devices incorporating pleated glass fibre paper purchased from Sofiltra. No advanced technology was involved in the assembly of the final product, which merely entailed the provision of a metal or plastic casing. The pleated glass fibre paper represented the major cost component and the key technical element in the finished product. Mitchell Cotts did not possess either the relevant technology or the research and development facilities necessary to manufacture the high-efficiency air filters. Sofiltra and Mitchell could not, therefore, be considered competitors at the manufacturing level.

In July 1984 Sofiltra and Mitchell Cotts entered into a Joint Venture Agreement and a Know-how Licence Agreement for a duration of 10 years. The Joint Venture Company undertook to manufacture air filtration devices using Sofiltra's technology, know-how and expertise under a royalty-bearing licence. Know-how was defined as secret technical data and other information relating to the design and manufacture of absolute high efficiency filters using small pleated paper media. A subsidiary company of Mitchell Cotts agreed to lease the production premises and to supply the commercial know-how. The Joint Venture Agreement and the Know-how Licence Agreement provided for the grant by Sofiltra to the Joint Venture Company of an exclusive licence to manufacture air filters in the United Kingdom and an exclusive right of sale in the United Kingdom, Ireland and seven non-EC countries. This was, however, subject to the right of Sofiltra and other licensees to sell the licensed products and spare parts in the United Kingdom when such sale was made under medium-term financial agreements, specifying country of origin, concluded between governments of customer and seller (it was expected that such agreements would be rare). A sum by way of compensation was to be made to the Joint Venture Company every time such a direct sale was made. At the same time, the agreement contained a provision prohibiting the licensee from manufacturing, warehousing, advertising or establishing any commercial sales branch or agency for sale of the licensed product outside its exclusive territory.

Passive sales were, however, permitted. The Licence Agreement prohibited the Joint Venture Company from manufacturing or dealing in competing products and from granting sub-licences without Sofiltra's consent. In addition, the Licence Agreement provided for the reciprocal disclosure and granting of non-exclusive licences for improvements and new inventions. It allowed Sofiltra to disclose any improvements and inventions developed or acquired by the Joint Venture to its other licensees. It also imposed an obligation on the Joint Venture Company to maintain confidentiality as to the know-how.

The market in which the goods competed was the high-efficiency air and gas filtration equipment market. Sofiltra's EC market share for the three years prior to the conclusion of the agreements was 15%. Mitchell Cotts' market share in the EC was negligible except in the United Kingdom and Ireland in which its market share was approximately 10%.

Main conclusions

Mitchell Cotts and Sofiltra were neither actual nor potential competitors for the manufacture of the complete finished product, since Mitchell Cotts lacked the requisite know-how and research and development facilities for the production of pleated glass fibre paper, which was the crucial component in the finished product and the subject of the technology transfer in this case. Also, due to the number of undertakings competing in the market and the relatively small market shares of the notifying parties in the relevant geographic market, the creation of the Joint Venture Company did not pose any risk in terms of the foreclosure of similar possibilities to other competitors. The agreement to undertake joint manufacturing did not, therefore, in itself fall within the terms of Article 85 (1).

However, as regards sales and distribution of the final product, Sofiltra and the Joint Venture Company were competitors. The exclusive right granted to the Joint Venture Company to sell the licensed products in the United Kingdom, Ireland and seven non-EC countries prohibited Sofiltra and any possible future licensees from actively selling in those territories. The ban on active sales was considered to fall within Article 85(1) since such a restriction resulted in the sharing of markets between Sofiltra and the Joint Venture Company, which had become competitors and were offering competing products. The Commission considered that trade between Member States would be affected by the Joint Venture arrangements as the Joint Venture Company's production would be marketed in Ireland as well as the United Kingdom. Also, Sofiltra's relatively strong position within the EC market made it likely that the effects on trade between Member States would be appreciable.

The Commission went on to find that the restrictions caught by Article 85(1) could be exempted under Article 85(3). This was the first time that Sofiltra's technology and know-how were being exploited in the United Kingdom. It was clear that in order to establish itself and to develop in a competitive market, the Joint Venture Company should not be subject to competition from other production units established by Sofiltra or from active sales by Sofiltra or from other licensees. Also, the territory allocated to the Joint Venture Company was sufficiently large to occupy its attention for a considerable period of time and it was in the interests of the Joint Venture Company not to be distracted from developing the market in its extensive territory by attempting to sell outside it. Such a restriction should enable the Joint Venture to concentrate its efforts on its exclusive territory, building on the experience of Mitchell Cotts' existing sales network. Also, the Joint Venture Company was free to make passive sales outside its licensed territory. The territory could be easily supervised with the result that there would be better market knowledge based on closer contact with consumers. Accordingly, the agreements contributed to an improvement in production and distribution.

Also, as a result of the agreements, the licensed products were manufactured by an integrated production process and technological improvements were made more widely and rapidly available to users and consumers. Competitive pressures in the market would ensure that consumers benefited from those improvements, while competition would not be eliminated for a substantial part of the products in question. The Commission considered that the restrictions were indispensable to the attainment of the benefits to which the Joint Venture gave rise, since without them the parties would not have been prepared to make the necessary effort or commitments.

The Commission granted an exemption for a period of 10 years to cover the duration of the agreements.

Referred to at Analysis Sections 8.5, 10.4

7.   Re the Agreement between Boussois SA and Interpane-Entwicklungs-und Beratungsgesellschaft mbH & Co KG (Case IV/31.302) [1988] 4 CMLR 124

Main facts

The German firm Interpane licensed to the French firm Boussois a body of technical information in connection with the sale to Boussois of a production plant for application of a fine thermal insulation coating to flat glass. Some of the information was patented but the majority was not.

The unpatented know-how licensed to Boussois was substantial, in that it comprised detailed information about Interpane's latest technology concerning:

1. the assembly, commissioning and operation of the production plant; and

2. the insulating coatings for which the plant could be used, covering the various stages in the production process. The licence also included any improvements made to that technology in the five years following the handover of the information.

The agreement allowed Boussois to manufacture and sell the insulating glass in France to the exclusion of any other licensee for the first five years after signature of the agreement and on a non-exclusive basis for an indefinite period thereafter. Interpane reserved the right to build and operate a similar plant in France itself but not before two years had expired from the date of the agreement. Boussois was prohibited from manufacturing any of the insulating coatings in any other Member State, although it was free to manufacture competing products and to sell the insulating coatings throughout the EC. This right to sell the insulating coatings in any country was understood by the parties as being without prejudice to the possibility of Interpane's later granting another licensee an exclusive sales licence for another territory.

The parties undertook to communicate to one another on a non-exclusive basis any improvements they made to the transferred know-how during the currency of the agreement. The licence for the improvements was on the same terms as for the original know-how transferred. The parties also agreed to preserve secrecy of the know-how and any improvements for five years following their communication, on the basis that the life cycle of technology in the industry was not generally more than five years.

The parties applied for negative clearance or exemption of the agreement. They submitted that their collective market position, though not insignificant, did not enable them to influence supply and demand conditions to their advantage and that the constraints placed on their conduct by the agreement could not be said to restrict competition. (The relevant product market was the market for double-glazing units made with "low-emissivity" glass plus that for conventional triple-glazing units.)

Main conclusions

The Commission held that the following three provisions had the object and effect of restricting competition:

1. the exclusivity of manufacture and sale in France granted to Boussois;

2. the prohibition on Boussois manufacturing outside France (which would restrict its potential sales in other EC countries); and

3. the prohibition on Boussois selling the products in another territory in which Interpane later appointed another exclusive licensee.

In view of the market share held by insulation-glass units made with Interpane's technology, the Commission held that the restriction of competition resulting from the agreement and the effect on trade brought the agreement within Article 85(1).

Block Exemption Regulation 2349/84 applied to patent licensing agreements, and to mixed patent and know-how licensing agreements where the patents are necessary for achieving the objects of the licensed technology and the know-how permits a better exploitation of the patents. However, the Commission held that this agreement did not fall within the exemption in Regulation 2349/84 due to the importance of the know-how element in the technology and because the use of patents was minimal. It said:

> "... until such time as there is a block exemption regulation specifically for pure know-how agreements or mixed agreements in which the know-how component consists of a body of knowledge that is crucial for the exploitation of the licensed technology and not just a factor permitting the better exploitation of the patents, the restrictions of competition involved in the agreement require individual exemption."

The Commission went on to find that the agreement fulfilled all the conditions in Article 85(3) for an individual exemption.

It held that the exclusivity granted to Boussois and the prohibitions on Boussois manufacturing outside France or selling in territories of other exclusive licensees appointed by Interpane in the future produced the following beneficial effects:

- Interpane was more willing to grant a licence for its know-how, which was of substantial importance;
- Boussois was more inclined to undertake the investment required to manufacture, use and market the insulating glass, thereby helping to disseminate and further develop a new product and promoting technical and economic progress in the EC;
- as a result of Boussois' building of the plant employing Interpane's technology and as a result also of the arrangements for the constant exchange of improvements to the technology, the number of

production facilities in the EC and the quantity and quality of the products had increased;

- in view of the investment undertaken by Boussois, consumers would be likely to enjoy a fair share of the benefits resulting from the agreement.

In addition, the provisions of the agreement would not allow the parties to eliminate competition in respect of a substantial part of the products in question, as there was effective inter-brand competition in the market in the EC and the parties had not taken any steps to prevent parallel imports of their products.

The Commission granted an exemption for a period of five years to cover the period of territorial protection provided for in the agreement.

Referred to at Analysis Sections 8.6, 10.4

8. Re the Agreement between Jus-rol Ltd and Rich Products Corporation (Case IV/31.206) [1988] 4 CMLR 527

Main facts

In April 1984 Jus-rol notified to the European Commission a know-how licensing agreement which it had concluded with Rich with a view to obtaining negative clearance under Article 85(1) or, alternatively, an exemption under Article 85(3).

Rich manufactured food products, including non-dairy creamers and frozen yeast doughs. It had production units in the United States and Canada which manufactured products for sale mainly on those markets. Jus-rol, a UK company, manufactured food products, in particular a range of frozen dough products all based on non-yeast doughs. All its production units were based in the United Kingdom.

Under the know-how licensing agreement, Rich granted Jus-rol an exclusive right to use its know-how for the manufacture of frozen yeast products ("the licensed product") in the United Kingdom in return for royalty payments. The agreement was for a 10-year period with a right to terminate by either party on written notice after five years. Rich Products had not previously manufactured or marketed, either directly or through distributors, the licensed product in the EC.

The know-how consisted of a body of written confidential non-patented information on the process for freezing the yeast used in the licensed product. It also related to the composition, preparation and processing of the licensed product and to production techniques, timing, apparatus and notes of oral discussions between the employees of both parties with a view to the delivery of technical information. Any improvements and other developments made by Rich to the initial know-how also formed part of the know-how under the agreement. Jus-rol granted to Rich a non-exclusive licence in respect of any improvements it made to the original know-how. Jus-rol undertook to purchase from Rich a pre-mix (whose composition was secret) for the manufacture of the licensed product and to use the pre-mix in the quantity and manner specified in the know-how.

Jus-rol was also granted a non-exclusive right to sell the licensed product in all Member States. Rich was free to sell the licensed product in all Member States, except the United Kingdom, or to appoint distributors or licensees. Jus-rol did not sell the licensed product direct to final consumers but made weekly deliveries by refrigerated lorries to stores such as supermarkets with in-house bakeries. In 1984 demand for frozen dough products was fairly limited but it was expected to increase considerably due to advantages, such as low capital cost, low labour costs, small surface area occupied, low hygiene risk and in particular, length of possible storage.

Although Rich had not granted licences for the product to any other licensee in the EC it reserved the right to exploit its know-how in other EC countries and was considering granting additional licences at the time of the proceedings. Also, during the proceedings the parties stated that any new licensees could export to the United Kingdom and that Jus-rol would continue to be free to export to the other Member States of the EC, including those in which Rich might appoint licensees.

Jus-rol undertook at all times during and after the term of the agreement to maintain the secrecy of the know-how and to use it only for the manufacture of the licensed product. It agreed not to grant sub-licences unless to a wholly owned subsidiary of Rich or of its own parent company, and with the written consent of Rich. Jus-rol also agreed not to use the know-how for a period of 10 years following the termination of the agreement (unless terminated through the fault of Rich) and to return all documents relating to the know-how to Rich at the end of the agreement.

Other firms in the United Kingdom and in other Member States had developed processes for freezing of yeast but they were not easily accessible. It could not be considered, however, that the licence agreement concerned the introduction and protection in the licensed territory of "new technology" within the meaning of the case law of the Court.

Main conclusions

The know-how supplied by Rich concerned a body of substantial technical knowledge which was not generally known or easily accessible and which had enabled Jus-rol to begin manufacturing the product immediately. This, in principle, was a factor favourable to competition. However, the exclusive manufacturing right granted to Jus-rol and the obligation imposed on it not to manufacture the licensed product outside the territory prevented, on the one hand, future licensees in other Member States from manufacturing the licensed product in the United Kingdom and, on the other, Jus-rol from manufacturing the product elsewhere in the EC. The Commission found that these clauses had as their object the restriction of competition within the EC and must be deemed liable to affect trade between Member States. They had to be assessed, therefore, on the basis of Article 85(3).

The non-exclusive right granted to Jus-rol to sell the product in all Member States did not restrict Rich's freedom to sell the product in the EC (except in the UK) either directly or through distributors and was not deemed to be contrary to Article 85(1). The obligation of secrecy in respect of the know-how did not infringe Article 85(1) as the commercial value of the know-how was dependent on its secrecy. The same assessment applied to the obligation not to grant sub-licences, as this clause merely protected Rich's right to use its know-how as it wished and to grant licences only to undertakings which enjoyed its confidence. The obligation not to use the know-how for a period of 10 years following termination of the agreement and to return all know-how documents to Rich Products on termination was regarded as inherent in this type of agreement because if the granting of a licence meant that the owner would lose the exclusive right to use the know-how on the expiry of a licensing agreement, the owner would be less willing to grant a licence, which would ultimately be harmful to the transfer of technical knowledge. The obligation on Jus-rol to purchase the pre-mix and to use it in the manufacture of the product was deemed to be necessary to ensure consistent quality in the licensed product and was not considered, therefore, to restrict competition under Article 85(1).

The obligation imposed on Jus-rol to grant Rich a non-exclusive and reciprocal licence for any improvement made to the know-how, whether patented or not, did not constitute a restriction of competition within Article 85(1) because it did not deprive Jus-rol of the possibility of using the improvement itself or of granting licences for this improvement to third parties, as long as it did not disclose Rich's know-how. Also, it was agreed that Rich's right to use the improvements made by Jus-rol would end at the same time as Jus-rol's right to use the original know-how so that neither party would be in a worse position than the other at the expiry of the main licence agreement.

Finally, the obligation on Jus-rol to pay a royalty throughout the period of the agreement, regardless of the fact that during the 10-year duration the know-how might have come into the public domain was not considered to be restrictive of competition. The agreement contained a five-year break clause which would allow either party to terminate if by that date the know-how no longer offered competitive benefits. Also, in view of the complexity of the know-how, the risk of it being divulged to third parties in its entirety and, therefore, losing its commercial value was considered unlikely.

The Commission then went on to consider whether the exclusive manufacturing right granted to Jus-rol and the obligation imposed on it not to manufacture outside the United Kingdom could be permitted under the terms of Article 85(3).

The exclusive manufacturing right contributed to promoting economic and technical progress. It was an incentive to Jus-rol to undertake the necessary investment for exploiting the substantial know-how in the United Kingdom, with a view to manufacturing and distributing yeast doughs that allowed fresh products to be prepared in a new way and offered numerous advantages to users, notably supermarkets. Restricting the exclusive manufacturing right to the United Kingdom obliged Jus-rol to focus its production and sales efforts and to concentrate on improving the quality of the products and increasing the quantity produced. If Jus-rol had not been certain that it would not encounter competition in the United Kingdom, it might have been deterred from accepting the risk of manufacturing and selling the product. This would have been damaging to the dissemination of a bakery product and would have prevented competition from developing between the licensed product and similar products within the EC.

Also, the exclusive manufacturing right did not enable Jus-rol to eliminate competition, as it had to compete with producers in the United Kingdom using similar processes which provided other means to manufacture frozen yeast dough.

The Commission granted an exemption pursuant to Article 85(3) for the 10-year duration of the agreement.

Referred to at Analysis Sections 8.1, 8.3, 10.1, 10.2, 10.7

9. Commission Press Release (IP(88)612) [1989] 4 CMLR 851

The Commission held that a prohibition on post-term use contained in a know-how licensing agreement between two unnamed companies was not caught by Article 85(1). The prohibition was part of a know-how licence agreement between two companies involved in the manufacture, sale and maintenance of heavy duty compressors. On termination of the agreement the licensor claimed back its know-how in exercise of its contractual right. The Commission considered that such a prohibition on post-term use was not restrictive of competition, since the alternative would be a permanent transfer of technology, which was a condition under which few companies would be prepared to disseminate their know-how.

In addition, the Commission found that Article 86 was not applicable. The refusal of the licensor to agree to the continuing use of the technology by the former licensee after the termination of the agreement would not normally constitute an abuse under Article 86. This was particularly true in this case, where the refusal was based on a contractual provision which did not fall under Article 85(1) and where the former licensee was claiming the right to use the know-how to the same extent as it had done under the terminated agreement.

Referred to at Analysis Section 10.3

10.   Velcro SA v Aplix SA (Case IV/4.204) [1989] 4 CMLR 157

Main facts

Velcro was a Swiss company which in 1958 granted Aplix of France an exclusive licence for the manufacturing and exploitation in France of Velcro's burr-type fastener, protected by a French patent. Aplix undertook to exploit the patent in accordance with Velcro's directions or generally to manufacture a technically equivalent product. It also agreed to pay royalties to Velcro in return for the patent rights and technical support. The fastener had a novel character when the patents were first exploited and required substantial technical and commercial development by the licensee. Aplix had the right to use the Velcro trade mark on all goods manufactured by it under the licence.

Aplix was free to sell the products covered by the agreement in countries in which Velcro had not yet granted exclusive licences but was prohibited from exporting directly or indirectly to any country covered by another Velcro licence. The agreement was expressed to last for as long as the patents covered by it and any further patents which might be obtained in the same field remained valid. The parties entered into three supplementary agreements between 1958 and 1973 which added three further patents to the original licence.

Aplix undertook to order all its requirements of manufacturing equipment, machinery and accessories from a nominated Swiss tape loom manufacturer and agreed not to use this equipment outside its licensed territories. Aplix also undertook not to manufacture or sell any fastener that might compete with the licensed product during the currency of the agreement. Velcro similarly agreed not to compete with Aplix directly or indirectly in this field and in particular, not to grant rights to its inventions to any competitor of Aplix. In addition, if Aplix made any potentially patentable invention in the field covered by the agreement which was subsequently patented in Germany, the United Kingdom, the Netherlands or the United States, such patent was to be obtained by Velcro or assigned to it with fair compensation being paid to Aplix. Velcro's other licensees would be authorised to use any such invention, just as Aplix would be able to use any inventions of other licensees or of Velcro.

In 1973 Aplix notified the licensing agreement to the European Commission.

In 1976 Velcro held a meeting with all its European licensees to discuss the fact that the licensing agreements contained a large number of clauses which were prohibited under EC law and that they would have to be substantially amended. In November 1977 Velcro told Aplix that its 1958 agreement would end with the expiry of the original French patent in December 1977. Aplix disputed Velcro's position and declared that it was entitled to withhold royalty payments. It alleged that it had suffered serious harm because Velcro had failed to pass on improvement patents to it. The parties entered into negotiations with a view to reaching an amicable settlement, but the negotiations were not successful.

In 1981 Velcro made a complaint to the Commission that the notified agreement infringed Article 85(1) and should not be enforced against it. The Commission initiated proceedings in June 1984.

Main conclusions

The Commission considered that there was no need to make a finding as to the validity of the 1958 agreement during the period prior to December 1977, during which time the parties had honoured the agreement in good faith.

The Commission found that since the expiry of Velcro's basic patents in France in December 1977, the notified agreement was caught by Article 85(1). The exclusivity granted to Aplix which prevented Velcro itself from exploiting its patents and trade mark in France and from offering licences to other firms, prevented competition in the contract territory. Assuming that the agreement was validly extended to 1989 (as claimed by Aplix) and that Aplix exploited until that time Velcro patents that were still valid, any exclusivity for such patents could only be considered compatible with Article 85(1) if it concerned the introduction and protection of new technology, which was not the case here.

Article 85(1) was not excluded by the fact that the goods were marketed by Aplix under the Velcro trade mark. According to ECJ case law the assignment or licence of a national trade mark did not permit either party to oppose direct imports by the other party.

The prohibition on Aplix exporting its products outside its licensed territory in countries where Velcro had granted exclusive licences was not an essential function of the patent rights and this protection of one licensee against competition by another licensee through a contractual ban on exporting and importing, especially after the expiry of the basic patents, constituted a restriction of competition within Article 85(1). This was true also of the obligation on Aplix to obtain equipment exclusively from the Swiss tape loom manufacturer and not to use such equipment outside the licensed territory.

The obligation to allow Velcro to acquire the title to patents in Germany, the United Kingdom, the Netherlands and the United States for improvements discovered by Aplix was an unwarranted extension of the licensed patents, in that the licensor was using his industrial property rights to appropriate certain foreign patents covering improvements and inventions that were wholly or partly the work of the licensee.

The Commission found that the above restrictions on competition were all likely to affect trade between Member States. It went on to consider the application of Article 85(3).

The exclusivity granted to Aplix made it easier for Aplix to take on the risk of investing in the exploitation of the Velcro patents and this facilitated the development of a new product, so contributing to technical and economic progress. The industrial exploitation of the Velcro patents through licensing provided the user industries with a new product which was suitable for particular applications and the user industries could be said to have received a fair share of the benefits resulting from the agreement. The territorial protection resulting from the licensee's exclusive sales rights and the related ban on the licensor exporting into the territory could be considered as indispensable for inducing the licensee to take on the commitment to develop and manufacture a new product, which when the agreement was signed was still at an experimental stage. The agreement did not eliminate competition for a substantial part of the products in question, since there were many other producers in France manufacturing competing products.

The Commission considered that there was no justification under Article 85(3), however, for the restrictions on marketing in France by Velcro after the expiry of the basic patents. Any exclusivity granted for patents under an agreement was indissolubly linked to the existence and continuing validity of the patents. The import of Velcro products into France could not be opposed on the basis of the use of the trade mark. Although the trade mark rights were not subject to a time limit, a trade mark owner or his licensees could not enforce the rights held in the mark where one of them exports to the other's territory within the EC unless special reasons such as the protection of the introduction of the mark into those territories justified such action. In this case it was accepted that exclusive user rights for a trade mark helped to promote the entry of a new product in a new territory, but such exclusive rights had to cease at the latest when the basic patents expired, which was in December 1977.

The Commission considered that the export ban on Aplix, the automatic extension of the term of the agreement, the obligation to obtain supplies exclusively from the tape loom manufacturer, the prohibition on Aplix manufacturing the patented product outside the licensed territory, the non-competition clause, and the obligation on the licensee to assign to the licensor its rights to improvements, were not justified since December 1977 by valid patents or by trade mark rights and they did not fulfil the conditions for exemption laid down in Article 85(3).

The Commission held that since not all the Article 85(3) criteria were fulfilled in respect of the period following the expiry of Velcro's basic patents in December 1977, the notified agreement could not be exempted after that date. It ordered the parties to bring to an end immediately the infringements of Article 85(1).

Referred to at Analysis Sections 9.1, 10.3, 12.6, Commentary Sections 2.2, 3.4, 8.5

11. Re the Agreement between DDD Ltd and Delta Chemie (Case IV/31.498) [1989] 4 CMLR 535

Main facts

Delta Chemie is a German company engaged, amongst other things, in selling a range of stain removers which are produced by Gisapharm, its wholly-owned subsidiary.

In March 1985 DDD, an English company, applied to the Commission for negative clearance or alternatively exemption of an agreement which it had concluded with Delta Chemie. Under the agreement, which effectively continued the operation of a previously existing oral exclusive distribution agreement, Delta Chemie appointed DDD as its exclusive distributor, for a period of 20 years, for the sale of a range of products for removal of stains from fabrics (called "Stain Devils" or "Stain Salts") in the United Kingdom, Ireland and Greece, as well as a large number of countries outside the EC. Delta Chemie sold its products in other Member States either direct or through other exclusive distributors. Delta Chemie undertook to refer to DDD all inquiries for the product received from any person or company in the licensed territory, but reserved the right to sell products in the territory to anyone who expressed a desire to purchase from the licensor rather than the licensee.

Delta Chemie also transferred to DDD its know-how for the manufacture, packaging and sale of the products in the same territory. The substantial know-how was described in formulae and technical documents disclosed to DDD. Delta Chemie also agreed to provide specialised technicians and advice on the correct application of the know-how. DDD undertook not to make any alterations to the formulae and methods of manufacture without the consent of Delta Chemie and to keep the know-how secret for the duration of the agreement and afterwards for so long as it was not in the public domain or generally known by the industry.

Both parties undertook to provide each other with all information relating to the know-how, including any modifications or improvements in respect of the manufacture and marketing of the products. This clause was modified at the Commission's request, so that the licensor's right to use the licensee's modifications and improvements, which could not be used independently of the original know-how, would cease with the termination of the agreement. This was effected in order to avoid the licensee finding himself unable to use his own improvements on the expiry of the contract because they were inextricably tied to the original know-how which he was no longer able to exploit, whereas the licensor would be able to continue using the improvements communicated by the licensee.

Main conclusions

The exclusive grant of the right to manufacture the products in the territory and the appointment of DDD as exclusive licensee would have the effect of restricting competition within the meaning of Article 85(1) and was likely to affect trade between Member States.

The Commission held that the notified agreement was not exempt under Commission Regulation 1983/83, the block exemption regulation which declares Article 85(1) inapplicable to certain exclusive distribution agreements. The exclusive distribution block exemption only covers simple resale agreements and could not extend to the manufacture of products under the licence.

The Commission went on to find that the agreement fulfilled all the conditions in Article 85(3) for an individual exemption. It considered that the manufacturing and distribution exclusivity contributed to promoting technical and economic progress because it encouraged DDD to undertake investments necessary to exploit substantial secret know-how with the aim of manufacturing and marketing a series of original stain removers which were different from universal stain removers. Delta Chemie and DDD were not competitors before the conclusion of the agreement, which enabled DDD to become a competing manufacturer.

The limitation of the right to manufacture to the licensed territory would oblige DDD to concentrate its efforts on manufacturing and marketing within that territory and to devote itself to improving the quality of the products and to increasing their quantities. Consumers could be expected to benefit from these improvements because the licensed products would be more easily available. Also, an increase in price as a result of the protection afforded to DDD would seem unlikely due to the presence of actual and potential competition. DDD was also exposed to parallel imports from outside the licensed territory and potential direct sales from Delta Chemie.

The Commission considered that the manufacturing and distribution exclusivity was indispensable to the attainment of these results because without the certainty that it would not be subject to competition from other licensees, DDD might not have accepted the risk of manufacturing and selling the licensed products. This would have been harmful to the distribution of stain removing products and would have hindered the development of competition between the licensed products and similar products in the EC.

Also, the products distributed by DDD would be in competition with comparable products sold in and outside the territory and the parties expected further competitors to enter the markets in the territory. DDD did not have absolute territorial protection from direct and indirect imports from Member States where Delta Chemie and its other exclusive distributors operated. As a result, the agreement would not give DDD and Delta Chemie the possibility of eliminating competition in respect of a substantial part of the products in question.

The Commission granted the agreement an exemption for the full 20-year period of exclusivity.

Referred to at Analysis Sections 10.4, 14.5, Commentary Section 7

12. Pilkington and Covina (European Commission Annual Competition Report 1989)

Main facts

A patent and know-how licensing agreement granted by Pilkington to Covina of Portugal on the float glass process was deemed to be in line with Commission Regulation 2349/84 on the application of Article 85(3) to certain categories of patent licensing agreements, only after it had undergone a number of amendments following intervention by the Commission.

In the version initially notified, the agreement prohibited the licensee, Covina, from exporting to certain Community countries for the whole period of the licence (10 years) and for 10 years after the agreement expired, irrespective of the protection afforded by registered patents in such countries. The Commission took the view that these provisions were caught by Article 3(10) of Regulation 2349/84 which does not permit any absolute sales ban on the licensee, beyond the period of five years permitted by Article 1(1)(6). The same would apply under Article 1(2)-(4) of the Technology Regulation.

The Commission also pointed out that a patent holder who had granted sales licences within certain protected territories to licensees producing within other territories could not be deemed to have reserved such territories for himself within the meaning of Article 1(1)(3) of the Regulation. This interpretation would apply equally to Article 1(1)(3) of Regulation 240/96, which permits an obligation on the licensee (for a period longer than the five years protection granted to other licensees) not to exploit the licensed technology in the territory of the licensor himself.

Main conclusions

After discussions with the Commission the parties amended their agreements so that the territorial restrictions applied only where the patents were in force in the territories concerned, and for the life of the patents, and so that the licensee was only restricted from pursuing an active sales policy in those territories. This brought the agreements into line with Article 1(1)(5) of Regulation 2349/84 which permits an obligation on the licensee not to pursue an active sales policy in the territories of other licensees, as does Article 1(1)(5) of the Technology Regulation.

A comfort letter was sent terminating the case.

Referred to at Analysis Section 9

13.   **Re the Agreements between BBC Brown Boveri and NGK Insulators Ltd (Case IV/32.368) [1989] 4 CMLR 610**

Main facts

BBC is a German electrical engineering company. NGK is a Japanese company whose main business is the manufacture of technical precision ceramics. These two companies set up a joint venture for the development of sodium-sulphur high performance batteries, intended primarily for use in electrically driven vehicles and for storing off-peak electricity for use during peak-load periods in national grid systems.

The joint venture company, NewCo, was set up in Japan with NGK holding a 60% stake and BBC holding the remaining 40%. BBC had brought the development of the sodium-sulphur battery to a highly advanced stage. However, the battery incorporated ceramic tubes and the problems inherent in the mass production of the ceramic tubes had not been solved. The co-operation with NGK was intended to reduce the cost of and speed up the development of mass production, which accounted for a large part of the battery development costs. The two companies continued their own research and development in the field of sodium-sulphur batteries regardless of the work of the joint venture but the results of each partner's own research was to be made available to the other through the joint venture, and new technical knowledge gained through the joint venture was to be passed on to the parent companies for their use. No production was planned within the joint venture. Each partner was to set up its own mass production facilities and market the product in competition with other battery manufacturers.

In June 1987 BBC notified to the Commission a set of co-operation agreements with NGK relating to the development of these high performance batteries. In order to enable NewCo to undertake research and development up to the manufacturing stage, BBC and NGK undertook to grant it an exclusive licence for their complementary technical knowledge. Since NewCo would not manufacture and market the battery it, in turn, would grant BBC an exclusive licence for a term of 15 years to use its technology for the manufacture and sale of the product in the EC, North America and others and grant NGK a similar licence for Japan and the Far East. After 10 years from the time when the product was launched in the EC or Japan, NGK would have the right to sell it in the EC and BBC would have the right to sell in Japan.

NewCo and NGK both undertook not to carry out any joint research and development with third parties in the field of sodium-sulphur batteries without the consent of BBC and each joint venture partner was prohibited from making available to third parties the technology provided to it by the other partner without its consent. This prohibition was to apply for a period of five years after the expiry of the agreements.

Main conclusions

The Commission decided that pursuant to Article 85(3), the provisions of Article 85(1) were inapplicable to the notified agreements. It held that all the conditions for an individual exemption were satisfied for the following reasons:

- the co-operation between BBC and NGK was aimed at developing a fundamental technological innovation which could be achieved more quickly and cheaply on a collaborative basis. In many countries the development of high performance batteries was promoted with the help of substantial public resources, as the authorities recognised that the overall benefits to be derived from the use of electrically driven vehicles and from the storage of off-peak electricity for use during peak times were great;
- the advantages of high-performance batteries would be of direct benefit to consumers;
- the restrictions were indispensable. The risk involved in marketing the product was unusually high. Consumers would not easily be induced to switch to electrically driven vehicles and resistance in the motor industry would have to be overcome;
- the period during which BBC was protected against exports by NGK into the EC was 10 years. To start with only relatively small quantities would be produced at a correspondingly high unit cost and there would be limited charging facilities and availability of exchange units and back-up services. The introductory phase was expected to be at least five years and during this time BBC would not be able to charge economic prices. At best a return on the investment undertaken by BBC could be expected during the latter half of the 10-year period. If BBC was exposed to competition from NGK and other licensees in the EC, the likelihood of it recovering its large research and development costs would be impaired;
- the duration of the protection granted to BBC through the reciprocal exclusive licences against supplies by other licensees into its territory was 15 years. It would probably be as much as a further five years after the grant of a licence to a third party before the development was complete, series production underway and selling the product became possible. Only then would the protection granted by the exclusivity take effect so that the duration of the protection would in fact be 10 years;
- there remained continued competition from rival manufacturers. The restrictions on competition did not result in the elimination of competition. A number of competitors were also developing high performance batteries to power electrically driven cars and store off-peak electricity. Also, electrically driven vehicles would compete with conventional vehicles.

The Commission granted BBC an exemption for the 15-year duration of the licensing agreements.

Referred to at Commentary Sections 7, 9

14. Re the Agreements between Moosehead Breweries Ltd and Whitbread and Company plc (Case IV/32.736) [1989] 4 CMLR 970

Main facts

In May 1988 Moosehead, a Canadian company, and Whitbread, a UK company, applied to the Commission for negative clearance or failing that exemption pursuant to Article 85(3) in respect of a number of agreements concluded between them.

The agreements concerned the manufacture of a beer in the United Kingdom which was sold by Moosehead in Canada and other countries under the trade mark *Moosehead*. Moosehead granted to Whitbread the sole and exclusive right to produce, promote, market and sell beer manufactured for sale under the name *Moosehead* in the territory (UK, Channel Islands and the Isle of Man), using Moosehead secret know-how. Whitbread paid a royalty for this exclusive right. Whitbread agreed that the quality of the beer and the type and quality of the raw materials would comply with Moosehead specifications and also agreed that it would not seek customers, establish any branch or maintain any distribution depot for distribution of the product, outside the territory. However, it was allowed to fill unsolicited orders from purchasers in Member States. During the term of the agreements Whitbread agreed not to produce or promote within the territory any other beer identified as Canadian.

Whitbread agreed to sell the product only under the trade mark *Moosehead* and to use the trade mark only on or in relation to the product. The property rights in the trade mark in the United Kingdom were assigned to Whitbread and Moosehead jointly. Whitbread was granted the exclusive licence to use the trade marks in relation to the product in the UK during the life of the agreement. Both parties agreed not to register any trade mark resembling the *Moosehead* trade marks in the United Kingdom. Whitbread acknowledged the title of Moosehead to the trade marks and the validity of the registrations of Moosehead as proprietor thereof. Whitbread undertook to observe all conditions prescribed by the terms of the registration of the trade marks. The agreement provided that on termination of the agreement Whitbread would re-assign to Moosehead all its rights, title and interest in the trade marks and desist from all use of the trade marks in future.

Under the know-how provisions of the agreement Moosehead agreed to provide Whitbread with all the relevant know-how necessary to produce the product and to supply it with all yeast which it required. Whitbread agreed to comply with all directions and specifications of Moosehead in relation to the know-how, and to purchase yeast only from Moosehead or from a third party designated by Moosehead. Whitbread agreed to keep all know-how confidential. The agreement was concluded for an indefinite period with variable periods of notice based on volume of sales by Whitbread. On termination of the agreement, Whitbread was obliged to cease producing the product, return all know-how to Moosehead, cease using the know-how and to keep the know-how secret from any third party.

Main conclusions

The exclusive trade mark licence, the prohibition on active sales outside the territory and the prohibition on marketing competing brands of beer were all appreciable restrictions on competition and therefore fell under the prohibition in Article 85(1).

The know-how provisions did not fall under Article 85(1) because the grant of know-how was not exclusive and the obligations imposed on the licensee were ancillary to the trade mark licence and enabled the licence to take effect. The exclusive purchasing obligation regarding yeast was necessary to ensure technically satisfactory exploitation of the licensed technology and a similar identity between the lager originally produced by Moosehead and the same lager produced by Whitbread. Trade marks were relatively new to the lager market in the territory and the maintenance of the *Moosehead* trade mark did not, therefore, constitute an appreciable barrier to entry in the market and was not, therefore, an appreciable restriction on competition under Article 85(1).

The Commission considered that the principal interest of the parties lay in the exploitation of the trade mark rather than the know-how. The block exemption (Commission Reg 556/89) for agreements relating to know-how was not, therefore, relevant, as the trade mark licence could not be considered as ancillary to that of the know-how. However, given the peculiarities of the UK beer market, in which at the time most public houses were operated by tenants tied by contract to purchase beer from one brewer alone and 75% of beer sold was in draught form, the Commission considered that the agreement was likely to contribute to the improvement of the production and distribution of the product in the territory and to promote economic progress. Consumers were also likely to benefit from the agreement as they would have a wider choice. Taking account of the existence of many similar competing beers and the ability of the parties to sell the product to other parties for export to other Member States, the parties to the agreement did not have the possibility of eliminating competition in respect of a substantial part of the products in question.

The Commission granted the parties an exemption pursuant to Article 85(3) for a period of 10 years.

Referred to at Analysis Sections 10.5, 12.2, Commentary Section 8.5

15. Re the Agreements between Akerlund & Rausing and Europa Carton AG (Case IV/32.681 – Cekacan) [1990]4 CMLR 170

Main facts

In 1988 Akerlund & Rausing (A&R) notified to the Commission a co-operation agreement which it had concluded with Europa Carton AG (ECA). The agreement concerned the use and marketing of a new method and a new type of packaging known as Cekacan in certain Member States and also in non-EC countries. The parties set up a new company, Ceka Europe, of which 74% was owned by A&R and 26% by ECA.

A&R is part of a Swedish group of companies whose activities comprise packaging, mainly for foodstuffs. A&R carried out research into new packaging systems based on materials composed of paperboard, aluminium and plastic, which were regarded as the new generation of packaging products compared with traditional glass and metal. ECA is a German company whose activities are chiefly in the paperboard and paperboard packaging sectors.

Ceka International (a division of A&R) had obtained ownership of the Cekacan patents, know-how and trade marks with its purchase in 1983 of the Swedish company Esselte Pac Aktiebolag. ECA had contributed financially to the development of a machine based on Esselte Pac's inventions, having obtained in exchange an exclusive right to exploit this machine in Germany under an exclusive licence agreement in 1982. Following the purchase of Esselte Pac by A&R, ECA became its licensee until the conclusion of the co-operation agreement between the two parties. The co-operation agreement provided for an amended version of the 1982 agreement to come into force in the event that the co-operation agreement terminated.

The Cekacan package was a completely new product made of paperboard laminated with plastic and aluminium materials and completely airtight, to be used chiefly for dry oxygen-sensitive foodstuffs. Other features of the product were its potential to carry advertising, its ease of opening and storage and the fact that it was a non-polluting recyclable waste product.

The new company, Ceka Europe, was to be responsible for marketing the product and installing Cekacan machines in customers' premises. It was to be the sole distributor for A&R and ECA, for supplying the materials needed to manufacture the Cekacan packages (if customers so wished) and providing customers with the necessary technical assistance.

A&R and ECA undertook not to compete with Ceka Europe in the relevant territory (which comprised Germany, the Benelux countries, France, Italy, Greece, Spain, Portugal, Austria and Switzerland) by manufacturing and/or directly or indirectly selling the products and/or Cekacan machines. In the original version of the notified agreements, ECA was also prohibited from manufacturing or selling similar products or machines but following discussions with the Commission the parties agreed to abolish this provision.

The notified agreements were for an initial period of three years to be automatically renewed unless notice of termination was given by either party. At the end of the initial three year period the contract would be prolonged for an indefinite period unless terminated by one of the parties on notice. The agreement could also be terminated without notice if it proved impossible for shareholders to reach agreement on a matter defined as a "major issue". In the event of termination the 1982 agreement would be revived and amended. Customers would be shared out between A&R and ECA, with ECA being allocated those customers in Germany and A&R taking all others. A&R would also have the right to purchase all ECA's shares in Ceka Europe. ECA would be free to supply Cekacan packages to customers outside Germany, either actively or in response to unsolicited orders and would have the right to respond to enquiries from other countries concerning the leasing of machines. The planned amendments to the 1982 agreement included a clause requiring ECA to purchase from A&R all its requirements for laminates used for the products. Following discussions with the Commission the parties agreed to remove this clause.

Main conclusions

The Commission considered that the setting up of Ceka Europe did not constitute a project for the development of long term co-operation between the two companies for the use of the processes concerned. As the agreement was concluded for only three years and could be freely terminated thereafter by either party giving 10 months' notice, it appeared to be aimed solely at co-operation in an initial phase for the purpose of introducing and marketing Cekacan technology in a number of European companies. The Commission concluded that the object of the co-operation did not go beyond what was required to introduce Cekacan technology on a wider market.

Outside the framework of the 1982 agreement the parties could not be considered as direct competitors for the purposes of using Cekacan processes or producing the basic materials for Cekacan packaging, but they were considered as potential competitors in the use of methods similar to Cekacan methods and as direct competitors as regards the cutting and printing of laminates used in the production of Cekacan packages.

The Commission concluded that the exclusive rights clauses and the exclusive supply clauses in the co-operation agreement did not have a restrictive effect as far as relations between A&R and Ceka Europe were concerned as they were deemed to be intra-group relations. However, the setting up of Ceka Europe would restrict competition from ECA as it was prevented from freely developing its commercial policy as regards use of the processes in the territory assigned to it (*i.e.* Germany). The clauses which required Ceka Europe to purchase materials and services exclusively from A&R and Ceka International had a restrictive effect on ECA because it was a potential competitor for the manufacture and sale of the materials covered by the clauses. Also, the termination provisions which provided for the revival of the 1982 agreement, the maintenance of ECA's exclusive rights in its German territory and the sharing-out of customers would result in restrictions of competition between ECA and A&R as A&R and Ceka Europe would be able to supply only ECA with machines in Germany and ECA would no longer be able to propose leasing such machines outside Germany.

The Commission found that the notified agreements fulfilled the conditions necessary for the application of Article 85(3) as they would help to improve production and distribution of the products concerned and to promote technical progress in the foodstuffs packaging sector. The object of the agreements was to extend throughout the Community the use of this new packaging, sales of which were initially confined to Germany. Introducing the products in other Member States would have been much more difficult for A&R to undertake without the co-operation of ECA who already had the experience of introducing the product in Germany. The users of the product (both the food manufacturers and final consumer) would receive a fair share of the benefits deriving from the agreements. The new product was regarded as an appreciable technological innovation and competition on the relevant market (glass, plastic, metal etc packaging for dry oxygen-sensitive foodstuffs) would become stronger due to the extensive marketing of the new methods which would have beneficial effects on packaging prices.

The Commission considered that the agreements did not impose any restrictions on the parties which were not essential to achieve the objectives of the co-operation. As the relevant market was that for all packaging of dry oxygen-sensitive foodstuffs, the agreements did not afford the parties the possibility of eliminating competition in respect of a substantial portion of the products in question.

The Commission granted an exemption pursuant to Article 85(3) for a period of 10 years.

Referred to at Commentary Section 9

16.   Bayer AG and Maschinenfabrik Hennecke GmbH v Heinz Sullhofer (Case 65/86) [1990] 4 CMLR 182

Main facts

In 1986 the Bundesgerichthof of Germany referred to the ECJ for a preliminary ruling under Article 177 a question on the interpretation of Article 30 and Article 85. The question was raised in proceedings concerning the validity of the licensing agreement between Mr Heinz Sullhofer, a trader in Dusseldorf, and the German companies, Bayer and Hennecke.

In 1950 Bayer obtained a patent (the Moroni patent) relating to processes and devices for the continuous manufacture of panels, lengths or sheeting from foamable substances, especially polyurethane substances. In 1965 Sullhofer applied for a utility model and a patent for a dual conveyor belt system for the manufacture of rigid polyurethane-foam-based panels. Legal proceedings were initiated between Hennecke and Sullhofer in 1967. Sullhofer, relying on the utility model had issued warnings to Hennecke and its customers. Hennecke for its part sought a declaration that the utility model was invalid. In addition, Bayer and Hennecke lodged oppositions to Sullhofer's patent application. The licensing agreement in question was concluded in 1968 to bring all proceedings to an end. Sullhofer granted a non-exclusive free licence to Hennecke and Bayer to use the utility model and patent, together with a right for both companies to grant sublicences. Sullhofer also agreed to grant the companies a licence subject to payment of royalties to use the corresponding industrial rights he held in other Member States, together with the right to grant sublicences. Bayer granted Sullhofer a non-exclusive non-transferable licence subject to payment of royalties for the manufacture of foam panels under a German patent it held, waived any claims against Sullhofer in respect of infringements of that patent and undertook together with Hennecke not to challenge the validity of the patent applied for by Sullhofer.

Some years later further disputes arose between the parties and Sullhofer terminated the 1968 agreement. On his application the Dusseldorf regional court declared the agreement invalid on the ground that it was based on wilful deception. On appeal, the regional appeal court considered that the no-challenge clause was incompatible with Article 85(1) which resulted in the whole transaction being void under German law.

On appeal, the Bundesgerichthof stayed the proceedings and asked the ECJ to rule on the following question:

> Is it compatible with Article 30 and Article 85 to include in a licensing agreement a contractual provision by which the licensee undertakes not to challenge the validity of technical industrial property rights granted to the licensor in several Member States which all have the same content and in respect of which licences have been granted?

Main conclusions

The ECJ held that Article 30, which relates to free movement of goods, was not relevant in these circumstances.

With regard to Article 85, the ECJ did not accept the Commission's view that a no-challenge clause in a licensing agreement should, in principle, be considered to be a restriction on competition, but may however be compatible with Article 85(1) when included in an agreement whose purpose was to put an end to court proceedings. The ECJ said that Article 85(1) made no distinction between agreements whose purpose was to put an end to litigation and those concluded with other aims in mind.

The ECJ held that a no-challenge clause in a patent licensing agreement may, in the light of the legal and economic circumstances, restrict competition within the meaning of Article 85(1). There would be no restriction on competition when the licence granted was a free licence, as in those circumstances the licensee would not suffer a competitive disadvantage involved in the payment of royalties. However, if the national court were to consider that the no-challenge clause, contained in a licence subject to payment of royalties, involved a limitation of the licensee's freedom of action, it would then have to verify whether, given the positions held by the undertakings on the market for the products in question, the clause was of such a nature as to restrict competition to an appreciable extent.

Referred to at Analysis Section 10.15

17. Kai Ottung v Klee & Weilbach A/S and Thomas Schmidt A/S (Case 320/87) [1990] 4 CMLR 915

Main facts

In October 1987 the Maritime and Commercial Court of Denmark referred to the ECJ for a preliminary ruling under Article 177 a number of questions on the interpretation of Article 85(1) with a view to determining the compatibility with that provision of certain clauses contained in a patent licensing agreement.

The questions arose in proceedings concerning certain clauses in a licensing agreement under which Kai Ottung, a civil engineer, granted to a licensee the exclusive right (which was subsequently assigned to the defendants in the main proceedings Klee and Schmidt (together "Klee")) to exploit two control devices which he had designed for use on brewery tanks. Under the agreement the licensee undertook to pay a royalty for each device sold for an indeterminate period. The agreement could be terminated only by the licensee giving six months' notice on 6 October of any year. On such termination the licensee was permitted to manufacture only a number of devices corresponding to the orders received at the date of termination.

The agreement was entered into after a patent application had been filed in respect of one of the control devices. Following the grant of the patent the licensee paid the agreed royalty when selling the devices developed by Mr Ottung. The Danish patent expired in April 1977 and the latest patent granted in respect of the same device in a Member State expired in March 1980. As from the end of 1980, Klee ceased paying the royalty on the ground that all the patents had expired. They did not terminate the agreement pursuant to the agreement, maintaining that the discontinuance of royalty payments was tantamount to termination. Ottung claimed that Klee should be ordered to pay him the royalty provided for in the agreement, or in the alternative, royalty of a lower amount to be fixed by the court. He argued that the licensing agreement had been entered into for an indeterminate period and could not cease to apply until Klee had terminated it according to the agreement.

The Danish Court asked the ECJ to consider whether a contractual obligation under which a licensee of a patented invention was to pay royalties for an indeterminate period, and thus even after the expiry of the patent, constituted a restriction of competition under Article 85(1) where the agreement was entered into after the patent application was submitted and immediately before the patent was granted, and was it of any significance that the grantor could not determine the agreement whereas the licensee could bring it to an end by giving notice of termination, after which he would not be entitled to exploit the patent?

Also, if the above question was answered in the negative, would a clause in a licensing agreement which prevented the licensee from manufacturing and marketing the products in question after definitive termination of the agreement constitute an infringement of Article 85(1)?

Main conclusions

An obligation to continue to pay royalties after the expiry of a patent could only result from a licensing agreement which either did not grant the licensee the right to terminate the agreement by giving reasonable notice or which restricted the licensee's freedom of action after termination. In that case the agreement may be restrictive of competition within Article 85(1). However, where, as in this case, the licensee could freely terminate the agreement by giving notice, there was no infringement of Article 85(1).

In answer to the second question, a clause in a licensing agreement prohibiting the manufacture and marketing of the products in question after termination would weaken the licensee's competitive position, as it would place him at a disadvantage in relation to his competitors who could freely manufacture the products after the patent had expired. To that extent the clause could restrict competition within the meaning of Article 85(1). It would be for the national court to verify, having regard to the information at its disposal, whether the licensing agreement was liable to affect trade between Member States. Such a clause would only infringe Article 85(1), if it emerged from the economic and legal context in which the agreement was concluded that it was liable to appreciably affect trade between Member States.

Referred to at Analysis Sections 10.3, 10.7

18.   Tetra Pak Rausing SA v EC Commission (Case T-51/89) [1991]4 CMLR 334

Main facts

Tetra Pak is a Swiss Company whose activities cover the sector concerned with the packaging of fresh and UHT-treated milk. They consist essentially of manufacturing cartons and carton-filling machines using the group's own technology. UHT-treated milk is filled by special machines into cartons which are sterilised, then sealed immediately after filling by the machines under strictly aseptic conditions. In the field of aseptic packaging, Tetra Pak supplies the "Tetrabrik" system. Fresh milk does not require the same degree of sterility and so less sophisticated equipment is required. In the field of fresh produce, Tetra Pak also distributes machines made by a number of other manufacturers.

In 1986, through its purchase of the Liquipak Group, Tetra Pak acquired an exclusive licence for patented technology relating to a new UHT milk-packaging process using ultra-violet light and hydrogen peroxide. The licence qualified for block exemption under Commission Regulation 2349/84 on the application of Article 85(3) to certain categories of patent licensing agreements.

Elopak, a Norwegian company whose activities were mainly in the fresh milk sector, had worked with Liquipak prior to its take-over by Tetra Pak to develop a new packaging machine incorporating the process protected by the exclusive licence. Following the take-over, Elopak ended its collaboration with Liquipak and made a complaint to the Commission with a view to establishing that Tetra Pak had infringed Articles 85 and 86.

The Commission concluded that Tetra Pak had infringed Article 86. It had abused its dominant position by the indirect acquisition of the exclusive licence which had the effect of strengthening its already dominant position, further weakening existing competition and rendering even more difficult the entry of any new competition.

In its decision the Commission considered in turn the application of Article 86 and of Article 85. With regard to Article 85, the Commission set out the reasons which would have entitled it to withdraw the benefit of the exemption from the exclusive licence for so long as there was an infringement of Article 86. Tetra Pak sought annulment of the Commission's decision in an application to the Court of Justice. Tetra Pak argued that Articles 85 and 86 together with the secondary legislation could not be interpreted in such a way as to contradict each other.

The question before the Court was confined to the issue of whether Article 86 could be applied where an exemption had already been granted under Article 85(3) or where the conduct fell within one of the block exemptions.

Main conclusions

The mere fact that an undertaking in a dominant position acquires an exclusive licence did not *per se* constitute an abuse within the meaning of Article 86. For the purpose of applying Article 86, it was necessary to look at the circumstances surrounding the acquisition, in particular its effects on the structure of competition in the relevant market. The decisive factor in the finding that Tetra Pak's acquisition of the exclusive licence constituted an abuse, lay quite specifically in Tetra Pak's position in the market and the fact that at the material time the right to use the process protected by the exclusive licence was alone capable of giving an undertaking the means of competing effectively with Tetra Pak in the field of the aseptic packaging of milk. Tetra Pak's acquisition of the exclusive licence had the practical effect of precluding all competition in the relevant market. In such circumstances the grant of exemption (whether individual or block exemption) under Article 85(3) could not be such as to render inapplicable the prohibition set out in Article 86. The Court went further and found that the application of Article 85(3) to offer an exemption from Article 86 was inconceivable in principle. There could be no derogation, by means of either primary or secondary legislation, from the prohibition of abuse of a dominant position.

The Court went on to consider whether, in practice, the granting of an exemption under Article 85(3) precluded application of Article 86. It considered individual and block exemptions separately. Where an individual exemption decision has been taken, characteristics of the agreement which would also be relevant in applying Article 86 may be taken to have been established, as the principle of effective competition underlies both the criteria for an exemption and the concept of abuse. Consequently, in applying Article 86 the Commission should take into account the earlier findings made when exemption was granted under Article 85(3), unless the factual and legal circumstances have altered. On the other hand, in order to qualify for a block exemption, an agreement has only to satisfy the criteria laid down in the relevant block exemption regulation. It is not subject to any positive assessment with regard to the conditions set out in Article 85(3). Block exemption regulations do not, in principle, exclude undertakings in a dominant position from qualifying for the exemption and do not take account of the position on the relevant markets of the parties to any given agreement. In addition, in certain of the block exemption regulations it is expressly stated that enjoyment of the block exemption does not preclude application of Article 86.

Tetra Pak argued that, according to the principle of legal certainty, those acts which had been established as legal and subject to the benefit of an exemption could not then turn out to be invalid according to Article 86. The Court accepted that one of the main purposes of block exemption was to secure legal certainty for the parties for so long as the Commission had not withdrawn the block exemption. However, this did not discharge undertakings in a dominant position from the obligation to comply with Article 86.

Tetra Pak also argued that the only interpretation of the relationship between Article 85(3) and Article 86 which was consistent with the principle of the uniform application of Community law, was to hold that Article 86 was incompatible with exemption. The Court held that the principle of uniformity was of secondary consideration and hypothetical importance and could be preserved in any event by recourse to Article 177 of the Treaty (which allows national courts to refer questions of interpretation of Community law to the ECJ). The Court dismissed Tetra Pak's application.

Referred to at Commentary Sections 5.5, 8.2

19. Re Odin Developments Ltd (Case IV/32.009) [1991] 4 CMLR 832

Main facts

In 1986 Elopak A/S of Norway and its subsidiary Elopak Ltd of the United Kingdom (together "Elopak") and Metal Box plc of the United Kingdom ("Metal Box") set up a joint venture company, Odin Developments Ltd ("Odin") to carry out the research and development of a new container (based on, but not competing with, Elopak's gable-top carton) with a carton base and separate closure that could be filled by an aseptic process with UHT processed foods. Odin was also to develop the machinery and technology for filling the new containers and, if successful, to undertake production and distribution of the containers and their filling machines.

In August 1986 the companies notified a shareholders' agreement, two know-how licences and two research and development contracts under the opposition procedure in Article 7 of Regulation 418/85 (the Research and Development Block Exemption) and applied for negative clearance or exemption under Article 85(3).

Elopak and Metal Box granted Odin exclusive licences to exploit all their respective intellectual property rights (patented and unpatented) relevant to the field of the agreements anywhere in the world. They also granted Odin licences for any new intellectual property rights they might obtain in the field. Odin agreed not to use these intellectual property rights for any purpose other than in the field of the agreement and to keep such rights confidential. Odin was to be the owner of any improvements made by it to the intellectual property rights. If Odin decided not to exploit the new technology in any particular country, both parent companies had the right to do so whenever Odin offered such opportunity to third parties.

Both parent companies had the right to obtain from Odin a non-exclusive licence (without the right to sub-license) for any improvement made by the joint venture company, provided that the use or exploitation of such improvements was unlikely to conflict with Odin (*i.e.* all uses outside the field of the agreement were permissible) or if Odin decided not to exploit the technology for its own purposes.

Both parent companies were free to carry out research and development or exploitation either independently or with third parties in the field of packaging systems for shelf-stable particulate foods, provided they did not use the know-how of the other partner in Odin or any improvements made by Odin (except as specified in the agreements).

Elopak and Metal Box agreed that they would carry out research and development work requested by Odin for a fee on a contract basis. Odin would be the owner of any intellectual property arising during such contract work and Elopak and Metalbox agreed to keep confidential all developments under such contracts.

The agreements contained specific provisions relating to the exploitation of the new product in the event of the break-up, sale or liquidation of the joint venture. In particular, neither of the parent companies would be allowed to use the know-how of the other parent or the improvements made by Odin with a competitor of the other parent for a period of five years after such break-up, sale or liquidation.

Main conclusions

The notified agreements could not benefit from the opposition procedure provided for in Article 7 of Regulation 418/85 as the Regulation did not at that time (it was amended in 1992) apply to joint undertakings such as Odin which not only extend to production but also to distribution. The joint venture was, therefore, considered under Article 85(1).

The relevant product market was difficult to define but it was considered that the new product may constitute an adequate technical substitute for the packaging of shelf-stable UHT-treated particulate foods (including semi-liquids but not liquids) filled aseptically. At the time of the conclusion of the agreements Elopak and Metal Box were not competitors, actual or potential, in the relevant product market and the development of the product by either party on its own was highly unlikely. Elopak's know-how was principally for cartons containing liquids and was not sufficient to enable it to develop the new product on its own. Metal Box had no experience with the type of cartons to be used as the basis for the new product. Both parties' experience and resources were necessary to develop the new product which would be a combination of their technical and commercial know-how. The technical risks involved in carrying out the research and development for a product which was not yet proven were great. There were also commercial risks involved in gaining consumer acceptance for the new carton and also in persuading food processors/packers to reinvest in the expensive new equipment necessary for the new product. Odin would need to provide a rapid after-sales and maintenance service. Back-up services were essential if breakdowns and delays, which could be very costly in terms of spoilt food, were to be avoided. Combining the know-how of each party reduced considerably the technical risks involved, thus diminishing the joint financial burden.

In activities outside the field of the joint venture the parties were not competitors and the creation of Odin would not, therefore, have any impact on any existing or potential competitive relationship between the parent companies. Also, the creation of Odin was not likely to lead to foreclosure of similar possibilities for potential competitors, as there were several other very large metal can makers with at least equivalent technical know-how to Metal Box, and Elopak was only one of several companies using that type of carton technology.

As the parties could not realistically be regarded as competitors and the creation of the joint venture did not entail a foreclosure risk, and the agreement did not involve the creation of a network of competing joint ventures, the agreements to establish Odin did not fall within the terms of Article 85(1).

However, it was necessary to consider the specific provisions of the other agreements to ascertain whether they restricted competition within the meaning of Article 85(1) or whether they were no more than was necessary to ensure the start-up and proper functioning of the joint venture. Also, it was necessary to consider the fact that the new product, if successfully developed and marketed, might compete to some extent with Metal Box's own output.

The grant to Odin of the exclusive right to exploit the know-how was a guarantee to each party that its partner would devote its full efforts to the project and would make each of them willing to bear the financial, technical and commercial risks involved as well as to divulge secret know-how. This was particularly important in this case where a significant proportion of the technical information was not protected by patents. The non-exclusive licences of improvements would ensure that Odin could exploit the know-how exclusively in the field of the agreement.

The know-how of both parent companies plus further research and development work by Odin were required to develop not only the new product but also the machinery and technology linked to it. There were no explicit restrictions in relation to price, quantity, customers or territory placed on Odin's activities and the exclusivity was limited to the field of the agreement, which was narrowly defined. In addition, the parent companies were not restricted in research and development or exploitation of closely related and possibly competing products, as long as each party did not use the other party's know-how or Odin's improvements. The Commission considered that these provisions and those relating to secrecy did no more than guarantee the confidentiality of secret know-how, and prevent the other party from using Odin as a vehicle to obtain know-how to which it would not otherwise have access.

The Commission also considered that the parties' obligations in relation to licensing of the technology at dissolution or break-up did not infringe Article 85(1). On such a break-up, both parties would be free to compete using all know-how including that of the other party in the field of the agreement and using their own and Odin's improvements in any field. The ease of break-up or sale (with the associated access to know-how) also ensured that Metal Box would not be able to use its joint controlling position in Odin to prevent the new product being fully and actively exploited if it considered that such exploitation might harm the products it produced. Metal Box could not impose any territorial restrictions on Odin's production or sales without either provoking a break-up of the joint venture if Elopak so wished, or without Elopak being entitled to exploit the new product in the territory in which Metal Box prevented exploitation by Odin. Elopak had no incentive to limit Odin's output or the geographical scope of its sales and there was no reason to believe that Metal Box would use its joint control of Odin in a manner incompatible with Article 85(1).

The obligation on the parent companies not to allow a competitor of the other parent to use that parent's know-how or Odin's improvements for a period of five years after the break-up of Odin was a necessary result of the creation of Odin, without which the two parent companies could not be expected to co-operate. Also, the provisions which relate to Odin's use of the parent companies' proprietary know-how and the obligation to keep such know-how secret were both necessary to avoid compromising or undermining Odin's purpose and existence. Such provisions were, in fact, recognised in Article 2 of Commission Regulation 556/89 (the Know-how Block Exemption: reflected in Article 2 of the Technology Regulation) as legitimate in the context of know-how licences.

The Commission held that neither the establishment of Odin nor any of the detailed provisions of the agreements fell within the scope of Article 85(1). In addition, the Commission considered that there could be no implicit anti-competitive impact on the activities of the parent companies outside of the joint venture because they were not even potential competitors at the creation of Odin and neither party could realistically have developed the new product without the full participation of its partner. There was no danger of implicit anti-competitive effects stemming from the potential competition created between Metal Box and Odin because of the facility with which a break-up or sale of Odin could be brought about and the wide post-term use possibilities for all parties that this implied.

As the establishment of Odin and the associated agreements and transfers of technology did not have as their object or effect any appreciable prevention, restriction or distortion of competition within the common market, it was not necessary to examine whether trade between member states had been affected.

The Commission granted the agreements in question negative clearance under Article 2 of Regulation 17.

Referred to at Analysis Sections 12.6, 13.10, Commentary Section 9

20. Re the Agreements between KSB AG, Lowara SpA, Goulds Pumps Inc, and ITT Fluid Handling Division (Case IV/32.363) [1992] 5 CMLR 55

Main facts

In August 1987 KSB, Goulds, Lowara and The ITT Corporation notified two co-operation agreements to the Commission.

The agreements, which were for a term of 10 years, related to the development and production of the wet end of a single-stage, single-flow radial centrifugal pump. The process used chrome nickel stainless steel, so as to withstand the greatest possible internal pressure with the thinnest casing and to be suitable for mass production. A number of manufacturers were already producing pumps using stainless steel. The use of chrome nickel stainless steel provided considerable advantages over traditional components, including resistance to corrosion, reduced weight, and increased flexibility. When the agreements were concluded KSB and Lowara, who were already co-operating on the development, had not yet solved the many problems associated with the development of the pumps.

The notified agreements were (i) an agreement for joint research, development and production (the joint agreement) and (ii) a production agreement. The aim and purpose of the joint agreement was the research, design, development and testing of the wet end components, the acquisition of patents in connection therewith and the provision of the tooling necessary for the manufacture. Work on the project was decided by the parties at joint meetings, but undertaken individually so that the research or development tasks were carried out and the necessary tooling was purchased by each party in its own name and on its own behalf. The manufacture of wet end units was carried out by Lowara to the specifications of each of the parties on the basis of individual contracts governed by the general conditions laid down in the production agreement. The parties then used these units as components of their own pumps to be sold under their own trade marks. The intellectual property rights to developments were owned by the developing party and on termination of the agreement each party would have a perpetual royalty-free, non-exclusive licence to use any of the intellectual property.

Each party had the right to withdraw from the agreement for good cause. In this case the participant would be entitled to retain on a confidential basis all information required to promote, advertise, apply, and sell the product and a perpetual royalty-free licence to utilise the technical know-how. The withdrawing party would not have the right to sublicense any of the technology and would also be subject to trade secrecy and would only be able to incorporate the components into pumps bearing its own trade mark. Subject to these conditions the party could, however, have the wet end components manufactured by a subcontractor. The parties agreed that the technology should be treated as a trade secret during the term of the agreement and be subject to strict confidentiality rules following termination of the agreement.

Main conclusions

The four undertakings were actual competitors in the manufacture of conventional pumps having the same field of application as the new stainless steel pumps. Also, contrary to their submissions they were considered to be potential competitors in respect of the chrome nickel steel components of the new pumps. Each of the undertakings would have been in a position to develop the components alone. The technology involved in developing the wet end components was available to other pump manufacturers and it was, therefore, conceivable that each of the undertakings could have acquired the technology by licence from other manufacturers. The co-operation on the research, development and use of the wet end components created a restriction on the freedom of action of the parties. Even if the other components of the pumps differed, so that the user had the choice of a number of brands, the fact remained that the new components would represent the key aspect of the user's decision to buy the new pumps.

The technical lead which the parties would gain over other competitors as a result of the co-operation was safeguarded by the way they chose to make joint use of the technology. Although the intellectual property rights to developments were owned by each party, the owner could not make free use of them due to the strict secrecy covering the process for the term of the agreement and for five years thereafter. Since the production of the individual units was carried out exclusively by Lowara for the parties and since, in addition, no provision was made for the production on behalf of third parties or for the licensing of third parties, the technology remained restricted to the co-operating parties. This constituted a restriction on competition which affected trade between Member States.

The Commission considered the applicability to the agreements of the block exemption contained in Regulation 418/85 which applies to joint research and development of products and processes. The activities of the parties fell within the above definition, with all the parties having developed technical knowledge which was either protected by a property right or was secret (know-how). The provision whereby Lowara manufactured the products exclusively for the parties which prevented third parties from having access to the new technology did fall within Article 1(3) of the block exemption, under which exploitation of the results is carried out jointly where the work involved is allocated between the parties by way of specialisation of production. It was also in line with Article 4(1)(c) under which exemption is also extended to any obligation on the parties to procure the contract products exclusively from the party jointly charged with their manufacture. However, contrary to the parties' submissions, the Commission considered that the parties' market share for water pumps in the EC exceeded 20% and that it was therefore necessary to assess the agreements under Article 85(3).

The co-operation in developing the new pump contributed to improving the production of goods and to promoting technical progress. It also concerned joint exploitation. Consumers would benefit through the improvement in the quality of water pumps at a price equivalent to the old iron pumps. Also, two aspects of the new pumps, *i.e.* energy conservation and the fact that fluids handled by the pump were not polluted, were environmentally beneficial.

The parties justified the need for co-operation on the grounds that development costs could be justified economically only if a minimum production of units was obtained. The not inconsiderable economic risk involved in introducing the new pumps onto the market led the Commission to find that the co-operation between the parties in development of the new pump was indispensable. However, as regards duration of any exemption it saw no reason to depart from the period provided for in Regulation 418/85, *i.e.* five years (where the parties are competitors). The Commission held that the joint exploitation of the results could not be considered indispensable beyond the expiry of the exemption, if the exclusivity of manufacture and sale remained reserved to the parties.

The arrangements did not afford the parties the possibility of eliminating competition in respect of a substantial part of the products in question, as they faced substantial competition from other suppliers of conventional pumps. The Commission therefore granted an exemption pursuant to Article 85(3) for a period of five years. As the parties' market share was close to the threshold provided for in the block exemption and the Commission considered this to be a borderline case for an individual exemption, it required the parties to submit periodic reports on how the co-operation was developing, including a description of the technical progress and a figure for annual turnover.

Referred to at Analysis Section 14.1, Commentary Section 3.3

21.   Re the Agreements between Fiat Geotech Technologie per la Terra SpA and Hitachi Construction Machinery Limited (Case IV/33.031) OJ 1993 L20

Main facts

In December 1988 Fiat Geotech and Hitachi applied to the Commission for negative clearance or alternatively exemption concerning a joint venture for the manufacture, distribution and sale of hydraulic excavators and related products which are used mainly in road construction, and in mines and quarries. An amendment to the notification was submitted in June 1992.

The notified agreements provided for the formation of a joint venture company, Fiat-Hitachi Excavators SpA (the JV), based in Italy. The JV started trading by taking over the existing Fiat range of excavators and cylinders, but developed a new range using Hitachi technology. The JV also organised the integration of the marketing structures and networks of Fiat and Hitachi in the countries indicated as exclusive JV countries.

The JV had an exclusive market covering Western Europe (including the whole of the EC), the Mediterranean basin and Africa. It had non-exclusive access to the USA (where Hitachi had a joint venture with Deere) and the former Comecon countries. It had no access to the rest of the world which was the exclusive territory of Hitachi.

Both Fiat and Hitachi licensed their relevant technology to the JV. The licences were perpetual and irrevocable while the JV lasted. After discussion with the Commission the parties undertook that, in so far as the EC was concerned, the agreements would allow passive sales by Hitachi.

The arrangements provided for the JV to buy all its motors from Iveco (which was part of the Fiat group) and all hydraulics which it did not manufacture itself from Hitachi. The arrangements also included a minority participation by the Sumitomo Corporation in the JV and provisions for the JV to purchase plant, materials and components through Sumitomo, but at the JV's option rather than exclusively.

Main conclusions

Fiat and Hitachi were actual competitors in Europe and world-wide prior to the JV agreements. Hitachi operated on the same product markets as the JV (although outside the territory of the JV) in Japan and the Far East and indirectly in the USA. Fiat continued to develop manufacture and sell its own product range based on its own technology. Both parent companies retained their technologies for production of hydraulic excavators and merely granted a licence to the JV which terminated in the event of liquidation of the JV. The agreements would have led to co-ordination of competitive behaviour between the parent companies, and between the parents and the JV, even if the parties had not included in their agreements restrictive clauses which were contrary to Article 85(1).

The Commission considered the application of Article 85(3) to the agreements. It considered that the JV would produce better excavators as each party would incorporate technically better components at its disposal. In addition the merging of the separate and largely complementary distribution systems of Fiat and Hitachi would improve the distribution of the resulting product.

The JV was expected to have 16% of the EC market for excavators which would not give it a dominant position in the market. It was expected to be more effective than either Fiat or Hitachi separately and the creation of the JV would therefore bring about a more balanced market structure in the EC.

The exclusive purchasing provisions foreclosed sales opportunities for third party manufacturers of motors and hydraulics. The Commission considered that these restrictions appeared to be reasonably necessary for the operation of the JV. In addition, the restrictions would not have the effect of eliminating competition in respect of a substantial part of the products in question. Following the amendment concerning passive sales, the provisions on distribution appeared to be no more than was necessary to allow the JV to function.

The Commission granted an exemption pursuant to Article 85(3) for a period of 13 years to cover the duration of the agreements.

Referred to at Analysis Section 14.2

22. Zera/Montedison (Case IV/31.550) and Hinkens/Staehler (Case IV/31.898) OJ 1993 L272

Main facts

Farmoplant SpA of Milan, a wholly owned subsidiary of the Italian Montedison Group was until May 1986 primarily a producer of agricultural plant protectants, including the herbicide Digermin. Montedison (Deutschland) Chemie Handels-GmbH was in charge of the distribution of Montedison Group products in Germany. Staehler Agrochemie GmbH & Co KG was exclusive distributor of Digermin in Germany under an agreement concluded with Montedison in 1980.

The active ingredient in Digermin was trifluralin, developed by Eli Lilly in the United States and the most successful active ingredient used in herbicides in the history of the chemical industry. Within the EC during the period 1975-82, Digermin had been registered in Italy, France, Spain and the United Kingdom as well as Germany, mostly for crops other than rape. It was not possible to establish which formulations were used in the applications for registration in Italy and Spain. However, it was established that a different formulation was registered in Germany than in all the other Member States. Digermin began to be distributed in the individual Member States following the expiry of Eli Lilly's patents for the active ingredient trifluralin, in 1979.

The 1980 agreement between Montedison and Staehler (which was annulled at the end of 1988 because of the expiry of Digermin's German registration) granted Staehler an exclusive distribution right for Digermin in Germany. It also contained an exclusive purchasing obligation, by which Staehler undertook to purchase Digermin exclusively from Montedison. In addition, Staehler undertook not to manufacture and distribute during the term of the agreement any herbicide of the same or similar chemical composition for the same application purpose, and not to request or demand any official registration of any such herbicide for itself or any third party.

In the period between May 1981 and August 1985 a series of meetings between Montedison and Staehler took place and on at least one occasion, a representative of Farmoplant was present. The subjects agreed at those talks included the co-ordination of jointly financed advertising for Digermin and an information campaign against an imported competing trifluralin product. Also, confidential talks were held on product strategy and parallel imports.

Under German Plant Protection Law, plant protection products could be imported or commercially distributed only if they were registered with the Federal Biologische Bundesanstalt (BBA). Where an already registered product was imported, its formulation had to correspond to the preparation formula lodged with the BBA. In 1983, Zera Agrarchemikalien GmbH (Zera) obtained from the BBA a subregistration to the existing registration, for Digermin imported from the Netherlands. The subregistration was issued on the basis of a satisfactory demonstration by Zera that the product was Digermin from

Farmoplant's production. Zera's products were sold under the name Zera-Trifluralin at 20% below Staehler's prices. Montedison wrote to the BBA pointing out that the German and Dutch formulations of Digermin were not identical. Montedison's claims, supported by an expert opinion, that the two products were not identical prompted the BBA to revoke Zera's subregistration. Following a complaint by Zera, the BBA allowed its subregistration to run until May 1985. Before the expiry of the subregistration, Zera-Trifluralin was given its own registration by the BBA. Montedison lodged a civil complaint against Zera seeking an injunction and damages on the basis that there was no identity between Digermin and the imported Zera-Trifluralin. The action was eventually dismissed. In addition, in 1984 a French firm sold the French-manufactured formulation of Digermin to two customers in Germany. Staehler complained to the Plant Protection Office and the goods were confiscated and administrative offence proceedings initiated.

In a series of memos between Montedison, Farmoplant and Staehler, and in some documents concerning the legal action against Zera, there were indications that the registration of differing formulations in Germany and other Member States had been pursued with the intention of preventing parallel imports into Germany, the market with the highest domestic prices.

Main conclusions

The Commission initiated proceedings in September 1989 after receiving complaints from a number of German undertakings. It was not concerned with whether the de facto exclusive distribution granted to Staehler under the 1980 agreement was permissible under Article 85.

The Commission found that when it took over the exclusive distribution, Staehler was required by Montedison and Farmoplant to pursue a high price policy in Germany. In 1983 intensive correspondence took place between Farmoplant and Montedison on the strategy for preventing parallel imports. They agreed that the prospects for the success of any moves against parallel imports depended on the maintenance of product differentiation. Staehler was brought into this strategy and two documents from 1985 were discovered which provided evidence of an agreement to the effect that Staehler was to be afforded territorial protection by ensuring that supplies to Germany had a different formulation to supplies to other countries. The Commission concluded that this agreement restricted competition pursuant to Article 85(1) and that trade between Member States was adversely affected. Despite the substantially higher level of prices in Germany, imports from other Member States into Germany were significantly impeded. Significantly, when parallel imports of Digermin appeared in Germany in 1983 and 1984, prices on the German market fell appreciably.

The agreement was not eligible for exemption under Article 85(3) as it was not notified and in any case it did not meet the conditions provided for in

Article 85(3). The arrangement did not contribute to improving the production or distribution of goods or to promoting technical or economic progress. Rather, the importation of cheaper Digermin into Germany was prevented. The maintenance of product differentiation made it possible in Germany to maintain a significantly higher level of prices with no compensatory benefits for consumers.

The infringement of Article 85 ended with the annulment of the distribution agreement by the parties. The Commission issued its decision recording an infringement, as is its practice if, as in this case, it is needed to clarify a point of law.

Referred to at Analysis Sections 10.5, 12.3

23. Philips International BV and Matsushita Electric Industrial Company Ltd (Case IV/33.847) [1993] 4 CMLR 286

Main facts

In November 1991 Philips notified a series of agreements for negative clearance or exemption relating to the development and exploitation of the Digital Compact Cassette (DCC) and the DCC player. The other five undertakings concerned included Matsushita, Thomson Consumer Electronics and Sony Corporation of Japan.

The DCC was a new type of magnetic tape cassette recording and reproduction system, producing digital sound as opposed to the analogue sound of traditional cassettes. The DCCs, unlike compact discs, were backwards, but not vice-versa, compatible with analogue cassettes, in that analogue cassettes were playable on DCC players.

The first of the series of notified agreements was the Multilateral Cross Licensing Agreement. In order to develop, manufacture and exploit DCC players and cassettes, the partners granted to each other during the term of the agreement (which was until the expiry of the last of the DCC patents included in the agreement), a non-exclusive, non-transferable licence of their DCC patents including the right to have made, use, sell or otherwise dispose of DCC players and cassettes.

The second set of agreements were bilateral agreements between Philips and each of the other partners. These agreements authorised Philips on an exclusive basis to grant licences in respect of all the partner DCC patents, to third parties for the purpose of using, manufacturing, selling or otherwise disposing of DCC products. These agreements would also remain in force until the expiry of the last DCC patent.

Arising out of the bilateral agreements, Philips granted licences on a non-discriminatory, non-exclusive basis to third parties for a period of 10 years to enable them to manufacture and sell DCC cassettes and/or players. The rights granted did not extend to manufacture of components.

Main conclusion

The Commission considered that while some of the agreements contained restrictions on competition contrary to Article 85(1) which could affect trade between Member States (*e.g.* pooling of patents and know-how, exclusive licensing and standardisation of specifications), they together would merit an exemption pursuant to Article 85(3) as they appeared to contribute substantially to technical progress and also to serve the interest of the consumer.

The Commission confirmed the suitability of the agreements for an exemption pursuant to Article 85(3) and closed the case by administrative "comfort" letter.

Referred to at Analysis Section 14.1

24. Quantel International (Continuum)/Quantel SA (Case IV/33.335) [1993] 5 CMLR 497

Main facts

Quantel SA (QSA), a subsidiary of Stefna which is a member of the French defence and aerospace group Aerospatiale, is a manufacturer of lasers for scientific and research purposes. Quantel International-Continuum (QLI) was a former US subsidiary of QSA. When Stefna acquired QSA, it directed QSA to sell QLI. QLI was purchased by Hoya Corporation, a Japanese company specialising in optics, optical fibres and lasers. The purchase was effected by a share transfer agreement in July 1985. The agreement was accompanied by a protocol which laid down certain arrangements for future production and sales by QSA and QLI. It included a section whereby the parties agreed a measure of technology transfer between themselves and envisaged some common further development of products being developed at the time of sale. For these products the protocol laid down a division of markets world-wide, with the European market being reserved for QSA. The protocol also contained a provision prohibiting QLI from using the know-how developed during the lifetime of the agreement in certain defined product areas.

The protocol was concluded for an initial three-year period with the possibility of renewal by mutual agreement for a further three years. However, it provided that specific provisions, including the allocation of territories, would continue to be applied, although it was not clear from the wording whether it was intended that these provisions would merely continue for the additional three-year period or whether they would survive the expiration of the agreements as a whole.

On the expiration of the initial three-year period, QLI gave notice to QSA that it did not intend to renew the protocol as it wished to enter the European market. A new agreement was concluded whereby the European market was partially opened to QLI. Acting on the new agreement, QLI entered into distribution agreements in various Member States. QSA then notified QLI that it was repudiating the renegotiated agreement and was invoking the provisions of the original agreements relating to territorial allocations, on the grounds that it had overlooked the fact that these provisions survived the expiration of the original agreements. QSA subsequently approached several of its European distributors warning them not to distribute QLI's products within the EC and claiming exclusive ownership of the trade mark and logo.

QLI complained to both the Commission and to the French competition authorities claiming that QSA's actions constituted unfair competition and amounted to a breach of contract, and it asserted that the provisions concerning allocation of territories contained in the original agreements breached Article 85(1) in any case.

In response to the complaint QSA maintained that the agreements did not fall under Article 85(1) because they were of minor importance. Alternatively,

QSA argued that they were legitimate covenants connected with a business sale or were exempt as research and development agreements capable of obtaining the benefit of block exemption under Regulation 418/85.

The Commission informed QSA that its preliminary view was that the agreements infringed Article 85(1) because they exceeded the turnover limits for agreements of minor importance and they could not qualify for exemption under Article 85(3) because the agreements had not been notified. Moreover, Regulation 418/85 did not apply because the primary object of the agreements was not co-operation in research and development.

Subsequently QSA notified the 1985 agreements and sent an explanatory note saying that it would limit its claims to territorial protection under the protocol to a period of five years from the time when the products were first put on the market within the EC, in order to comply with Regulation 418/85. QSA acknowledged that there had been delays in finalising development of products for which it was responsible but alleged that these were partly due to QLI's failure to transfer technology to it in accordance with the protocol. QSA also claimed the benefit of the opposition procedure in Article 7 of Regulation 418/85. The Commission informed QSA by letter that the agreements did not prima facie satisfy the tests of Regulation 418/85 and did not therefore qualify for application of the opposition procedure. The Commission's letter was the subject of an appeal by QSA to the Court of First Instance.

Main conclusions

The 1985 agreements relied upon by QSA had the effect of depriving European consumers of access to QLI's lasers on the EC market. The sharing of markets between the parties was contrary to the wording of Article 85(1). Although some degree of territorial protection may have been justified following the sale of QLI, the duration of the protection in this case was excessive and could not be considered necessary to ensure the transfer of the undertaking sold.

Contrary to QSA's arguments, the agreements' effect on competition was appreciable. In addition, its claim that the agreements were capable of benefiting from the block exemption in respect of research and development agreements was not acceptable. The block exemption only applied to agreements entered into by undertakings for the purpose of joint research and development of products and processes and joint exploitation of the results of that R&D. It was clear in this case that the purpose of the agreements was the transfer of a business and the joint development provisions were purely ancillary to that sale.

The Commission found the agreements to be incompatible with the application of Article 85(3). QSA had not put forward any arguments to demonstrate that the improvement and distribution of the products in question which would result from the agreements were sufficient to compensate for the disadvantages which they would cause in the field of competition. The

Commission concluded that the restriction of competition resulting from the application of the territorial allocations in the agreements constituted a barrier to market entry which was not compensated by any technical and economic benefit deriving from the agreement between the parties in developing, manufacturing and marketing the products concerned. The fact that QSA had said that it was limiting the territorial restrictions to a duration of five years was not enough to resolve the difficulty because it was one of absolute sharing of markets, while Article 4(1)(f) of Regulation 418/85 which is the inspiration for the five-year period, is considerably more limited, allowing only an obligation not to pursue an active marketing policy and only in respect of products resulting from joint R&D.

Although the parties reached a settlement, the Commission considered it appropriate to adopt a formal decision in this case. It held that the 1985 agreement and protocol between QSA and QLI infringed Article 85(1) in as much as they established the sharing of markets and they did not fall within the scope of the block exemption of Regulation 418/85.

Referred to at Analysis Section 13.10, Commentary Section 5.1

25. Ford of Europe Inc and Volkswagen AG (Case IV/33.814) [1993] 5 CMLR 617

Main facts

Ford, a UK registered company and Volkswagen of Germany notified to the Commission an agreement relating to the setting up of a joint venture company (JV) for the development and production of a multi-purpose vehicle (MPV) in Portugal. An MPV is one that can carry up to seven persons, with the ability to remove seats adding flexibility.

The agreement provided for the setting up of the JV which was owned in equal shares and jointly controlled. All costs relating to the development, engineering and manufacture of the MPV were shared equally. It was intended that the JV would last at least as long as the MPV's projected life cycle of 10 years. The product development was predominantly carried out by VW in Germany while Ford was mainly responsible for the manufacturing and plant engineering. Both partners supplied engines and transmissions whilst most of the remaining parts were purchased from external suppliers. The parties agreed to differentiate their MPVs in order to preserve their brand image and make their versions distinguishable to their customers. They each committed to purchase fixed quantities of MPVs and parts from the JV on a "cost plus basis", with shortfall penalties being payable if minimum quantities were not purchased. The partners independently distributed their respective MPVs through their own networks and under their own brand names.

Main conclusions

Ford and VW were important competitors in the European and world car markets. In view of their financial, technical and research capacities, either company was capable of producing an MPV on its own. The development of new models was one of the key elements of competition in the car sector and a determining factor for the success of a manufacturer in the market. Any agreements between competitors likely to restrict this activity had to be regarded as serious restrictions of competition under Article 85(1).

The co-operation between Ford and VW led to an extensive exchange and sharing of technical know-how which could have affected the competitive behaviour of the two partners on neighbouring market segments such as light vans or estate cars. The agreement would appreciably affect trade between Member States as it was concluded between two internationally active car manufacturers concerning the joint development and production of a product which was sold throughout the EC.

The Commission considered the application of Article 85(3). The co-operation made available an advanced vehicle designed to meet the requirements of European consumers. Both companies had at their disposal extensive know-how in the field of research as well as car automation. The co-operation allowed the partners to pool complementary engineering resources and technical expertise. This would result in an improvement in the production of goods through a rationalisation of product development and manufacturing. Technical progress would be promoted and production of MPVs in the EC would be improved by the establishment of a new and modern manufacturing plant using the latest production technology. The vehicle would also be improved considerably with respect to environmental requirements.

The European consumer would benefit directly. Due to the sophisticated production technology and the economies of scale, the consumer would be offered two versions of a high quality and reasonably priced MPV which would be distributed throughout the EC through the extensive sales networks of the parties. Ford and VW would be forced to pass on the benefits to the consumer, because as a result of their entry, along with that of other manufacturers into the MPV market segment there would be increased competitive pressure on all suppliers leading to a more balanced segment.

The Commission held that the restrictions were indispensable to the functioning of the JV. Neither party had a sufficient capacity at its disposal for a production of the size projected for their JV. Also given the investment required for separate development and production of an MPV as well as the unit production required for profitability, it could not be expected that the companies, acting on their own, would achieve a reasonable return in view of their anticipated sales and with regard to the low volume of the MPV segment in comparison with other market segments.

The co-operation between Ford and VW would not lead to an elimination of competition in the MPV segment. Having regard to the leading market position of Renault's MPV, the Espace, it would stimulate competition through the creation of an additional choice. There would also be increased competition concerning price and quality with further penetration of the segment by Japanese producers as well as other new entrants. The Commission also considered that the product differentiation and profit margins in the MPV segment would leave sufficient scope for a degree of competition between Ford and VW.

The Commission also considered Article 86. However, in this case the parties did not hold a joint dominant position in the MPV segment and could not be in breach of Article 86.

The Commission granted an exemption pursuant to Article 85(3) for a period of 10 years but made the exemption subject to a number of conditions. These included *inter alia* an obligation on the parent companies to establish procedures to ensure that all competitively sensitive, non-public information did not reach employees of the other parent company; a prohibition on the expansion of the range of products to be produced by the JV without prior approval of the Commission, and an obligation on the parties, in the event of termination of the JV agreement, to grant or procure the granting of all technology licences (patented or not) necessary to enable the other parent to continue making the MPVs separately.

Referred to at Commentary Section 9

26. Albert Pestre and another v Oril SA and another [1994] 2 CMLR 515 Judgment of the Paris Appeals Court

Main facts

Following the discovery in 1954 of an antibiotic called "Fusafongine" and the method of its preparation, Mme Couchard, its inventor, obtained a patent in 1958. In 1959 Mme Couchard entered into licensing agreements with two companies for the exploitation of the existing patent, any foreign patents and any further patents which might arise. She agreed to supply the licensees with sufficient quantities of the product and to provide them with all information relating to its manufacture. In return the licensees agreed to pay royalties to Mme Couchard. By 1961 Mme Couchard was unable to supply the required quantities of the product to the licensees (which by then included the company Oril). It was agreed by all the parties that the product would thereafter be manufactured by Oril with Mme Couchard supplying all necessary information and providing essential technical assistance for a period of several years. In 1966 the parties entered into a new agreement for a duration of 50 years.

In 1982 the French tax authorities decided that the patent had passed into the public domain in 1978 and that the supposed royalty payments were in fact gratuities and taxable as such. As a result Oril refused to continue to perform the contract on the grounds that the tax authorities' decision had completely distorted its economics. Mme Couchard's successor in title, Mr Pestre, brought actions against Oril in the French domestic courts seeking enforcement of the contract and payment of damages and interest.

At first instance the court considered that the basis of the agreement consisted of the monopoly conferred under the patent and that this could only exist from the licensee's point of view for as long as the patent endured, and the provision of information necessary for the manufacture of the product could not by itself justify continuing with the royalty payments. On appeal Pestre asked for the judgment to be overruled and for Oril to pay damages. Oril, in support of its request that the judgment should be upheld, argued that the clause in the agreement under which it was obliged to pay royalties after the expiry of the patent was invalid as contrary to Article 85(1) in that it increased the manufacturing costs without economic justification.

Main conclusions

It was common ground that know-how essential for the exploitation of the patent was of considerable importance and it was clear from the facts that the agreement covered not only the exploitation of the actual patent but also the transfer of the know-how. The stipulated royalty was paid equally for the grant of the patent licence as for the know-how transferred and the demise of the monopoly effectively conferred by the patent could not reduce to nil the value of the know-how transferred. Contrary to the findings of the tax authorities, the stipulated royalties, which were payable over a defined period in respect of a contractual obligation fulfilled by the licensors, could not be treated as gratuities.

As for Article 85(1), the 1966 agreement did not restrict competition because the product concerned did not by itself cover the entire sphere of application of antibiotics of that type and it competed with other similar products on the market. In addition, as the agreement was equally concerned with the exercise of the patent and the transfer of the know-how, its validity could not be confined to the duration of the patent. The agreement fell directly within the block exemption for patent licences provided for in Regulation 2349/84.

The Court of Appeal overruled the first instance judgment and ordered Oril to pay damages with interest.

Referred to at Analysis Section 10.7, Commentary Section 3.4

27.   Re the Agreement between Pasteur Mérieux Sérums et Vaccins and Merck & Co Inc (Case IV/34.776) [1994] 5 CMLR 281

Main facts

In June 1993 Pasteur and Merck notified to the Commission a set of agreements establishing a jointly controlled company, Pasteur Mérieux MSD SNC ("the JV").

Pasteur, a French company, specialises in the manufacture of human vaccine products, blood, proteins and other related biological products. Merck, a major US company, is active world-wide in pharmaceuticals. The JV's primary purposes and objectives were:

- the creation and development of new multivalent vaccines which would result in significant public health benefits;
- the distribution of existing and new products in countries where they were not yet marketed; and
- future research in new vaccines, concentrating on specific European requirements.

The business scope of the JV was to facilitate the research of, oversee the development of, register, arrange for the manufacture of (in principle either by Pasteur or Merck), distribute, market and sell in the EC and EFTA ("the territory") human vaccines, specific immunoglobulins, in-vivo diagnostics and sera ("JV products").

The JV was set up under French law. Each party transferred to the JV its existing product registration rights and exclusively licensed to the JV the existing patents and know-how owned or licensed by it, except for any rights retained (i) to permit the continued manufacture of products solely for sale to the JV in the territory and (ii) for sale for use outside the territory. All other existing product rights such as copyrights, trade dress and tradenames were licensed or transferred to the JV. In addition, Pasteur transferred or licensed certain tangible assets and both parents transferred their respective rights and obligations under distribution agreements.

In relation to new vaccines, each parent agreed to transfer or license to the JV the product rights necessary to make the pipeline products (*i.e.* those vaccines at late development stage) in any country of the territory as they arose, and if the JV elected to commercialise the product, the originating party would permit the JV to obtain registrations for the product in the territory. If the JV elected not to introduce such a product to the market, the JV could transfer or license the product rights to a third party. If the JV did pursue development of the product, any patents and know-how resulting from the development work funded by the JV would belong to the JV for the territory, whereas the party engaged in the relevant development work outside the territory would own the patents and know-how there. With regard to future pipeline products (*i.e.* those at any early stage of development) each parent agreed to offer such products to the JV at a certain stage of testing. If the JV accepted the product it would receive an exclusive licence, subject to third party rights in the territory, for the product rights. If the JV elected not to pursue development of the product, the parent with whom such product originated could transfer or licence all rights to a third party in the territory on terms no more favourable than those offered to the JV.

The agreement was to terminate automatically at the end of the year 2023 unless extended by mutual consent. However, Merck was given the right to sell its interest at any time after 2001, with Pasteur having the first option to purchase. The parents agreed not to sell or supply, nor to license to a third party, prior to termination, a JV product or a competing product for use in the territory. Merck agreed that for a period of five years following the sale of its interest it would not sell, supply or license to a third party a JV product.

In addition to the agreements between Pasteur and Merck, the parties concluded a set of ancillary agreements with third parties, including agreements for distribution of vaccines in France and Germany and exclusive manufacturing licences in respect of particular vaccines. A technology transfer licence agreement was concluded with Behring for development of multivalents for sale in Germany. This was a pure know-how licensing agreement with ancillary provisions relating to other intellectual property rights. It contained an obligation on the JV not to license other undertakings to exploit the licensed technology in the licensed territory and an obligation on Behring not to exploit, market or advertise the technology, or establish any branch or distribution depot in countries within the EEA which were reserved for the JV.

Main conclusions

The Commission considered that the creation of the JV breached Article 85(1) in respect of its effects on various vaccine markets and in the field of R&D for future pipeline products. The JV and related agreements limited to an appreciable extent the access of competitors to existing and imminent vaccines and vaccine technology. The ancillary distribution agreements and manufacturing licences also fell foul of Article 85(1).

However, the Commission considered that through the JV the parties would avoid R&D overlaps and benefit from each other's technical strengths which would lead to qualitative promotion of technical progress. The JV would also improve distribution of vaccines as Merck had a very limited presence in the EEA markets (with the exception of Germany). These improvements responded to a genuine public health concern and would be of benefit to consumers as the JV would be able to stimulate and speed-up the development of new vaccines adapted to the needs of each EEA country. Such development required far reaching co-operation between the parties to enable them to adapt to unforeseen and new circumstances resulting from the continuous exchange of information between them. It was considered that only a joint venture would provide a mechanism which was flexible enough to achieve this and the JV was, therefore, indispensable. In addition, it was considered that it was indispensable for the proper functioning of the JV and for the achievement of all the anticipated advantages, that the scope of the JV was extended to the joint distribution of the existing and future vaccines by the JV. The Commission did not believe that the creation of the JV would lead to elimination of competition on the vaccine markets of the EEA.

A number of the ancillary agreements were found to fulfil the conditions laid down by Commission Regulation 1983/83 granting a block exemption for exclusive distribution agreements.

The multivalent technology transfer licence with Behring could not benefit from the know-how Block Exemption in Commission Regulation 556/89 because the restrictions in the agreement lasted for a period which might be longer than the 10 years allowed by the Regulation. However, the Commission considered that the agreements could lead to a new series of multivalents which would constitute an important element of technical progress on the German vaccine markets and could also be beneficial to consumers. The fact that the agreement guaranteed a minimum commercialisation period of five years for each multivalent developed did not prevent an individual exemption in this case, as this provided a further incentive for Behring to continue its R&D work for the creation of such multivalents.

In view of the fact that (i) the JV would not terminate automatically before the year 2023, (ii) the Commission retained an ability to review the actual effect of the JV on competition in vaccine markets and (iii) account had to be taken of the characteristics of the agreement and of the fact that the nature of the markets involved meant that it would take a longer time before the advantages of co-operation could be fully realised (*e.g.* the R&D work leading to the introduction of a new vaccine on the market usually takes in excess of 10 years), the Commission concluded that an exemption until the end of 2006 was appropriate.

The Commission granted exemptions pursuant to Article 85(3) to the JV and related agreements and to the multivalent technology licence until 31 December 2006.

Referred to at Analysis Section 9.5

28.   Securicor Datatrak (Case IV/M561) March 1995, EMCR B289

Main facts

In February 1995 the Securicor group of the UK and two Dutch undertakings, Centraal Beheer Pensioenverzekering NV (Centraal) and Parcom Services BV (Parcom) notified to the Commission the creation of a joint venture to provide vehicle tracking services within the territory of the Netherlands.

Securicor's main activities, carried out in the UK and internationally, included express parcels, freight haulage, document delivery and mail services, security guards and patrol, and installation and maintenance of communication products, electronic surveillance and alarm systems. Centraal was active in both life and non-life insurance. Parcom was an investment company belonging to the banking and insurance group ING.

The parties first created a holding company Security Datatrak Europe BV (SDE) which held all the share capital of an operating subsidiary, Security Datatrak Netherland BV (SDN). SDN was to carry out a vehicle tracking system in the Netherlands, using new technology which would provide operators with real time information on the position and status of all vehicles under their control.

SDN was to be jointly controlled, through SDE, by each of the parent companies holding one third of the share capital. Major decisions concerning the activities of SDN required consent of all the parents. However, SDN would be an autonomous full function undertaking with its own assets and personnel and would not give rise to the co-ordination of the competitive behaviour of the parents, since only Securicor would be active in the JV services market, although in a different geographic area. (NB Changes to the Merger Regulation in 1998 have removed the test of "coordination" so that a transaction can be treated as a concentration as long as it creates a full function autonomous entity.)

The parties notified the following ancillary restraints:

- Securicor would enter into an exclusive supply and licence agreement for the Netherlands to supply SDN with all infrastructure and vehicle equipment. However, SDN could purchase equipment from a third party if better conditions were offered provided that no know-how of Securicor was used in the manufacture of such equipment.
- The supply and licence agreement also dealt with the exclusive licence for SDN to use the know-how, software and other rights owned by Securicor in connection with the vehicle tracking system.

Main conclusions

The service provided by SDN would be a new one in the Dutch market and the Commission approved the concentration. The Commission also considered that the supply and licence agreement between Securicor and SDN was directly related to the concentration. However, the exclusive nature of the agreement went beyond what was strictly necessary for the implementation of the joint venture. It could not be considered as ancillary to the proposed concentration and, therefore, it had to be assessed separately under Article 85. Nothing has been published to suggest what was the outcome of the assessment under Article 85.

Referred to at Commentary Section 9

29.   Voest Alpine Industrieanlagenbau and Davy International (Case IV/M585) July 1995, EMCR B323

Main facts

In June 1995 the Austrian company, Voest, and Davy, a UK company, notified to the Commission their proposal for the creation of a joint venture company, Conroll Technology GmbH (the JV). The JV was to supply engineering and construction management services in connection with the supply and construction of equipment for hot connect systems for steel manufacturing plants. The technology for a hot connect system involved both slab casting and rolling mills. Voest specialised in slab casting and Davy specialised in rolling mills. The JV was to be under joint control of both parents. It would have its own management, secretarial and other staff but the parents would contribute experienced personnel, the necessary exclusive royalty-free intellectual property licences and capital. The JV would not be a supplier or customer of either parent.

The parties requested that certain restrictions be considered as ancillary to the concentration. These included:

- the agreement of the parents that for the duration of the JV they would not operate in the field of activity of the JV;
- the grant to the JV of exclusive intellectual property rights necessary for its activities;
- the agreement of each parent not to use any know-how which it obtained from the other parent to design, use and sell plant other than hot connect systems and not to disclose the know-how;
- the agreement of the parents and the JV not to sublicense the design or manufacture of hot connect systems except for the purpose of the joint venture agreement and not to sublicense the design and manufacture of components without prior approval of the executive committee of the JV; and
- the agreement of the parties that, for the duration of the JV, they would not supply specified components to other companies which designed, manufactured or supplied hot connect systems.

Main conclusions

The relevant product market was the design and installation of hot connect systems. More than 40% of the relevant global market was held by a competing German undertaking. Accordingly, the proposed concentration would not create or enhance a dominant position and the overall effect would more likely be the enhancement of competition, since only by creating the JV could Voest and Davy compete effectively on the market.

The Commission considered that the participation of the parents in the JV did not appear likely to lead to the co-ordination of their activities in other areas (NB see comment on Case Note 28).

In relation to the ancillary restraints including the technology licences, the Commission found that these were directly related to and necessary for the successful implementation of the concentration and could be cleared together with the merger. One exception was the provision relating to the supply of components, which could not therefore be treated as ancillary. Nothing has been published to suggest either that this provision was deleted by the parties or that it was subsequently considered under Article 85.

Referred to at Commentary Section 9

30.   Re a Co-operation Agreement between Banque Nationale de Paris SA and Dresdner Bank AG (Case IV/34.607) OJ 1996 L188

Main facts

In January 1993 Banque Nationale de Paris (BNP) and Dresdner Bank (DB) notified to the Commission an exclusive world-wide co-operation agreement of indefinite duration. The four areas of co-operation were:

1. in organisational matters and through exchange of information;

2. in the field of international financing;

3. in information on activities outside France and Germany; and

4. in the French and German markets.

With regard to the question of the banks' activities on each other's home markets, the co-operation agreement did not restrict access to such markets by existing subsidiaries or by the creation of new subsidiaries or branches or by the acquisition by one bank of a competitor on the other's domestic market. However, it did limit the extent to which one bank may operate on the other's domestic market in co-operation with a competitor of the latter, by providing that such agreements may only be concluded with the latter's express consent. The agreement as initially notified gave the latter the absolute right to withhold approval. In response to a request by the Commission the parties agreed to limit this right of refusal to cases where a co-operation agreement would involve the utilisation of know-how or business secrets received from the other party as a result of the co-operation.

Main conclusions

Co-operation in organisational matters and the exchange of information would not only improve the internal performance of the two banks from a management standpoint. It would also lead to an exchange of know-how on customer electronic banking instruments, as a result of which the electronic systems of the two banks would be improved, harmonised and interconnected.

In the field of international financing, the relative size of the two banks would not enable them to restrict competition appreciably. On the contrary, the co-operation was likely to be pro-competitive as it would strengthen the position of the two banks internationally so that they would be better able to compete against the large international banks, particularly American and Asian banks.

Trade between Germany and France would be affected because the banks would not have any financial interest in competing against each other with regard to products and services on their respective home markets. This applied both where they exchanged know-how in order to develop new services and products and to areas where they would make products available to each other for distribution on their respective home markets.

The Commission considered that the co-operation would lead to an improvement in the production of financial services provided to individuals and undertakings as a result of the fact that the two banks would co-operate to improve their organisation, in particular by introducing new data processing tools and expanding their sources of financial data. By transferring existing know-how they would be able to provide improved or new services, such as new electronic banking services and new forms of information and financial advice, to their customers. The co-operation would also improve the distribution of services and products supplied by the two banks. Interconnection between the data-processing systems would also improve banking services across frontiers, especially cross-frontier payments. Consumers, especially those in France and Germany would benefit from qualitative and quantitative improvements in banking services and their reciprocal distribution via the branches of both and from the setting up of new forms and means of electronic banking.

The clauses relating to the exchange of know-how and to the distribution of one partner's products by the other on its home market were indispensable in order to obtain these benefits.

The Commission did not consider that the two banks would be able to eliminate competition in the various areas of banking on the French and German markets. The new banking products which the two banks would provide were not protected by intellectual property rights. It was therefore likely that other credit institutions, some of which had also concluded co-operation agreements, would also be offering new products.

The Commission granted an exemption pursuant to Article 85(3) for a period of 10 years.

Referred to at Analysis Sections 10.1, 10.18, 12.2

· Index ·

Rights. *See* Exhaustion of rights, Patent
    rights
    sales rights, exclusive, where, 86
Risk,
    allocation of, 29
Royalties,
    additional, linked to capacity, 67
    duration of, 63, 64, 146, 147, 188, 189
    gratuities, whether considered as, 216
    minimum amounts, payment of, 65,
      66, 71
    obligations regarding, 190,191
    payment of, 19, 24, 60, 61, 146, 147,
      171,188,189
    production, where dependent on, 113

Sales activity,
    inadvertent sales, licensee by, 49
    organisation of, rights to, 158
    passive sales activity, where, 163, 164
    restrictions placed on, 47, 48, 103, 126
    sales, active pursuit of, 49, 50
Sales policy,
    restrictions affecting, 47, 179
Secondary sourcing,
    provisions as to, 147
Secrecy,
    know-how, requirements as to, 15, 27,
      70, 114, 127, 131, 132, 154, 155,
      170
    obligations as to, 154, 170
    secret, definition of, 31, 132
Selling price. *See* Price
Services,
    improved, provision of, 224, 225
    provision of, regulation affecting, 38
Single market,
    competition law, protecting, 1
Site licences,
    protection afforded to, 139, 140
Software,
    protection of, regulations affecting, 15,
      137, 138, 139
Sole traders
    position of, 4, 100
Sources of law,
    competition law, 2
Subcontractors,
    agreements relating to, 101, 102
    goods supplied by, 101, 102
    licence-back, arrangements for, 101,
      102
    opposition procedure, involving, 102

Sub-licences,
    provisions affecting, 88, 154
Sublicensing,
    restrictions placed on, 58
Substantiality,
    know-how, requirements as to, 15, 27,
      70, 114, 127, 131, 134
    substantive, definition of, 31
Supply,
    exclusive, agreement for, 220
    refusal to, where, 92
    single customer to, 68, 69
    sources of, 68, 69, 105

Technological progress,
    agreements promoting, 17, 187, 207,
      218
Technology pools,
    operation of, 28, 84
Technology Transfer Agreement,
    definition of, 37
Termination. *See* Agreement, Patent
    licences, Post-termination ban
    agreement of, basis for, 70, 111
    challenge, licensee by, 70, 71
    unnecessary patent, grounds for, 70,
      71
Terms and conditions,
    agreement, contained in, 4
Territorial protection. *See also* Territorial
    restriction
    licences, afforded to, 103, 105, 106
    patents, afforded to, 128, 129
    restrictions on, 209, 210
Territorial restriction,
    agreement, as to, 113, 114, 179, 184
    common market, operations within,
      44, 45, 46, 47
    duration of, 78, 79, 211
    effect of, 124, 156, 157, 159, 167,
      170, 175, 176
    exploitation on, 144
    know-how agreements, affected by,
      127
    mixed agreements, contained in, 128
Territory. *See* Territorial protection,
    Territorial restriction
Third parties,
    enforcement action, involving, 63, 110
    equipment, purchased from, 220
    facilities constructed for, 24, 139, 140
    know-how, communicated to, 22
    licences granted to, 156